CONVERSATIONS
ON *Success*

INSIGHT PUBLISHING
SEVIERVILLE, TENNESSEE

Published by Insight Publishing Company
P.O. Box 4189
Sevierville, Tennessee 37864

10 9 8 7 6 5 4 3 2

Printed in The United States

ISBN: 1-932863-40-0

Table Of Contents

A Message From The Publisher

Some of my most rewarding experiences in business, and for that matter in my personal life, have been at meetings, conventions, or gatherings after the formal events have concluded. Inevitably, small groups of ten to fifteen men and women gather together to rehash the happenings of the day and to exchange war stories, recently heard jokes, or the latest gossip from their industry. It is in these informal gatherings where some of the best lessons can be learned.

Usually, in informal groups of professionals, there are those who clearly have lived through more battles and learned more lessons than the others. These are the men and women who are really getting the job done and everyone around the room knows it. When they comment on the topic of the moment, they don't just spout the latest hot theory or trend, and they don't ramble on and on without a relevant point. These battle scarred warriors have lessons to share that everyone senses are just a little more real, more relevant, and therefore worthy of more attention.

These are the kind of people we have recruited to offer their insights and expertise for *Conversations On Success*. The book is filled with frank and powerful discussions with men and women who are making a significant impact on their culture, in their field, and on their colleagues and clients. It is ripe with "the good stuff," as an old friend of mine used to always say. Inside these pages you'll find ideas, insights, strategies, and philosophies that are working with real people, in real companies, and under real circumstances.

It is our hope that you keep this book with you until you've dog-eared every chapter and made so many notes in the margins that you have trouble seeing the original words on the pages. There is treasure here. Enjoy digging!

Interviews conducted by:

David E. Wright
President, International Speakers Network

Chapter One

THE INTERVIEW

David E. Wright (Wright)

Today we are talking to Johnny Wimbrey. He is a young dynamic motivational success trainer known nationally for his record breaking achievements. He trains and encourages thousands through seminars and events throughout the world. Johnny's inspirational story of overcoming life's adversities has empowered masses for greatness. The author of his best selling book *From the Hood to doing Good,* Johnny was marked with one of his first memories in life, of living in a battered women's shelter, to growing up on the hard core streets as a young drug dealer. After several near death experiences he decided it was time to flip the switch and refuse to let his past determine his future. At the age of twenty, he became a temporary licensed insurance agent with no experience and within six months of being in the insurance industry, he received recognition as a top fifty producer in a national marketing agency. In less than a two year period moving from senior agent, to district manager, to regional manager, on to regional vice president, over seeing the states of Texas and Oklahoma, Johnny found himself in the position of training experienced regional managers to recruit manage and teach sales developmental skills for well known national agencies. After

1

recognizing the high demand for his services, Johnny decided to use his skills for a higher purpose. His passion is to create success stories by helping others experience financial, spiritual and emotional wealth. Johnny Wimbrey has been interviewed on national radio talk shows and television networks as a young success story. He has been featured as the special guest speaker for the Zig Ziglar Training Systems and has shared the stage with other world famous speakers such as, Les Brown, Bill Bailey and Jim Rohn, to name a few. His message is to expose the reality, your past doesn't determine your future and, "If I can do it, anyone can." He is also a professional member of the National Speakers Association. Johnny, welcome to *Conversations on Success.*

Johnny Wimbrey (Wimbrey)

Thank you so much, David. It is definitely an honor and a pleasure to be here.

Wright

Johnny, you are sought after by popular demand as a motivational trainer. How would you describe your perfect audience?

Wimbrey

David, I would have to say that my perfect audience is an audience that's hungry for more. Whether I'm speaking at an elementary school, a prison ministry, leadership retreat, Corporate America, or for a network marketing company on the other side of the world, my perfect audience is an audience that's hungry for increase, that's hungry for success, and is willing to open their hearts and humble themselves to the proven principles and information that's going to get them there. I'm a motivator of wealth, which means I empower individuals to tap into their own "Inner Winner Within," which will allow them to experience the true manifestation of wealth. True wealth is being able to experience physical, financial, emotional, and spiritual success. A lot of speakers are guilty of speaking to just the audience, but great speakers understand that you have to be a great communicator while possessing the unique gift of being able to speak to the audience that's inside the audience. I don't have a Cookie Cutter message! I design my speeches, trainings, or workshops around my audience so that it caters to their specific environment or situations. If I stop and think about it for a second, is there really a perfect audience? When you're dealing with people there will never be perfections and those who understand that make the best coaches and students.

Wright

Many people call you a young success phenomenon and it has been said that you're the youngest, wisest, personal development guru of our time. What sets you apart or makes you different from most speakers?

Wimbrey

Well first, David, I have to say that even if one person has said that, it humbles me. It is very humbling to hear that has been said about me. People ask me that all the time and I find that people are amazed at how I answer that question. Many people are looking for a very deep response or an incredible response of revelation. So when I'm asked that question, I love to make the person get ready to take some notes, as if I'm going to say something that's going to blow their mind. You should see their eyes as I began to say, "Are you sure you want the answer? Do you really, really want to know? Are you sure?" Then I looked them square in the eyes and I say, "I do what I'm told to do! I'm a great student. " And it amazes me how big of a challenge it is for some people to follow people who have proven success track records. I believe the only thing that really makes me different is I'm coachable, trainable and teachable. What I mean by that is, I believe if you find a person that's coachable, trainable and teachable you can make them unstoppable, whether it be in their finances, or their training abilities or their abilities to be a better husband, a better father, a better wife, a better family member, a better church person, a better pastor, what ever it may be. I believe that everybody in the world must stay under the umbrella of a mentor. I believe that none of us is as smart as all of us. And I believe the thing that has made me different, the thing that has made me achieve, top production, being the top money earner in every company I've ever been a part of and sought after all over the world as a wealth trainer is, I'm still a student. I haven't arrived; I believe that the day we believe that we have arrived is the day that we will begin to fail. I will never arrive in my own eyes, but I can say that I'm constantly on my way. I'm constantly a student.

Wright

Your best selling book, *From the Hood to doing Good,* has reached a very respectable level of success. Tell us about the book and how you came up with the title.

Wimbrey

Well, thank you so much for recognizing my book. It's available in any major book store across the world. A lot of people think it's a book on my life, well I'm only twenty-nine years old, so I can't have a book on my life yet. The subtitle is what I really focus on: *From Adversity to Prosperity through Choices you Make.* What I did in this book is I talked about the principles that I used in my life to help me overcome a lot of the obstacles, a lot of the life or death situations in my life, and I talked about how I actually overcame them. From my earliest memory in life being in a battered women's shelter, to an ex-drug dealer with a felony conviction and with all those negative labels that were hanging over my head I have still managed to become victorious by becoming a very successful individual, at a very early age in life. I talk about the principles that I used to help me overcome. I'm a firm believer that your past doesn't have to determine your future. Where you come from has nothing to do with where you're going. You're in complete control of your end result regardless of your past results. In my book people will find their own "Inner Winner Within." My book has been bought all over the world, from different people and from different walks of life. A lot of people, after reading my book, come to the realization that it has nothing to do with the hood or a neighborhood. I'd like to break down the word H.O.O.D. When you break down the word hood, h-o-o-d, the reason I used the word hood is because hood stands for Hazardous Obstacles Of Destruction. I teach people how to come from their HOOD and how to do good. How to overcome the obstacles in life, persevere, press through and make it happen. One of my favorite quotes in the world is by William Ward, he said that adversity causes some people to break, but it causes others to become record breakers. I teach people how to break records and how to go against and be victorious against all adversity.

Wright

You talk openly about your personal life, your living in a battered women's shelter to selling drugs on the street as a teenager. Why are you so willing to share your personal downfalls in life? Don't you think you might jeopardize your potential to have a wider audience?

Wimbrey

Well, David, I battled with that internally. Should I share my story? The moment I began to share my story was the moment my audience began to broaden across the world. I've come to the conclusion to believe that people are looking for real people with real messages that can be transparent about their previous life. Why? Because everybody in the world deals with everyday people. Unless your hearing from someone who can be candid about the situation, that can be open about where they come from, how else can you learn from someone else's experiences? If you look in the Bible, you look at Paul, who was Saul, if we didn't know where he came from, if we didn't know that he killed and persecuted Christians before he became the number one author in the New Testament, we learn so much from individuals like that. I've come to the conclusion to believe that I have turned my "mess" into a "message." I have victory over the past Johnny Wimbrey. I have victory over my past life style. Not only do I have victory over it, I have conquered it. I now leverage off my story to help other individuals. Now my mess has truly become a message to the world.

Wright

Here's one of your quotes, "Everyone wants to be successful but only a few must be successful." Could you tell us what that means?

Wimbrey

I believe that everyone wants to be successful. I believe that everybody wants true victory. But only a few people must be successful. I believe that people get caught up into their wants, but are never compelled to take action . They have the desires, they have these dreams, but even a dream is over when the person wakes up. I believe there's nothing wrong with wanting something, but if you can't find your WHY, your W-H-Y behind all of your *wants*, you will never ever attain the mentality that you *must* have it. A good example would be this, David. I want to eat healthy so I can live longer. What I did was, I attached something to my want that was much bigger than me, and that's life itself. It's not that I want to eat healthy, it's I must eat healthy so I can live longer. And I think that's a gap that a lot of individuals have in their lives, because they constantly want things, but they never train themselves to think that they must have it. When you want something it's optional, but when you must have something it's nonnegotiable. I have never heard a person say I want to pay my taxes. You'll hear them say I must pay my taxes. Their "WHY" behind paying their taxes is they don't want to go to jail. I have found that it is possible to train yourself to have a WHY for every one of your desires, which will turn your wants into your musts. So it's not that I want to be successful, I must be successful! Why? Because I must leave an inheritance for my children's children. You must make it bigger than you, and then it's no longer about what you want. So when people say, I want to be successful, I will walk them through and personally coach an individual on how to take those "wants" and turn them into "musts." So stop wanting to be successful and say, "I must be successful. "

Wright

You talk about the importance of having mentors. Can you tell our readers the characteristics of a mentor as you see them?

Wimbrey

Absolutely. I believe that none of us is as smart as all of us and iron sharpens iron. You need someone in your life that can hold you accountable. A mentor is someone that can hold you accountable. A mentor is someone that can coach you; they can walk you through situations in your life that can help you make the right decisions. I can say this, if I didn't have mentors in my life, I would not be where I am right now. If I didn't have personal coaches in my life to help me out through my life development skills, and guiding me in the midst of important decisions, I would not be where I am right now. You have to have a mentor. A mentor is someone that's in your life, that can hold you accountable, and ultimately, is someone that can tell you no. I believe that you chose your mentor, your mentor doesn't choose you. Your mentor has to be someone that you have access to. Your mentor has to be someone that you can go to and you can just really put all your cards on the table, your not ashamed to tell them anything because they're the person that you trust, that will tell you yes or no. And if they tell you no and you don't listen to them, then they're not your mentor. A mentor is someone that can say no and you listen.

Wright

Someone told me years ago that a champion could best be defined as that person who gets up one more time than he falls down.

Everyone of course will face good and bad in their lives, why do you think so many people fall down and fail to get back up?

Wimbrey

I believe that people fall down and refuse or fail to get back up because they haven't identified the true enemy. What I mean by that, David, is this. I believe that a lot of times when we make mistakes, fall down or obstacles come in our way, I believe that we can get to a point in our life where we almost get into a pool of pity. You start feeling sorry for yourself. I think its ok for other people to feel sorry for you, but when you begin to feel sorry for yourself it is a very dangerous and life threatening trap. Failing to get back up is the internal struggle. It's the war within one's self that disables him to get back up. Everybody is looking for the enemy, David, everybody is trying to find the person or entity that's against them. "This thing is holding me down, this person is holding me down, this or that is against me!" The true enemy, which is IN-A-ME, the true enemy is inside me, it's the in-a-me, it's inner me, it's inside me! So I've got to find the thing that's inside me, that's holding me down, that's refusing to let me up. Because the only thing in life that can hold you down is you. It's a choice to stay down. What you have to do is you have to go inside and do self inventory and figure out, what the things are that are holding you down. What is in your life that you have allowed to come inside and manifest inside to the point where it's causing you to become mentally, spiritually and emotionally crippled and you can not get up from this situation. Before you can even attempt to get up from failing or making a mistake, you've got to figure out the thing that's inside you, that caused you to make that mistake and the thing that's causing you to stay down. It can be guilt, it can be shame, and it can be a lot of things. Those are mental things that can overcome you and cause you to stay down. You've got to tap into yourself, you've got to find the inner winner within and in order for you to do that, you've got to tap into the enemy that's inside you and destroy it.

Wright

I've heard you introduced as Johnny, the Record Breaker Wimbrey, why do they call you the record breaker?

Wimbrey

Well, I got that title in my very early twenties, probably right around the age of twenty-one. It started out in the insurance industry. When I first got involved with insurance I was selling health and life insurance for a national agency on a temporary license. I literally didn't even know what a deductible was. I had no idea what I was selling, but what made me different was this: I was still coachable, trainable and teachable. I attached myself to a guy, who was where I wanted to be. He was a top agent in our office. He was also one of the top agents in the nation. I rode with him and I did exactly what he told me to do. I said exactly what he said, I mimicked him to the T. And because I did that, I began to break the production records for this national agency. Within three years, I became the youngest Regional Vice President ever. Then I got involved in network marketing. I always had the fastest growing organization in every company. I was the first person in a company to reach six figures in three months. That is where it started; Johnny, the Record Breaker Wimbrey, he always has the fastest growing organization. He always has the top production and he's always breaking records and is always the youngest person to achieve a level of success. It really came from my age, my determination and my personal growth.

Wright

Johnny, you must endure challenges, periodically, from relationships from your past. Are there people and situations from your past that come back to haunt you? And if so, how do you handle it?

Wimbrey

You know, David, those are things that I think about on a daily basis. You have to be conscious of the fact that your past can come knocking on your door every now and then and you have to be prepared for it. I talk about this in my book and also my audio series, *Think and Win Big*. I talk about the ability to identify your friends from your foes that are in your life. You've got to be able to identify these entities because if you don't, when these things come up against you you're not going to know how to respond. My definition of a friend is this, a friend is someone who is for you, and a friend is any person, any place or thing that's pushing towards your destiny. And a foe is anything, any person, or any place that is pulling away from your destiny. So once you identify who your foes are, it can be a person, place or a thing, it can be a family member, it can be a TV show, it could be a memory, it could be anything that's holding you back. So the way that I handle the obstacles, people, places, things, temptations, that I've overcome from the past, I immediately identify it as a foe. Once you identify your foes, once you figure out what a foe is in your life, then it is your responsibility to immediately take action. What I do is, I cut that thing off! As I realize that I am in the presence of a foe, then it's my responsibility to take action and I cut them off, I'll leave, I'll make an excuse, I'll do whatever I need to do to get out of that situation. Because I know that I'm human, I know that I can make mistakes, I know I can fall into temptations and I know that the things that are in my past can come back to haunt me and if I don't take immediate action over those things, then once again I become my enemy.

Wright

Success has been defined many ways, depending on whom you ask. What is true success for Johnny Wimbrey?

Wimbrey

True success for me is the definition of the word wealth, which would be spiritual, emotional, financial, and physical success. I believe that there are many people that think that they have true success but they're not happy with whom they are. They're not happy at home; they're not healthy, so true success for me is being able to be successful in your personal life, your spiritual life, your emotional life and your financial life. And I think to me that is a true definition of success. Many people ask me what are my goals, what are my aspirations in life, or what could truly define you as a successful person? I want to empower the masses for greatness. I want to do it in such a way that maybe even streets are named after me, not because of a selfish desire, it's because I will have empowered and touched so many people around the world to be a better person, to truly find the victory in life, that in some shape or form of fashion that I've empowered so many people that in such a great way, that streets one day may be named after me. To me that's a success, leaving a legacy behind you, leaving a good name for your children and their children's children to be honored, for what you brought to the world, that's my definition of success.

Wright

You spoke of your audio series a few minutes ago, *Think and Win Big;* it's been an incredible hit for you, with corporations and the direct sales industry, across the world. Why do you think that is?

Wimbrey

Well, when I produced the audio program, *Think and Win Big,* the whole concept was to teach individuals to tap into the inner winner within, how to have the mindset of a winner. And corporations deal with this on a daily basis. You may be dealing with things internally or your employees are having identity crisis or they're just having challenges of tapping into a successful streak. So what I did was I put together a series, with the principles I used in my life to build agencies, to build an incredible financial structure, to build my training company and my training team. I teach companies and corporations how to walk to the beat of one drum, how to speak the same language, how to become victorious against your competitors and how to use your competitors as a leveraging edge to become number one in your industry. I think the way that I came up with the title *Think and Win Big,* was almost off the, *Think and Get Rich;* I believe that if you can begin to learn to think like a winner on a daily basis, on a hourly basis, to constantly program yourself to think as a winner, I believe that you will begin to win. The evidence has manifested even since the series has come out. I'm getting incredible responses around the world, people ordering the series across the globe and individuals are having life enhancing experiences after listening to it. It also features my good friend and mentor, Les Brown, as well as Jerry Cark, who is an unbelievable individual that's known around the world as a network marketing guru. Vince Lombardi said "winning isn't everything but wanting to win is." I teach people how to win!!!

Wright

Johnny, if you could tell our readers in a nut shell, a message that would help them on their life's journey, to change for the better, what would that message be?

Wimbrey

My message would be that you can not allow your past to determine and dictate your future. You do not have to let your past experiences dictate the rest of your life. Sigmund Freud said that you become a product of your environment, and I do believe that. But I also believe that you're in control of what your environment is. Every single day, every moment of our lives, we are in a character building process. And I believe that you can't stop that process, you cannot stop the process of character building, but you can control what's building your character, where you go, who you hang around with, what you're listening to, the things that you entertain most, that's who you really are. They say you can always judge the size of a man's character by the size of the obstacle that it takes to overcome them. And my message to the world is this; you are in control, by the choices that you make in your every day life. There may be obstacles and enemies around you every single day, but your choices to entertain those obstacles, your choices to participate with your enemies, your choices to participate with the very entities in life that are holding you down, is your choice. And I believe when people really, really understand that they are in complete control of the choices they make, that's when they will begin to win. My message is this, if I can overcome obstacles in my life that held me down, if I can overcome society and all the things they said that were suppose to hold me down, being a ex drug dealer, born in the projects, earliest memory in life, being in a battered women's shelter, having a felony conviction, being multi racial, not suppose to know who I am, I'm suppose to have an identity crisis and according to statistics, according to society, I'm suppose to be put into this box of failures. I'm suppose to be a drug addict, I'm suppose to be in prison, I'm not suppose to be able to have a successful marriage, I'm not suppose to be able to tap into true success. Why, because of where I come from and the things in my life that I participated in, that wasn't so good. My message is this, your past doesn't have to determine your future, you are in control of your life and if I can overcome all the obstacles in my life, you can too. There is an "Inner Winner Within"!!!

Wright

Today we've been talking to Johnny Wimbrey. He's a young dynamic, motivator, known nationally for his record breaking achievements. He trains and encourages thousands of people through seminars, events, through his writings, his inspirational story of overcoming life's adversities, has empowered many, many, people throughout this country and throughout the world. Johnny, thank you so much for being with us today on *Conversations on Success*.

Wimbrey

It has been an honor and a pleasure; let's win big together!

About The Author

Sought after by popular demand by entities all over the world! His message has encouraged thousands across the globe for greatness.

Johnny is the President and CEO of "Wimbrey Training Systems." He has graced the stage with world famous leaders like Les Brown, Jim Rohn, Zig Ziglar, and many others. Johnny has been interviewed on national radio and television networks as a young success story because of his incredible life enhancing messages.

Mr. Wimbrey's best selling book, *From the Hood to Doing Good* is available in every major book store across the globe. From homeless, to street drug dealer, to a success phenomenon; Johnny Wimbrey has transformed his "MESS into a MESSAGE" and now encourages the masses around the world to "NEVER let your past determine your future."

Tap into your "Inner-Winner-Within" with Wimbrey Training Systems!

To request Johnny to speak at your next event, or to order products, please contact us at:

Johnny Wimbrey

Wimbrey Training Systems

Phone: 1.800.505.7851

www.JohnnyWimbrey.com

Chapter Two

JIM ROHN

THE INTERVIEW

David E. Wright (Wright)

It's my sincere pleasure today to welcome Jim Rohn to *Conversations on Success*. Jim has helped motivate and train an entire generation of personal development trainers, as well as hundreds of executives from America's top corporations. He's been described as everything from "master motivator" to a "modern day Will Rodgers," to a legend. Jim has been internationally hailed over the years as one of the most influential thinkers of our time. His professional development seminars have spanned 39 years. He has addressed over 6000 audiences and four million people worldwide. He has authored 17 different books as well as dozens of audio and video programs. There simply are not enough superlatives when introducing Jim Rohn. Jim, thank you for taking time, to visit with us today.

Jim Rohn (Rohn)

Hey, my pleasure.

Wright

Before we dive into some pretty deep subjects, I know our readers would appreciate an update on your current focus. What kinds of projects are occupying your mind and your calendar these days?

Rohn

Well, I'm still involved in world travel—from Asia to South Africa, South America, to Europe, across the United States—which I've been doing for the last 40 years and enjoying it very much. I'm 74 but haven't slowed down!

Wright

I've belonged to a political discussion group called Great Decisions, for the last 15 years. Every year we discuss conditions in Africa and every year we come away with our hands in our pockets, saying we don't know what can be done about it. Is it as bad as we believe?

Rohn

It's a complex continent and who knows what it will finally take. You know, there are some good signs but you're right.

Wright

The problems are just voluminous.

Rohn

I have lectured in all the major cities in South Africa. I've gone there several times over the last 20 years. When I first went they still had Apartheid, now that's all gone. There are some good signs that recovery is under way and I love to see that.

I first lectured in Moscow in Russia, starting about 10 years ago and fortunately that was after the walls came tumbling down. They were changing from communism to capitalism, I've made about five lecture tours in Russia in the last 10 years, teaching capitalism and personal responsibility and entrepreneurship, all of that during the last 10 years. It's exciting to go back and see so many of them doing it. They still have a long ways to go—there's still push and pull between the old ways and the new ways.

Years and years ago when I went to South America, every country had a dictator. Now they're all gone, for the most part. So there are a lot of improvements that have been made around the world but there is still a long ways to go. But I'm hopeful and since my career, of course, takes me around the world, the changes are exciting to watch as different parts of the world go through change for the better.

Wright

Do you appreciate the United States when you come back in?

Rohn

No doubt about it. This is the place where you can start with so little and still—with some good advice and coaching and a bit of training and personal responsibility and a whole lot of courage—you can start with pennies and make your fortune. That's extraordinary.

Wright

I spend a lot of time with professionals from all types of industries and I often give, when I'm asked, career advice. Would you mind looking back over your career and sharing a story or two that demonstrates some relevant success principles? In other words, to what do you attribute your success in life?

Rohn

I met someone when I was 25—his name was Earl Schoff—this is in most of my recordings and writings—and I worked for him for five years. He died at the early age of 49 but during those five years I worked for him, he gave me really a lot of the fundamentals— especially the economic and personal development principles—that really revolutionized my life.

When I met him I had only pennies in my pocket, nothing in the bank and creditors calling once in a while saying, "You told us the check was in the mail." That embarrasses me.

I think what triggered my search to find him was what I call "the Girl Scout story." I was at home alone and heard a knock on my door. I go to the door and there's this Girl Scout selling cookies. She gives me this great presentation—it's the best organization in the world, she goes on and on and she describes the several different flavors available and that the cost is only two dollars and then she politely asked me to buy.

No problem, I wanted to buy—big problem, I didn't have two dollars. I can remember today that embarrassing moment—I'm a grown man and I'm 25 years old, I've been to one year of college, I've got a little family started, I live in America and I don't have two dollars in my pocket.

I didn't want to tell her that, so I lied to her and said, "Hey look, we've already bought lots of Girl Scout cookies, we've still got plenty in the house we haven't eaten yet.

She said, "Oh, that's wonderful! Thank you very much," and she leaves.

When she leaves, I say to myself, "I don't want to live like this anymore. I mean how low you can get, lying to a Girl Scout? That's got to be the bottom, right?

I called it "the day that turns your life around." Everybody can look back at some of those days when you made a unique decision at a particular time and you were never the same again. That was one of those days.

Shortly after that I met this incredible mentor that I went to work for—Earl Schoff—and using the things he taught me, I was a millionaire by the age of 32.

It doesn't take much if you get the right information and put it to work and are willing to accept refinement, keep up your studies, and engage primarily in what we call "personal development"—becoming more valuable. For economics personal development makes you more valuable to the marketplace. Personal development also makes you become more valuable as a father, a mother, a parent, a friend, a business colleague, and as a citizen.

Personal development is the subject I have talked most about during the last 40 years—seeing how valuable you can be to yourself, to your community and to those around you.

I've got a little economic phase I use that says, "We get paid for bringing value to the marketplace." And the first part of that is the value you bring such as a product, but the biggest part of what you bring how valuable you become through personal development. I say, "To climb the ladder of success, work harder on yourself than you do on your job." If you work hard on your job you can make a living, if you work hard on yourself you can make a fortune.

I learned those very fundamental ideas when I was 25. Fortunately I discovered them at 25 rather than at 55—55 is okay and 75 is still okay but gosh, it's good to learn them at the age of 25 when you can really put them to work. These ideas revolutionized my life. And it formed the foundation of what I've shared now all these years in so many forms.

Wright

I've only heard that name Schoff twice. You just mentioned it and when I was in junior high school in seventh and eighth and ninth grades, one of my mentors was a coach named Schoff. He was a real mentor. This guy was just a fine, fine, man.

Rohn

The same man, Earl Schoff, influenced Mary Kay—who started Mary Kay Cosmetics—and me back in 1955-1956. Those were the early, early years and she went on to become a superstar. What he shared with me just transformed my life.

Wright

You're known throughout the world as a personal development expert. In practical terms what does that really mean?

Rohn

Well, there's a phase that says, "Success is not something you pursue, success is something you attract"—by becoming an attractive person. Currently I'm sharing it like this: to really do well—and the opportunity of the 21st century is number one: you need multiple skills. If you've just got one skill, it's too risky economically. For example, a guy has worked for a company for 20 years and the division he works for goes out of business. Now he's lost his job, he tells us he's in financial trouble and the reason is, even after 20 years working, he only had one skill. If he would have taken an accounting two nights a week or something—there's so much available that can double your value to the marketplace.

I started learning these extra skills: finding good people, sales, finding a product I could believe in, and talk about its merits until somebody said Yes, follow up and get referrals. Then I learned to build an organization, and then I learned organization—getting people to work together.

I need to get to learn to get a team and work together. Then I learned recognition—I learned to reward people for small steps of progress.

The biggest skill I learned was communication. I got involved in training, showing people how the job works, and then I got involved in teaching. I taught setting goals, personal development leadership, and communication skills. My theme for that was, "You need both job skills and life skills"—because just learning how to set goals revolutionized my life—it's not usually top on the job, or in school.

Then the ultimate in communication is learning to inspire— helping someone to see himself or herself as better than they are— transport them in to the future, paint the possibilities, and then use your own testimony. Say, "Hey if I can do it, you can do it."

So you're starting with pennies, you're behind, the creditors are calling; but that's not really what's important. What's important is the decision today to start the journey of self-improvement. I think that theme has been paramount in all of my teaching and training during the last 40 years—work harder on yourself than you do on your job.

In leadership, I teach that to attract attractive people, you must be attractive. So it's a constant pursuit of self-development and personal development.

The theme during my career, teaching and training during the past 40 years is: communication, managing your time, managing your money, and learning to inspire.

Wright

You know I have my own opinion about how difficult it is for people to change whether it's in regards to a health issue or dieting for example. Do you believe that people can really change and why is change so difficult?

Rohn

Give easy steps. For example, if you want to change your health and you say, "I've got to do something that will make me healthy. My momma taught that an apple a day was healthy," why not start there?

If you don't start with something simple, you can forget the rest of the complicated stuff. Sometimes it's good to do it with someone else. I've found in all my entrepreneurial business projects during the last 40 years, it's more inspiring to say, "Let's go do it," than to say, "I'm going to go do it." Get together with someone and say, "Let's get healthy, let's exercise, let's go to the gym, let's climb a mountain." The "let's" is what's very powerful. A lot of things are pretty tough to do all by yourself.

Wright

In the past few years there've been some major scandals in corporate America. I know you've counseled many high profiled executives over the years. Is there a leadership crisis in America? What do you think has contributed to this kind of moral failure?

Rohn

No, it's always been such from the beginning of recorded history, when there were just four people on earth. You know there was the great scandal of brother who killed brother (Cain and Abel). So it's not a year 2000 or 2005 phenomenon. It's not a 21st century phenomenon. Even the Old Testament records good kings and bad kings—those who "did right in the sight of the Lord" and those who led the people into idolatry. You know, it's just not unusual.

My best explanation is the great adventure started back according to the Storyteller, God created all these angels and then gave them the dignity of choice, and a third of them decided to go with Lucifer and make a run on Gods throne. They didn't win but it started what I call "the adventure of the Creator and the spoiler." And then I further describe it with the concept that the adventure of our life seems to be opposites are in conflict and we are in the middle. But that's what makes a great adventure.

Illness tries to overcome your health but if you work on your health you can overcome your illness. But if you let up the least little bit, sure enough, illness creeps up and takes away some more of your health.

Liberty and tyranny in the world—for a while there's more tyranny than liberty. Now it's turned around, since the walls came down in Berlin about 14 to15 years ago and now there's more liberty than tyranny.

But whether its politics or whether it's corporations, it doesn't matter, the temptation is always there—the drama is always there. Should we do the right thing or would it be okay to cross the line? I use this illustration sometimes: when I was a little kid I saw this cartoon of a little boy and this little boy had an angel—a little angel—on one shoulder and a little devil on the other shoulder. And both of them were whispering in his ear. And the little devil said, "Go ahead and do it, it will be okay," and the little angels says, "No, no, it *won't* be okay." The little devil says, "Yes, yes, go ahead, it's okay, nobody will know." Little angel says, "No, no, no." That little cartoon appeared back when I was a kid. It describes this concept of opposites in conflict and that's what makes an adventure.

There wouldn't be positive without negative it doesn't seem like. And you couldn't win if you couldn't lose. If you took a football today and walked out to the stadium and we followed you and in the football stadium you took the football and walked across the goal line, would we all cheer and call it a touchdown? And the answer's "No, that's silly." It's not a touchdown until you face the 300-pounders. If you can muscle by them—they want to smash your face in the dirt—and if you can dance by the secondary, on a special day, we call it a touchdown and maybe you win the championship.

That's the deal—opposites are in conflict. We're tempted every day, whether it's the slight little things or whether it's something big and major. You come to the intersection and the light is yellow and it starts to turn red, some little voice may whisper to you, "Go ahead you're late—you can make it." But if you try running that light you may wind up dead. If you say, "No, I'll be more cautious, then you live a little bit longer."

So it's not that we're not involved in this push and pull. It happens at the high echelons of corporate America—little voices whisper in a collective way around the boardroom, and the board members decide to cross the line, they think, "It looks like we can get by with it—we can put it off shore or we can play some games here and we'll be okay," or, "If we want this stock to grow and necessity demands it, we probably skate the line a little bit." That happens in the poorest of homes and it happens in the riches of homes. It happens in the boardroom and it happens on Main Street and it happens in the back alley. So it doesn't really matter where it is—temptation is always there. But that's what makes the adventure—to see if you can handle the temptation—do more right than wrong—have a longer list of virtues than mistakes—then you win.

Wright

I recently read an article you wrote about attitude. In it you said attitude determines how much of the future we're allowed to see. This is a fascinating thing to say. Will you elaborate on this thought?

Rohn

Well, it's attitude about four things:

1. How you feel about the past. Some people carry the past around like a burden. They continually live and dwell on their past mistakes. They live in the past—past failures—and it just drains away all the energy they could apply to something much more positive. We have to have a good healthy attitude about the past. The key on that is just to learn from it. Hey, here's where I messed up, I've got that corrected now, and I'm going to make the changes for the future. We call that "drawing on the past" as a good school of experience to make corrections in errors in judgment or whatever that puts you in a bad place.

2. Then the other attitude is how you feel about the future. We need to look back for experience but we need to look ahead for inspiration—to be inspired by the goals we set for ourselves and for our family, the goals we've set for friendship, lifestyle, becoming wealthy, powerful, and influential, and as a unique citizen—those goals that that get us up early and keep us up late, fire up the fuel of our imagination, and how can we accomplish them.

3. Another attitude is how you feel about everybody, because you can't succeed by yourself. It takes everybody for each of us to be successful. Each of us needs all of us. One person doesn't make an economy; one person doesn't make a symphony orchestra. So you have to have that unique sense of the value of everybody and that it really does take everybody for any one person to be successful.

4. Then the last attitude that's the most important is how you feel about yourself. At the end of the day evaluate yourself—"I pushed it to the limit, I did everything I could, I made every call, I stretched as far as I could—and then you lie down and sleep a good sleep. Solomon wrote, "The sleep of the laboring man is sweet..." (Ecclesiastes 5:12). This is describing somebody who puts in the work—who works hard either with his hands or with his mind or with his ability to communicate, whatever it is—so at the end of the day he feels good about himself. Nothing is more powerful than high self-esteem. It builds self-confidence, which builds success.

Those five attitudes really do give you a promising look at the future. But if you're always being pulled back by the past or distracted because you find it difficult to manage your life with people you have to associate with, that's tough. And the better we can handle that, and realize the law of averages says I'm going to be around some good people and some bad people, I'm going to be around some ambitious people and some not so ambitious. I've got to learn to take that in stride.

Then knowing that you're on track for better health, you're on track for becoming financially independent. You haven't quite got it solved but you're on track for the management of your time and your money. And your attitude toward that really creates high inspiration that the future's going to multiply several times better than the past.

Wright

I don't normally like to frame a question in the negative but I thought it would be interesting to get your prospective on mistakes that people make in life and in business. If you had to name the top three on a list of mistakes that people make that kept them form succeeding or living a fulfilled life, what would they be?

Rohn

Well, number one mistake economically is not to understand that people can make you wealthy. And all you have to do is just figure out how to do that. For example: Johnny mows Mrs. Brown's lawn and she pays five dollars. One day it occurs to him, "If I get my friend Paul to mow this lawn, Mrs. Brown would pay five dollars, I would give Paul four dollars and keep one for myself because I got the job." Now, instantly he has now moved to that higher level of economics that says this is how you become wealthy.

A little phrase that philosophically and economically changed my life is: "Profits are better than wages." Wages make you a living but profits make you a fortune. You don't have to be General Motors, you don't have to be high in the industrial complex society to understand this concept, that's why it's so powerful to teach capitalism, how to buy and sell and how to sell and buy.

I've got so many stories of people who I've helped in my seminars who started with pennies and now they're rich. That's the key—learning how to employ other people. First do it yourself—learn how to do it yourself—then find a need someone has and get someone else to render the service, and then someone else and then someone else. Teach them the same and the principles of economics and capitalism and how to go from pennies to fortune are so simple.

When I taught it to the Russians they couldn't believe how simple it was. I said, "Capital is any value you set aside to be invested in a enterprise that brings value to the market place hoping to make a profit"—that's capitalism. They couldn't believe I could put it in one sentence.

Wright

I can't either.

Rohn

Any value you set aside to be invested in an enterprise whether it's, I teach kids how to have two bicycles, one to ride and one to rent. It doesn't take long to make a profit, if you're halfway bright, if you get just a little advice to give you a chance to start.

I see capitalism in two parts—one is capital time, the other is capital money. If you wisely learn to invest capital money you can make a fortune. And then together with that if you can learn to invest capital time. You set aside time to be invested in an enterprise. I started that part-time when I was 25 years old, all those years ago in 1955. I took about 15 to 20 hours a week part-time and invested it in a capital enterprise and by the time I was 32 I was a millionaire. It didn't take much money because I only invested $200, which I borrowed. That was my capital money, but the other was my capital time and once I learned how to invest both and then learn how to teach and train and inspire other people to do the same it totally changed my life.

I don't have to worry about social security; I developed my own social security. It's interesting that they're not teaching that today when Social Security is the main topic. We've got to let our young people put aside some of that withholding and put it in a personal account. How about teaching them how to be financially independent. Who's doing that? John Kennedy said," Don't ask what your country can do for you." Don't ask what Social Security can do for you—that is so small and so little in the long run. Why not ask what can I do for my country? Could I mow Mrs. Brown's lawn and collect five dollars and do it part-time? Then could I get someone else to do it and then someone else to do another job and finally work my way from the pennies in my pocket to the fortune that I could have because this is America—the land of opportunity.

It's startling how simple it is in concept and how really easy it is in practice; but the results can be phenomenal. I got such great early results that I never did look back, from age 25 until today.

Wright

We've got time for one more question.

Rohn

For me it's fun to teach it. Because I've been teaching it now for all these years and I've got some testimonials where I helped people start, just like I started with pennies and now they're rich. It's just exciting. One of the great exciting experiences is to have your name appear in somebody's testimonial—"Here's the person who found me, here's the person who taught me, here's the person who wouldn't let me quit, gave me more reasons for staying than for leaving. Here's the person that believed in me until I could believe in myself," then they mention your name. I call that big time, and you can't buy it with money. You have to simply earn it by sharing ideas with somebody that makes a difference in their life. And I love to do it.

Wright

This is the definition of great mentors.

Rohn

Yea, I love to be that. Hopefully my books and tapes and my personal appearances have done that during the last 40 years.

Wright

I'd like to go back to the issue of personal development and change. Considering the issues most Americans face in this modern era with all of our technology, where would you advise most people to focus their energy if they could only change one thing about themselves?

Rohn

The current advice I'm giving is start figuring out to how to learn another skill, and then another skill, then it would be good to learn another language. People who know more than one language now are getting some good pay. Some of my business colleagues who speak three or four languages make three or four million a year. Not that that's a guarantee but that's just an idea for self-improvement. Learn something beyond what you now know because that could be something that you can cash in on, maybe sooner than you think.

Wright

Not to mention the fact that you're talking for the first time to another whole culture and look what you could learn. I've always been fascinated by the Chinese culture.

Rohn

Then develop wise use of your time and then wise use of your money. I teach kids to not spend more than 70 cents out of every dollar—10 cents for charity or church, 10 cents for active capital (i.e., two bicycles, one to ride and one to rent), then passive capital 10 percent, let someone else use it (you provide the capital that will pay you dividends, increase in stock or whatever), I call it "seventy-ten-ten and ten." Then I teach not to buy the second car until you've bought the second house. Cars won't make you rich but houses will make you rich. I love to teach that.

A lady called me from Mexico not long ago and said, "Mr. Rohn, and I'm now shopping for third car because I just finished paying for my third house." She started listening to my training ten years ago. She not only uses it, she teaches it. Down in Mexico she makes about $40,000 a month, which down there is just staggering.

But it's fun—it's been fun for me over the years to have stories like that. My own story I use as an inspiration not only for myself but also for the people that listen to my lectures. And then it's fun to watch people actually grab a hold of something and turn it into success.

Wright

Jim, it's been a sincere joy having this enlightening conversation with you today. I really appreciate and thank you so much again for taking the time to be with us on *Conversations on Success*.

Rohn

I appreciate it, thank you for calling; I'm in Beverly Hills, California enjoying the California sunshine. It's a beautiful day to have a great conversation. Thanks a million.

Wright

Thank you so much.

About The Author

Jim Rohn is a philosopher, motivational counselor, business executive, and best-selling author. He has been recognized as the greatest motivational speaker of all time. He is one of the world's most sought-after success counselors and business philosophers with some of his most thought provoking topics being: sales and entrepreneurial skills, leadership, sales and marketing, success and personal development.

Jim Rohn's conducted seminars for over 39 years and addressed over 6,000 audiences and 4 million people worldwide. He is a recipient of the 1985 National Speakers Association CPAE Award. He's authored over 17 different books, audio, and video programs. Rohn's been internationally hailed over the years as on of the most influential thinkers of our time.

Revealing contemporary success secrets in a way that is both accessible and practical, Jim ignites enthusiasm and a can-do attitude in all who hear him speak. He approaches the subjects of personal and professional success by asking four questions: Why? Why not? Why not you? Why not now? He answers these questions and reveals practical, perceptive secrets for success and productivity. His special style laced with witticisms and anecdotes captivates listeners. Among his most thought-provoking topics are: sales and entrepreneurial skills, leadership, sales and marketing, success and personal development.

Jim Rohn

www.jimrohn.com

Chapter Three

BARRY DONALSON

THE INTERVIEW

David E. Wright (Wright)

Today we're talking to Barry Donalson, an internationally recognized trainer, speaker, mentor, and author in the direct sales and professional networking industry. Few people have impacted the industry of direct sales and professional networking as Barry Donalson. Barry built a direct sales organization of over 150,000 representatives that produce over $50 million in sales for the company of his affiliation. In addition to having the largest organization in the company, Barry also has been featured in issues of *Upline Magazine, Networking Marketing Lifestyles, Money Makers Monthly, Networking Times, Work at Home Solutions* and several business related periodicals. He is the author of over fifteen audio training programs and is sought after to train and to speak worldwide. Barry's international acclaimed monthly audio training program entitled, *The Win Series,* is sold worldwide to sales professionals seeking a direct and proven approach to developing systems for immediate results. Barry is a nationally recognized trainer, speaker, author and mentor for high achieving direct sales professionals. He has conducted over 2000 high energy speeches and sales seminars throughout the United States and abroad, in which he has trained tens of thousands of representatives in the areas of prospecting, business development, leadership, strategic planning, professional and personal development in all levels of marketing. Barry, welcome to *Conversations on Success*.

Barry Donalson (Donalson)

Thank you David, how are you?

Wright

I'm doing great. Every time I talk to someone about success and ask them to define it for me, I get a different definition. I'm going to ask you the same question, what does success mean to you?

Donalson

Well, I tell you David, I'm sure success means different things to different people. I have a definition of success for me and I think that it really hones in on what I feel success has done for me. I think success is a person who lives well, laughs often, enjoys life, who has gained the respect from their children, who leaves the world a better place than they found it, one who's never lacks an appreciation for what they do, who never fails to look for the best in others, and also gives the best of themselves. I feel that's what success is.

Wright

So, unlike many other people that I talk to, you take a global look at success, don't you?

Donalson

Yes. I think success is so many different things to so many different people, but I can only describe what it is for me.

Wright

Are there any secrets to success?

Donalson

I personally don't think there are any secret to success. I believe that success means so many different things to so many different people. I think that for some people success is money. For some people success is time. For some people it's money and time. For me, David, success is choices. I like to have choices, having extra money does help to have choices, but I like the fact that I can do what I want, when I want. That's why I've worked so hard to achieve the success I've been able to achieve. My mother used to tell me as a kid that I never liked people telling me what to do. Well, that's probably true today; I like the fact that I can get up when I want to and do what I want to. I like do the things that I enjoy doing, like this book, speaking across the country, and events in different parts of the world.

Wright

How important do you think goal setting is in becoming successful?

Donalson

Well, here's something, David, I found out the hard way. I found that setting goals wasn't a necessary thing that you have to do to become successful or do whatever it is you're trying to do. I read a book and it really helped me out a lot. I stopped setting goals and I started choosing a result. So now I don't have goal setting workshops, I have result oriented workshops. If people say they are going to do something, they should set a natural game plan to make it happen to get that particular result. If you want a new car, then get the new car. I had a goal sheet a mile long, and I didn't even accomplish half of them. But when I started choosing a result, I started seeing exactly what I put on that sheet and I started taking the steps to make it actually happen. So I started teaching people to choose a result and stop setting goals. That works for me.

Wright

What do you think are the biggest obstacles that people face when they decide to pursue their dreams?

Donalson

There are several things that are definitely going to happen to you when you're on to something great. The first thing that starts to happen is something I call circumstances. Circumstances start coming into play, such as negativity, job situations or a financial setback. All of these are circumstances that can plague your success. You know when you are on to something great when more circumstances get in your way. What you have to do is understand how to overcome each circumstance, and each circumstance differs.

If you can understand how to overcome those circumstances, and you've decided that you're going to pursue this result no matter what, then you'll start getting past them.

Wright

Do you believe that negativity plays a role in any of this?

Donalson

Absolutely. What I've found was that when I started telling people that I was going to do something, they began to tell me how I couldn't. If I told people I was going to build a business, they'll start giving me negative information about how businesses fail; no positive reinforcement. The funny part about it was, it was coming from the people that I loved and cared about the most. This bothered me so much that I created an audio series about negativity. Even when I told a few of my mentors that I was going to create this CD, I was told by them that it would not sell, because it was negative. I did it anyway and it's entitled, *Caution! "The Negative Signs to Look For."* I created this CD series because a lot of people don't expect to get negativity from the people that they love the most. A lot of times that's where a lot of the negativity comes from, the people that your closest to. I have sold thousands of these CD's, David, I can't keep them in stock! People buy them from all walks of life, and even in different countries. This CD series has helped so many people overcome negativity from others in regards to their success. I am glad I did it!

Wright

Most people that I talk to have had humble beginnings. What was yours like?

Donalson

If you can imagine this, David, I grew up in a household with very little means. My grandmother raised me and she was a maid. She made about sixty-five dollars a week, and that's all she ever made. She cleaned a local plumber's house in the small town I grew up in. I know what it's like to go to the grocery store and ask my grandmother, why does our money have different colors. I'm originally from Arkansas, and we use to stand in a hot line to get free cheese that didn't melt. I was brought up in very humble beginnings. I had a pair of jeans I wore throughout the winter, maybe two pairs I wore throughout the winter, and a couple pairs of shoes. We got a lot of our stuff on credit, or on time, that's what they called it back then.

To go from that to driving a Mercedes and a Lexus, to living in multiple homes, traveling to the best vacation destinations all over the world, it has been an incredible journey for me. When I tell people what I have done, and who I have met in my life, they still don't believe me. I have to show them pictures for them to believe me. You have to see where I came from to know what I mean. Sometimes, I can't believe it myself. I'd never forget my humble beginnings because my grandmother kept me grounded on all the different things I talked about pursuing. She made sure that I was in Little League, and I was in karate, and I was in those things with very little money. Somehow she made it work until I got through college. Man, what a incredible lady she was!

Wright

Do you remember the defining moment that inspired you to go out on your own, and who supported you the most?

Donalson

That's an interesting question. I do, and as funny as it may sound, it was a situation at my job that motivated me the most. I remember back, it was 1996, and I was working for a gentlemen in the company that I worked for, He and I didn't get along very well because I felt really underemployed and under-appreciated. I was in sales. I worked hard and out produced everybody in our division of the company. This guy made my life miserable that year. He was micro managing me to the point where it became unbearable. It was almost like a harassment situation. I remember, I did not have one choice in my life then. I had to work, I had to pay bills and my businesses were not successful at the time. I remember sitting in my car one afternoon at lunch, and I was literally at tears wondering why it was that I'd allowed myself to be treated this way. I decided that particular moment that was it. I call it threshold. I decided that I was no longer going to be a slave to the corporate environment. I was no longer going to allow anyone to dictate my future. I was no longer going to sit there and take that from anyone. I started pursuing my life then. That day is when I started, I mean I can tell you, David, I got my hands on everything I could get my hands. That's one of the reasons I fell into the industry of professional networking. I saw an industry that I could get in with this desire that I had, not a whole lot of money, because I didn't have a whole lot of money, and with hard work and dedication I could be successful. Within one year of that date, I walked away from that job. I have not had a job since I was 28 years old. I am celebrating my 38th birthday this year, so almost 10 years ago. I had to hit that point, I guess. I work hard to never be put in a situation where I'll allow someone to belittle me or tell me what my worth is. I have a friend name Chadd. Chadd is my best friend, I'm the godfather of his son, and Chadd has been an inspiration in my life. He's been the guy that no matter what I said I was going to pursue, he's always said to me Barry you can do it.

Even to this day when I come up with different ideas of businesses—I just came up with a business today that will make me a hundred thousand within months—I'll say, "Chadd, I got this idea. What do you think?" And he always says, "That sounds like a phenomenal idea and if anybody can do it you can do it." He also tells me if I should think about it more, but the point is he is never negative. I cherish our friendship and he's been an inspiration to me. He was actually working for the company that I worked for, and he ended up selling everything, leaving the company and going to law school. He's now a practicing district attorney, well actually an assistant judge in Florida. When he did that it made me feel as if I could do whatever I wanted to pursue. He's told me, "Barry, you've always been the guy who has done what he said he was going to do. I admire that in you." He's been a great inspiration for me, my really close friend, Chadd.

Wright

It seems that you went through a process to become successful. Could you tell our readers a little bit about the journey?

Donalson

Yes. The process failed several different times before I found out exactly what I was put on earth to do. The journey started very humble. I started out taking very small steps as I went to pursue my businesses. I remember when I was getting started, I wasn't making very much money, but I can remember thinking about what the end result would be. I can remember thinking about the amount of money I wanted in the bank. I can remember thinking about the car I wanted drive and the type of house I wanted to live in. Finally, I was able to take the car off my refrigerator and put it in my driveway based on a solid amount of vision inspired focus that I pursued on this journey.

You know what it's all about? It's about having to start at humble beginnings, going through the ups and downs, the obstacles. I went through them all. I still have obstacles, but what I've come to realize is, that's part of it. I understand some people will embrace your success and some people won't. People will even try to sabotage it, and that's part of it. I know in my subconscious mind that I can get through it because I will do the very best I can. This continues to shorten my curve to success.

Wright

Could you explain a little bit about *"The Win Series?"*

Donalson

Sure David, *The Win Series,* is a copulation of CD's that I recorded for the professional direct sales industry. How *The Win Series* came about was, I felt there was a need out there in the direct sales industry to understand exactly what it was going to take to create income. Now, *The Win Series* is not motivational. *The Win Series* is techniques and strategies that will work. So each month, each CD walks you through a process that's going to help you get closer to what you're trying to pursue in the direct sales industry. I know that there's a need out there because a lot of the CD's I was listening to were great, they were wonderful information, and it was motivational. No one really taught me how to go into a new city and build a business without knowing anyone. No one taught me the difference of understanding what it was going to take to keep me working and what would allow me to leverage my efforts. I teach people these techniques in *The Win Series. The Win Series* is a year's worth of training. I come to a person's home via audio training once a month to give them another technique to master. The reason I titled it *The Win Series* is because, each month you get a CD to listen to over and over and over and over again until you win, until you win on that topic. By the time you do all twelve topics you should be in the position to make at least a six figure income in the industry.

Wright

Is there a philosophy behind it?

Donalson

The philosophy is that you can win if you know the rules. You can win this game of business if you know the rules. The game has changed and so have the rules. You see, doing business in 1968 or 1975 is different than doing business in 2004. There's different technology, there are different ways we think. We are a much faster economy now, a global economy. The philosophy behind **The Win Series** is for you to find out what you need to do today, to make money. Not what happened twenty years ago, which was great information, and motivational, but what you need to do today. That's the philosophy behind *The Win Series.*

Wright

What are some of the most important attributes to having a successful business?

Donalson

Well, being a trainer and producing training materials today, there are several different things that I think are critical in having a successful business. I would say one is to produce a high quality product that people want. Produce products that people can use, and they want more of. I think this is so important in your strategy in building a successful business. Also, I think it's important for you to serve your customer, to understand that your business has to be customer driven. Whether you're in the service business or hospitality business, or product business, you still have to deal with people and people are your customers. Also, you have to value the people that you're working with. You have to recognize the good associates and the team you surround yourself with. This is so important in the success of your business. It's so important to practice teamwork with your associates.

Another attribute is you have to be able and easily adapt to change. Business is always changing, something's always going to be moving and shaking. If you're willing to move and shake with the environment to make it work for you, you will be absolutely ok. You've got to also continue to learn, and teach the correct principles of business. I'm always a sponge, looking for more information. I'm hoping that people that read this information can get something out of what I'm telling you in this interview. Consistent learning is the key. I think you can be only as successful as your extent of learning. The more you learn, the more successful you are going to be. If you stop personal development and professional development, you're going to stop in your income growth. You've got to continue that process of on going educational learning to make you successful. I think that's important.

Wright

If you had one minute to give someone a single piece of advice on becoming successful in life, and in business for that matter, what would that piece of information be?

Donalson

One minute? Ha, David,

Wright

We're in a one minute society, you know!

Donalson

We are, everything's fast and in a hurry. Isn't that right?

Wright

That's a shame; I miss some of the old days.

Donalson

Absolutely. I would say this. I would break it up into two parts, David. I would take life and I would take business, but both of them would have the same common denominator, and that common denominator is the right partnership. I think that in life, if you don't have the right life partner in your life; your life is going to be miserable. A lot of people get the wrong life partner. And what happens is that they find themselves in a struggle, chaos, and in conflict all the time. It's tough if you and that life partner are not on the same page in trying to pursue excellence. That's one part of the equation. The other part is the business partners that you associate yourself with. If you don't get the right partners that have the same work ethnic as you, they will steal from you, and they will take from you. The hardest thing to do is find the right people that understand your proposed results and your dreams of what you're setting for the company and organization. It is hard to find people to want to buy into that, to have the same tenacity, honesty and work ethic to build it with you. However, we can't do everything by ourselves, as much as we want to as business owners, right, David? So if I had one minute, a bit of single advice, to anyone reading this chapter that would be get the right life partner and the right business partner to be successful. And if you're lucky it will be both.

Wright

Let me ask you one final question. Down through the years as you have made your decisions in your business and your personal life, and knowing now that you are successful, did faith have anything to do with your decision making process?

Donalson

Yes, absolutely. A lot of my vision and a lot of the things I've done, have been because I stepped out on faith, because I didn't have anything to measure it by. I had to go out and believe in what I was doing, it was based on faith and that's not knowing, but believing that it was actually is going to happen.

I can give you an example, I said to myself about a year ago, that I was going to be published in a book or write a book. As you know, David, today we're sitting here having this phone interview for this book. I had no idea how it was going to happen and I even put it on my result-oriented goal setting sheet. I was even going to be working on my second book within the same year my first book was published. I did not have a publisher, content, nor contacts in the publishing industry. I had nothing. I was speaking at a seminar and when I got through training at the seminar, a guy walked up to be and said,"Hey, would you like to be in a book?" That was faith and belief that I spoke to existence. I had an opportunity to meet your staff and one of your staff members said, "Hey, once you finish this book would you like to do another one with us." Isn't that faith?

Wright

That is. And we're glad that you did by the way.

Donalson

And I'm glad I did, too. I'm responsible for five other authors being in this book.

Wright

That's great. One thing about success is it just spreads in other people's lives.

Donalson

It does and when you collaborate with the right people, everyone can win. Everyone can win; everyone has attributes that they can contribute to the whole entire project and we all win, even the readers.

Wright

Barry, it's always a pleasure to talk to you. I always learn a lot and I'm always energized by your conversations. I am sure people listening to this or reading this chapter will feel that same thing. I do appreciate you taking all this time to talk to me today.

Donalson

Thank you, David, I'm looking forward to more projects with your company. I'm looking for the collaboration to last a lifetime.

Wright

Today we've been talking to Barry L. Donalson. He is a nationally recognized trainer, speaker, author and mentor for high achieving direct sales professionals. He has conducted over 2000 high energy speeches and sales seminars throughout the United States and abroad and he trains tens of thousands of representatives in the areas of, prospecting, business development, leadership, strategic planning, professional and personal development in all levels of marketing. We have found out this afternoon that he knows what he is talking about. Thank you so much, Barry, for being with us today on *Conversations on Success*.

Donalson

Thank you, David.

About The Author

Few people have impacted the industry of Direct Sales, and Professional Networking as Barry Donalson. After a broad experience in Marketing, Accounting, Finance and training for one of the largest automobile companies in world, he began and launched a successful direct marketing company, focusing on the sales of information material.

Barry turned his attention to Network distribution. Within five months of joining his last company, the company became the first in US history to obtain $1Million/month in sales within it's first year, in which Barry's organization produced over $600,000/month of that record's sales volume.

Prior to starting MMG, Barry owned and operated DIH Communications Group, in which he managed and grew his personal sales organization of over 150,0000 representatives reaching from California to New York, from the mountains of Portland Oregon to the beaches of Virginia, as well as Canada and Puerto Rico. DIH has produced over $50Million in sales for the company of its affiliation. In addition to having the largest organization in the company, Barry also has been featured in issues of *Upline Magazine*, *Networking Lifestyles*, *Money Makers Monthly*, *Networking Times*, *Work at Home Solutions*, *Home- Business Connections* and several business related periodicals

Barry L. Donalson is currently a nationally recognized trainer; speaker, author, columnist and mentor for high achieving direct sales professionals. He is the author of over 15 audio training programs and is sought after to train and speak worldwide. Barry's international acclaimed monthly audio training program entitled, **THE WIN SERIES**, is sold world-wide to direct sales professionals seeking a direct and proven approach to developing systems for immediate results. He has conducted over 2000 high energy speeches and sales seminars through out the US and abroad in which he trains ten of thousands of representatives in the areas of prospecting, business development, leadership, strategic planning, professional & personal development, in all areas of marketing.

To book Barry Donalson for next event....

Barry L. Donalson, President

Momentum Marketing Group, {MMG}

7115 W. North Ave. Ste. 264

Oak Park, IL 60302

Phone: 708-366-5214

Fax: 708-366-5313

Email: barryd@bdonalson.com

www.bdonalson.com

Chapter Four

TODD FALCONE

THE INTERVIEW

David E. Wright (Wright)

Today we are talking with Todd Falcone. He began his sales career as an account executive in the broadcast industry. For the past 14 years he has worked as a successful network marketing professional, building sales organizations numbering in the thousands. He attributes his overall success to sheer commitment, consistent work habits, and a focus on personal development.

Todd has found that although prospecting is the key component to successful selling, many struggle with it. Having a passion for teaching and wanting to share the principles that have helped to create abundance in his own life, he began sharing his strategies for success with others. Todd is now a trainer, personal coach, and public speaker to network marketing and direct sales professionals worldwide. Todd, welcome to *Conversations on Success*.

Todd Falcone (Falcone)

David, I'm happy to be here with you today.

Wright

You began your career in direct sales and for the past several years have worked as a successful networking marketing professional. Can you explain the process you went through to achieve success in these ventures? Was it easy for you from the beginning?

Falcone

It's been an ongoing process. In fact, it is still going on! No matter what occupation an individual decides to pursue, there is a process of going from being average to being exceptional.

From the beginning I wanted to make it, wanted to be successful. I always liked the idea of performance-based careers. Working in an industry where I could be in control of my own destiny versus working in a salary-based environment was appealing. When choosing between the two the performance-based career spoke to me.

In the beginning it wasn't easy; I was not remotely close to being an overnight success in either my direct sales or network marketing business. Like everyone else, I went through a process. David, I think the process for me began with dedication and focus. I made a commitment.

If you think about it, commitment is a pretty big word. You've got to truly focus on your objective and pledge to see it through to completion. Too often I see individuals get involved in an enterprise, or jump into an opportunity, business venture, or sales job and really not make the commitment to seeing it through. They adopt the "I'll just give it a shot" kind of attitude. Personally, I was never the "I'll just give it a shot" kind of guy. When I made the decision to pursue a career in the direct sales and network marketing industries, respectively, I focused on my commitment. I was going to make it happen. It wasn't easy the first week, the first month, or even the first year, but I was focused. Dedication and focus was first and foremost.

Secondly, I had a desire to learn from other people. If I hadn't done something before and knew somebody that had, I emulated that individual. I just simply started following other successful people. That is a philosophy I've lived by for many years; find somebody who has what you want and simply do what they do.

For example, if you want to learn how to become a master billionaire in the software business, who are you going to strive to be like? Are you going to emulate Bill Gates or are you going to copy the guy who collects your trash every Thursday morning? You're going to emulate Bill Gates; it's a pretty simple philosophy. And, that's a philosophy that I've stuck with and has served me well over the last decade.

Wright

Many years ago a sales trainer told me one of the most intelligent statements I have ever heard in my life. He said, and you reminded me of it when you were talking about commitment, "that 98 percent of all failure comes from quitting."

Falcone

That is so true. It really doesn't matter if it's traditional selling or a network marketing sales model, most people quit. It's a sad fact because 98 percent of the people that don't make it have the skills or, at least, the innate ability to figure out how to do it. They just give up. The reason they quit is that we live in a society with a microwave mentality. We have fast food, we have microwaves, we have digital cameras; everybody wants it NOW. And unfortunately, a performance-based profession like a traditional sales or marketing occupation takes some time to develop. It doesn't happen overnight. People need to be a little bit more patient and allow success to happen over time because it doesn't happen immediately.

Wright

Do you find that you need to continually evolve? How do you nurture your professional growth?

Falcone

David, there's no question that you need to continually evolve. Obviously, if you look around things are always changing and we need to always be growing. We need to embrace change and not be resistant to it. In a prior occupation, when I was working in corporate America for a brief period of time, there were some pretty monumental conversions that were taking place. The company which had been a small family-run operation for many years was going to transform into a very large corporate-owned operation. The employees were very resistant to the dramatic modifications that were inevitable by this transition. Several of those people became statistics and ended up having to leave or go find another job just because they couldn't deal with the changes. For me, it was something I embraced.

Change happens every day, every moment, every second; things are always changing. As entrepreneurs we have to be visionaries. Anybody in a performance-based occupation, whether it's traditional sales or network marketing, has to be willing to embrace change. What I do is consistently strive to keep an open mind and accept the fact that things do change. I look for the opportunity and identify the positives rather the negatives; continually being an optimist versus a pessimist.

To nurture and continue personal growth, I collect new books and audio series, and attend seminars. I invest in myself. I haven't counted, but over the years I've probably paid out hundreds of thousands of dollars in my personal development. I have an ever-growing library. I love to go to the book store and buy books. I take my infant son, throw him in a little Baby Bjorn and run around the store checking out books, usually buying four or five. I might do that a few times a month. And while I may not absorb every single word of every book as soon as I get home, I'm constantly picking them up, reading, and scanning through chapters to obtain new information, new ideas, and new concepts so that I can implement them into my business.

As a very good friend of mine says "when you're green you grow and when you're ripe you rot." To be successful you need to stay green and have a willingness to learn. I've got to tell you that I've seen people who are extremely successful, think they know it all, and the next thing you know they're getting eaten up by someone else who knows more than them. Why does one thrive? Because the individual willing to stay green and learn doesn't fall into the trap of believing that he or she knows everything about success. You always have to be growing.

Wright

Is there anything in particular that you can point out that led you to success?

Falcone

There were several factors that led me to success. Like I mentioned earlier, I make sure that I remain humble and have an openness to learn and grow. I love to learn from other people. As we start experiencing a little bit of success, our ego starts to take over.

I'm a humble guy. I may have had some great success in my life, thus far, but I know it can be snapped away in an instant. Things change, as we just talked about. So living a life of humility, always having the willingness to learn, and referring to experts and people that know more than you do or that are more successful will lead you to greater success in your business. It's really a commitment to personal development.

The other factor that has led me to success is to refuse to give up. Don't quit. Go at it, work hard, write down goals, stay focused on those goals, and then pursue those goals. Develop a game plan. My game plan has always been having a consistent work ethic, setting specific goals to achieve the things that I want, and looking for resources that will help me get from where I am to my required destination.

Wright

That is an interesting way to put it...required destination! It seems that you don't leave yourself any room for failure.

Falcone

Not at all David...there's simply no room for failure in my life.

Wright

You're known as an expert in the area of prospecting. Why do you think it is that so many people have such a difficult time with the overall sales process in either traditional selling or network marketing?

Falcone

We all know that the majority of people that try performance-based professions like sales, network marketing, and commission-based occupations seem to fail. Let's look beyond the reasons we discussed just a few minutes ago. Obviously, people fail because they quit. So, let's look at why people fail when they're willing to commit.

First of all, many people don't make it simply because of fear. It could be fear of failure, fear of success, fear of commitment, fear of rejection, or fear of the unknown. There are a lot of factors that paralyze people; that stop them in their tracks and prevent them from moving forward. If someone can get beyond the fear, and anyone can, they will find success. Fear is both real and imaginary. It exists but doesn't exist. We create fear in our own minds. And, we can decide to make it go away whenever we want.

I certainly had a significant level of fear during the early days of building my business. Fortunately, I didn't have fear to the point of paralysis. But, I did have fear to the point of being extremely nervous and scared about everything I did and what was going to happen as a result of my actions. I would get so afraid of making phone calls or making cold calls that my mouth would dry up, my heart would pound, I would sweat, and my palms would get clammy. I was very nervous in the beginning. Over time I learned that the nervousness I had experienced was primarily self-induced. I discovered that all of the different little things that I was afraid of were really nothing to fear.

I'm a firm believer that selling is a learned ability. It's not something that you're born with. You've heard the saying, "that individual is a born salesperson." To this date, I've never meet anybody who's come out of their mother's womb as a professional salesperson, making a six-figure salary or six figures working in a home-based business. It's something that is learned.

The crucial areas of the sales or prospecting process where people tend to lose it are in their ability to establish a connection with their prospect and in their inability to ask for the business. Learning how to effectively build rapport and establish a relationship is critically important. It doesn't matter what you're selling, people in any area are not going to buy from you unless they feel good about you and trust you. They don't have to like you. We're not necessarily in the business of making friends. But they've got to feel good about the situation. In any business relationship you have to learn how to effectively connect with a human being. They're not going to give you their money; they're not going to do business with you unless you connect with them and build up that rapport. Many people have the inability to do that or lack the simple discipline it takes to learn how to do it. Not that they can't do it, they certainly can and have the ability to learn how to do it, but a lot of people just get in and go through the motions. They don't really take the time to learn how to connect.

Learning how to close is the other prime area where people fall short. If you've interviewed other sales people, you know that most of them have a difficult time closing. Why is that? Is it because they're just simply not asking for the business? There are a lot of things that go on psychologically when it comes to asking for money. I've trained many sales people who could get the meeting scheduled, sit down with the decision maker, give an incredible presentation, and convince the buyer she's ready to buy, yet they never <u>ask</u> for the business. And, if you don't ask, you don't get. As it says in the Bible "ask and ye shall receive."

In summary, the primary areas I believe people have a difficult time mastering in the overall sales process are, first and foremost, the inability to connect, and beyond connecting, just being able to close the business.

Wright

It will take me the rest of the day to get rid of the mental image you gave me; I picture myself in the birthing room and out pops a little baby with a pinstriped suit and briefcase. Thanks a lot! Is there a specific approach that can assist people in getting better results?

Falcone

When it comes to prospecting, I do believe there is a specific approach to getting better results. In fact, I created a training series around what I call the Five Critical Elements that lead to understanding prospecting. These five elements provide individuals with a guideline that enables them to transform themselves from persons who don't produce results to persons that produce very consistent results. It doesn't necessarily mean they're going to be the top performer, but at least they'll be able to produce consistent results.

Some people never want to be number one while others always have to be number one. We have great salespeople at all levels that are producing. The bottom line is that you've got to produce. What I have found by studying top athletes and top performing people in traditional sales and network marketing is that what separated these folks from people that weren't able to perform were basically five elements. I also looked at myself and reflected on the past decade or so, and thought about what I have done to get good at prospecting because when I started I wasn't very good. I didn't produce results. I spent 18 months in my first business venture closing virtually nothing and with very little to show for it. Over time, by studying other successful people, doing things in the field, and really looking around I discovered there are five critical elements to prospecting. I'll now share those five elements with you.

The first critical element is called prep time. Prep time primarily involves the mental side of the picture. It involves making sure that your attitude is in check by asking yourself the following questions. How are you approaching your business? Are you approaching your business with a level of enthusiasm and a level of conviction? Do you believe in what you're doing? Do you believe in the company, the product, service, or element that you're bringing to the marketplace? Where is your head? Where is your attitude in relation to your opportunity or your business? Are you really committed to it? Have you made the firm decision that you're really going to do it?

It all begins with the six inches between your ears. It doesn't mean you can't do business in the prep phase. You can actually be in action conducting whatever it is you're involved with while you're in this phase. But, just make sure that you're going through an attitude check. Am I in the right zone? Am I enthusiastic, excited, and feeling good about what I'm doing? If you want to attract people and business, you're not going to attract either by having your head in the wrong place. People want to do business with good people that are fun to be around. You know what I'm talking about David. So, the number one element is prep time.

The second critical element is practice. Tiger Woods, for example, is without a doubt one of the greatest golfers that's ever lived. Does he not have to practice because he's naturally so good? Vijay Singh is one of the winningest golfers on the PGA. Vijay hits more golf balls than probably any other player. I think I read in *Golf Magazine* that he hits something like 25,000 golf balls a year. The calculation ends up being about 500 a day. Can you imagine hitting 500 golf balls a day? In addition, he plays every weekend.

Vijay and Tiger are consistently ranked at the top of their game. Why? They practice. So, if you've got these top two athletes that are constantly practicing to perfect their game, shouldn't we as home-based business professionals or sales people practice our routine to reach the top of our game?

What do we practice? We practice our opening call prior to attempting to get an appointment if we're in traditional sales. You may be practicing your prospecting script if you're involved in a home-based or network marketing opportunity. Practice getting that script ingrained into your head and really making it a part of you so that it becomes conversational. What's your approach beyond the introduction? Where are you going to take the person? How are you going to book your next appointment? Those are all things you want to practice. Practice it with your spouse and practice it with a business associate. Practice it until it becomes natural. The worst thing that somebody can do in their network marketing business is to start making phone calls without practicing their script or approach ahead of time. Typically what happens is that when they call their friends they end up sounding like a mechanical robot, reading off of a piece of paper. I guarantee you that you're not going to get business that way. So, number two is practice.

The third critical element is that you've got to play the game. It's game time in the trenches. You're never going to get good at anything without playing the game. The same goes for golf. You can't read a golf book and expect to become a great golfer. The way you're going to get good at golf is by preparing, practicing, and playing the game; doing all these things consistently. The same goes for prospecting. The way you're going to get good at prospecting is by setting aside prep time, mentally preparing yourself, practicing, and playing the game. You might be a little wobbly the first time you step out into the marketplace; it may be a little tough or even nerve racking. It certainly was for me. But, I went out and simply started prospecting. I went out and did it and missed out on a lot of business because of my lack of skills early on. But that's okay...it's all part of the developmental process. In the short term you make up in larger numbers what you may lack in skill. There are plenty of people out there that will buy our products and services, so don't sweat it if somebody says no to you.

The fourth critical element is working with coaches. I'm a very firm believer in working with a coach. Look at the top athletes: Tiger Woods, Michael Jordan, Barry Bonds and Marion Jones, just to name a few. All of the top athletes in every sport have coaches that work with them. Why? A coach can figure out what is affecting your performance, or lack thereof, and tweak it individually. It's a whole lot different than going to a seminar and listening to a tape series. Working with a coach provides focused attention on you and only you.

I work with coaches myself. I also provide personal coaching and personal prospecting coaching to help people really begin to solve their problems and make changes. What often happens is that if you're on your own and not working with a coach, you don't have the advantage of someone checking in on you to see what's happening. Therefore, you could be making the same mistakes over and over again and not be able to make the necessary change to improve your performance. Worst of all, you might have a great month where you obviously did something different that led you to increased production only to have it followed by an incredibly poor month. There are a lot of people who can't string two good months together. They've got no duplication. The question; why weren't you able to duplicate it? Because you didn't know what you did the month prior that led to your record-breaking production. You see, a coach can help you identify the good things that you're doing and the bad things that you're doing. They keep you on an even keel and make sure you're producing each and every month.

The fifth critical element is conducting self examinations. Not only do you want to work with a coach, but it's great to examine yourself. I teach people to do two different types of self checks, qualitative and quantitative. A qualitative self check examines the quality of what you are doing. How are you coming across? What do you sound like when you are talking with your prospect? Do you sound like you're on the ball or do you sound like you're constantly struggling, scrambling, not knowing what to say, stuck, and not in a flowing position? You want to be in a comfortable, flowing type of situation when you're communicating with your prospect. You want to engage in a nice, relaxed, flowing, focused business conversation where you are listening to the prospect. You've got to be interacting. If you listen to yourself, if you actually take the time to record calls, if you record those things that you're doing, you can listen to it. You can put yourself on rewind, replay, and review those critically important times in your life when the money is made. And...in sales or network marketing, it is only made when you get out there and talk to people! Doing this will absolutely help you on the qualitative side.

On the quantitative side, it's simply a matter of numbers; being able to track the quantity of calls. Track the quantity of presentations that you make; the quantity of clients, customers, or potential distributors that you may be calling or speaking with on a daily, weekly, or monthly basis. Whether you are involved in traditional sales or network marketing, they're both numbers games. However, they are also both people businesses. If you aren't working the numbers and you're not producing, that's a pretty good sign that you're not doing enough to make it happen. If you are truly working the numbers on a consistent basis and you're still not producing well, it might be something on the qualitative side. So, you can use those two self checks to balance things out and really help you focus on getting good at prospecting.

David, those are the five critical elements that I teach in many of my seminars and to my coaching clients. Incorporating those five critical elements into your business approach will lead to greater success in your prospecting efforts.

Wright

So what advice do you have for individuals thinking about entering the network marketing or direct sales industry?

Falcone

Simply put, success is not that difficult. People make it much more difficult than it really is. When you get involved in something and make a commitment, don't make the commitment unless you believe in what you're doing. If you don't believe in the product, services, or whatever it is that you're involved with, don't do it. You've got to have belief and you've got to have conviction in what you're doing. When you do make the commitment, utilize whatever resources you have to help shorten the learning curve, increase your skills, stay focused, and work harder on you than you do on anything else. You know the old saying: "work harder on you than you do in your job or in your occupation." If you can become more, if you can increase the value that you bring to the marketplace, you are going to earn a whole lot more money and be more successful.

The last bit of advice I have is not to quit. Pure and simple, we all learn at different paces. Comparing yourself to another person's success can absolutely wreck you. Don't compare yourself to others in terms of the pace at which you succeed. Someone else in your organization or company may blow you away. I've known people who were much faster than me and I've know people who were much slower. It doesn't matter. If you stay focused, if you have a willingness to learn, if you have the right kind of work ethnic, if you're paying attention to things as they happen, and you're really learning from mistakes and successes, you'll make it.

Wright

Often times we see people in business that are so focused on the money, the fame, the power, and all that success can bring that they forget about the other important things in life. How do you feel about working hard and playing hard as well?

Falcone

I love it. Balance is critically important. In business, sometimes you've just got to bust it. Whether it's being at the top of your sales game or being at the top of your network marketing company, you've got to put the peddle to the metal. That's called business in today's environment. Sure, I suppose you can do it haphazardly. But, I like to push the petal to the metal when I'm working and also do the same thing when I'm not working. I strongly believe that individuals need to focus on having balance in their lives. If you don't, work can eat you alive. You'll burn yourself out. You need to take some time for yourself, take some time for your family. Life's too short to just work. Have some fun. Balance yourself. Work hard, then take some time off and go enjoy yourself and your family by doing something that you love to do. If you re-energize yourself by taking a little time off every now and then it's going to make life more enjoyable and it will be much easier to give your business the focused attention it needs in order to prosper.

Wright

Tell our readers a little bit more about how an individual's mindset affects their ability to succeed.

Falcone

I think mindset greatly affects your ability to succeed. If your attitude is in the wrong place, you're not going to cut it. Mindset is everything. If you're looking at the glass half empty with a grumpy attitude and a crinkle in your forehead, it will never happen. First of all, you're no fun to be around. Secondly, you're not going to succeed with that kind of attitude. We all have bad days; we're emotional beings. Sometimes we get rejected, have a bad day, or something disruptive happens in our life. It doesn't feel good. Who wants to have a low production day? A no production day? Who wants to hear the word no from a prospect? Nobody does. But, some days are good and some days are less productive. Regardless, you have to maintain that positive mental attitude. The more you can stay focused in good times as well as bad, the more productive you will be in the long run.

If you look around, if you look at the leaders in your company, if you look at the super successful producers, it doesn't matter if they are having a good month, a bad month, a great year, or a poor year. They pretty much stay on an even keel. Their ability to stay in that zone is what enables them to pull themselves through the poor times.

There are cycles in every type of business; you have good months, bad months, good seasons, bad seasons, slow times, and fast times. You've got all these different situations. The key is to maintain a positively consistent attitude so you can increase the likelihood of attracting good people.

Personally, I prefer to expose myself to materials that are of a positive nature. I avoiding watching the negativity of what happens on the news at night and exposing myself to the abundance of toxic information available in today's society. I avoid negative people. If you hang out with negative, grumpy people, you'll become negative and grumpy. If you enter a new business or new occupation and you've got a bunch of glum people surrounding you, you might need to start hanging out with some other people. Have you ever heard the saying "you become like those you hang around"? Well, it's very true. If you hang around with a bunch of beer-drinking, unmotivated people that just sit around and do absolutely nothing, then that's probably what you're going to do. If you hang around with fun, entrepreneurial, excited, motivated, successful people, that's probably how you're going to end up.

Wright

My wife has that one all figured out. She went to church yesterday and I guess someone thought that maybe she wasn't feeling very well. That person asked if she woke up grumpy. She said, "No, I just let him lay there and sleep." Todd, what do you ultimately look to accomplish in your business endeavors?

Falcone

That's an interesting question. Ultimately, I'm looking to impact as many people as I possibly can who really want to make changes in their lives. I simply want to assist others in making positive changes towards helping themselves produce more business and getting more out of life.

Most people have to work for a living. Some people don't have to work. For the majority of us that do, we might as well make the commitment and enjoy it rather than stress out and jump from occupation to occupation. I think we need to focus on doing something that fulfills us and while we're at it, do as well as we can from a financial standpoint. Everyone should be in a zone that allows them to create a level of enjoyment, not only for themselves, but for others as well.

I think most people like to play. I certainly do. I love to work and I love to play. Ultimately, if I had the choice to never work again but instead play golf everyday, ski, fish, travel, and spend time with my family, loved ones, and friends, I'd probably do that. But you know what? We've got to go out there and create something that enables us to have the free time to do the things in life we want to do. I chose network marketing as a venue because it provides me with the ability to create a recurring stream of income rather than having to be reliant on the next deal, the next close, or the next sale. That's why I got started in the network marketing industry.

Ultimately, what I'm looking to do is share with people the strategies that have worked well for me and brought me success. I certainly have a passion for helping those that are having a difficult time producing; who are putting forth the effort and energies in their business, yet are not getting out of the business what they want. Sometimes all it takes is a little bit of tweaking and a little bit of coaching from somebody else in order to begin to make the changes that will lead them to production. I want to help people out in their businesses, spend quality time with my friends, loved ones, and family, have as much fun as possible, and eventually go on to eternity feeling good about what I contributed on planet earth.

Wright

I'm probably like you. I would love to be independently wealthy with a trust fund and not have to work, but when I really think about it, in my lifetime I've known three people who had large trust funds and were independently wealthy. And without exception, and I'm not just saying this to affirm what you said, this is a true statement, they were the three most miserable people I've ever met in my life and the most worthless, as far as I was concerned.

Falcone

Yes, I agree. I have a few friends that are in the same situation. Three guys are coming to mind right now. They'll never have to work a day in their whole lives. To me, there's more reward in making the money and creating the wealth rather than just having it dished out. The growth process that one goes through in making the money is probably the most rewarding part of having it.

Wright

Well, it's been very interesting. I really do appreciate you taking this time to talk with me and answer these important questions. I've learned a lot here today and know our readers will too.

Falcone

Thank you David. I appreciate the opportunity to participate in this project.

Wright

We've been talking to Todd Falcone. He is a trainer, personal coach, and public speaker to network marketing and direct sales professionals worldwide. As we have found out today he knows a lot about what he's talking about. Todd, thank you so much for joining us for *Conversations on Success.*

Falcone

Thank you very much David.

About The Author

Todd Falcone began his career in Network Marketing in 1990. He was introduced to the profession by an unexpected cold-call. Intrigued with the concept of working for himself and having unlimited earning potential, Falcone decided to take a serious look at the unique business opportunity. Over a decade later, Falcone attributes his success in the industry and reputation as a respected prospector to the following three key factors: commitment, consistency, and personal development.

From the start Falcone treated Network Marketing like the serious business that it is. He has always worked with an extremely high level of commitment and consistency to the industry. Personal development has been equally important and a strong focus in his career development. Continuous exposure to successful individuals through the utilization of books, tapes, and CD's in addition to the attendance of seminars provides Falcone with the knowledge and inspiration needed to continuously grow and prosper.

Falcone has devoted over a decade to mastering the principles of success in Network Marketing. He clearly understands the theories and strategies one needs to apply in order to achieve consistent results in the business. Having a passion for teaching and sharing the principles that have helped to create abundance in his own life, Falcone is a sought after personal coach, trainer, and public speaker.

Prior to entering the Network Marketing industry, Falcone worked as the top sales representative for his family-owned radio station located on California's Central Coast. There he led the sales staff in making the station one of the top revenue producing in the market. After overseeing the multi-million dollar sale of the radio station, Falcone was able to fulfill his desire of working as a fulltime network marketer.

Falcone has published a number of training articles and has been featured in several magazines and books relating to the Network Marketing industry including *Networking Times*, *Six Figure Income*, *Home Business Connection*, and Zig Ziglar's *Network Marketing for Dummies*. He is also the author of *Success Tips*, a nationally recognized training newsletter and that embodies his mission to support, educate, and inspire home business owners. Falcone is the author and host of *Dynamic Divas of Networking*, *How to Win in the Game of Prospecting* and *The Cold Market Lead Mastery Course*, all of which are audio CD programs. Falcone lives in Seattle, WA with his wife, Carla and son, Gianni.

Todd Falcone

Reach4Success, LLC

P.O. Box 18071

Seattle, WA 98118

Phone: 800.259.1177

Email: Todd@ToddFalcone.com

www.ToddFalcone.com

Chapter Five

MICHAEL PODOLINSKY

David E. Wright (Wright)

Today we are talking to Michael A. Podolinsky. He is Asia's leading expert in developing people and people skills. He authored the Pearson / Prentice Hall book, *Mining for Gold, Facilitation Skills to Unearth a Wealth of Ideas from Your Team*, as well as *Smart Leadership, Go for Your Goals, From Stress to Success, Winning at Work,* and *E-Mail and Voicemail Tools*. Michael was his state chair for President George W. Bush's Small Business Advisory Council. He was awarded the Ronald Reagan Gold Medal for Business Leadership in 2004, the first year this prestigious award was ever given.

This 24-year business owner (serving Asia Pacific since 1989), has served over 500 clients, addressed over 1800 audiences across six continents in 23 countries impacting over 11 million people worldwide. Michael, welcome to *Conversations on Success*!

Michael A. Podolinsky (Podolinsky)

Thank you David. It's good to be here and included in this book with such prestigious colleagues.

Wright

It is our pleasure, Michael, and an honor to have you on the program. Right up front Michael, let me ask you, how do *you* define success?

Podolinsky

I define it a lot differently than most people would. It's simply, "Being at peace." It's not exactly a journey. It's not exactly a destination. It is a state of MIND. If you are really at peace, aren't you successful? It doesn't mean you don't aspire to more. It doesn't mean you don't want to *do* more. When you are successful, you are at peace with yourself *right now* in where you are, as well as where you are going.

I got this definition from a friend of mine, Krysta, Eryn Kavenaugh, several years ago. Since then, I found one word that even sums it up better than the phrase. It is the Jewish word *Shalom* that translates to mean you are to be in a total, complete state of peace. That is, you are personally, spiritually, physically and mentally in a state of peace, love, fulfillment and satisfaction. It is all about being at peace with God, your family, work, yourself and life in general.

Face it, David, in order to be at peace, you need to feel you are doing the right thing, you are using your talents, you are serving God in the right way, and you are doing what really is important for you, for your community, for your family in your life. That is being at peace. That is success.

Wright

That's incredible Mike. I have never heard it put so well. Does that mean that anyone can be successful?

Podolinsky

Well, I believe anybody has the capacity to be successful. I would say that very few people actually reach that state. I've heard it said that as many as 80% of the people working dislike what they do.

Wright

Right. Boy that's horrible. How would you like to get up every morning and go to a place you don't want to be?

Podolinsky

Sure, a place you don't want to be or doing something in general that you do not want to be doing. The problem is that many times people think that if I change my location that is going to change my feeling.

Wright

Yes, but the change of scenery does not help. Why do they think that way?

Podolinsky

We have all heard, "It is always greener in the other pasture." I figured out a long time ago *why* it's always greener in the other pasture. It's because they use more **fertilizer**. Maybe, just maybe, we need to plant ourselves into the pasture that we are in as better seeds and then bloom, blossom, and grow where we are planted, but we've got to cultivate the soil. We've got to work that pasture a little bit better. Create habits for success and be perpetual students of work and of life in general.

Wright

That is so true. Tell me, who are some of the most successful people that you have ever met and why did you think they were successful?

Podolinsky

The people I thought were most successful were the people I believed were at peace and loved what they were doing. Sometimes it was some very simple people. Somebody that was cleaning a building with incredible pride and who really enjoyed what he or she was doing. I can think back to when I was a kid growing up. I got my first job as a janitor when I was 14 years of age. I was working at my local church. One of the people I admired and to this day believe was really successful was old Father Francis Burn. The man was a jazz musician and he got the calling from God to become a priest and to get involved in the church. I used to go up to church to clean and sometimes I couldn't clean for two hours at a stretch because he was just sitting or kneeling by the alter and praying. As a 14-year-old, I thought, "Now here's somebody who really loves God with his entire being."

I also thought my father was quite successful and really at peace because he loved what he did. He was a salesman and he loved it so much. He just lit up any time he could help people and help them solve a problem. He thought that was absolutely incredible, particularly when he could take an account away from one of his competitors. The best part for him was being able to help his customer make a lot more money at the same time.

There were speakers and trainers that I met in this industry, people I really admire, like Nido Qubein, who has made a success out of his life or one of my first mentors, E. James Rohn (also featured in this book), back in the late '70s. And when I listened to him and his stories on the platform, you could see and experience that he just *resonated*. While he claimed to be better in the boardroom than on the platform, well, on the platform it was hard to get much better.

Another successful individual I can think of was a guy named Carl Luther. I used to carry his bags and help him out in his programs before I even got started in this business just to learn from him. He was 92 years of age and still doing seminars. Carl had worked in over 86 countries and asked me if I wanted to distribute his materials as he felt he still wanted; no, he NEEDED to do more. David, now THAT is PASSION for what you do. Carl Luther was a huge success in my mind.

Wright

Goodness!

Podolinsky

I went to pick him up one day. He'd been in an automobile accident. He was driving up until he was 90, and if that isn't a scary thought. The poor man got in an accident. (Of course, it wasn't his fault. But if you're standing still at an intersection, it's amazing what will happen.) Anyway I went to pick him up one day and I thought I had better go down the stairs before him, just in case he falls down. He takes one step and *falls backward* and lands down hard.

I shouted to him, "Are you okay Carl? Are you okay?"

He replied, "Oh, I'm okay. Nothing hurt but my pride." Now, I'm really nervous and upset out of worry that he might be injured. I bring him to my car and get him safely inside, and tuck him in the seatbelt. After he is secured, I got in on the driver's side.

As I sat down, Carl says to me, "You know what I need, Mike?" I'm thinking, "What? A hospital? A doctor?" "No! I need more power in my presentations!"

David, here is a man, a professional, who loved what he did so much and yet he had the pride to say I can do it even better... even when he was 90+ years of age.

Wright

Amazing story. Obviously, that was a long time ago. When you started your business, was it successful right away?

Podolinsky

Are you kidding me? I had so much of a struggle when I got started, and I wasn't at peace on the inside either because I was trying to do what other people told me I needed to do. I remember I had gone to an NSA convention and I had not one, but two different mentors tell me, "Don't tell them what they *need* to hear, tell them what they *want* to hear." Reality, it worked great for getting standing ovations, but I felt like a trained barking seal. Performing tricks for little "fish" clients would throw to me. I also wasn't getting the responses from audiences that I wanted.

So to answer your question, it was very difficult at the start, but something happened along the way that really changed my life. Is it okay to get into this?

Wright

Absolutely!

Podolinsky

Wonderful. I was asked by a teacher to speak at her school, and I thought, "Great! Two hundred kids or whatever, filling up the auditorium. I'll motivate them." And she says, "No, I need you to talk to my *classes*." I said, "Classes?" She says, "Yes, I teach seven classes and I want you to give seven talks, one to each class." And I said, "Well, okay. How much are you going to pay me?" She said, "Well, it comes out of my pocket. How is $15.00?" And I said, "Okay." Hey...at the time for me I saw $15 as a tank of fuel for my car.

So I gave them...all 7 talks. They went okay even though I remember being sicker than a dog that day. The fourth talk though, changed my life forever. In comes this young girl, into the class. She's got an interpreter. She is deaf and the interpreter is signing for her.

As I knew a little sign language from dating a deaf woman, I sign over to her, "Sorry I sign slowly. I am a big dummy." She laughed.

And then I just motioned to her in sign language, "YOU, are a beautiful girl," She beamed.

That was all I knew in sign language. But she got my brief message and then I went on and did the talk as per usual. Afterwards, her interpreter came over and said, "Can I talk to you for a moment, please?"

I was nervous because I thought, "What? Did I make the wrong sign or something?" Her interpreter shared, "Well, you know, she always felt different in this class, but today you made her feel *special*. I just wanted you to know you changed her life."

At that moment, everything changed because I had never *changed* anybody else's life before. What I did after that was, I drove home and I erased all of the financial goals and material plans from my board in my home office. I erased all of those superficial goals the gurus told me I needed to be "successful."

All the financial goals others told me I needed were replaced with a new and heartfelt mission for my life. I put at the top of my goals board, "I will serve God and humankind, and the success and the money will follow." And guess what? It did!

From that moment on, everything was completely different. The reason? The focus was totally different. For the first time since starting my business, I was at peace with what I was doing. Does that make sense?

Wright

Absolutely! That was a long way from where you are today. Now, you have settled in Asia. What brought about that amazing shift in your business?

Podolinsky

David, a couple of things. One was getting married to my bride, Sarnai, whom I love with every cell in my body. For years, I had my speaker buddies say, "Mike, you're never going to find a woman who wants to travel that much with you going all over the world." At the time, they might even have seen justified in their cynicism. As I had already been working in 23 countries on six continents, it seemed most unlikely I WOULD ever find someone who would travel the world with me. I prayed really hard and very specifically to God requesting a woman who would love me and cherish me and travel with me. He provided! I found, and *married* an amazing and beautiful Mongolian woman. Hey… they are traditionally a nomadic people! So I found (was given by God) somebody who was willing to travel with me and it was just fine with the two of us.

Then we got (thank the Lord) our first child, Anna Maria, and that began to change things. When she was an infant, she traveled easily. As a toddler wanting to go here, there and everywhere became a little more difficult. My wife was saying, "Well, I don't really care which side of 'the pond' we're on as long as we stay on one side."

We were struggling with what to do for some time. Most of our business was in Asia. Most of our family and friends were in the USA. Then, I heard Allen Weiss say something that stuck in my mind. He said, "You know, you can't move on to bigger business until you let go of the smaller business that you already have."

I thought about it, and in reality I was hanging on to the U.S. because I liked the environment and I had a little bit of business there, and there were my family and friends. And we talked about it and we prayed about it, and we just decided to leave everything. So we sold 95% of our material possessions—house, cars, furniture, everything—and moved to Asia to our home here in Singapore. It's quite an adjustment to go from 3200 square feet and five bedrooms on freehold property to a three-bedroom 1350 square foot condo.

Wright

Yes, Michael, I can imagine.

Podolinsky

But it has been wonderful; good for business, good for perspective, understanding what it's like to live in another culture, another environment. More over, the business side of it has just been amazing. We really are at peace about it and we've got a good plan and we're hitting all of our numbers and things are going great. The best possible decision to make. We have also launched the Professional Speaking and Training Institute where we offer certificate and diploma programs for people in how to become professional speakers and trainers AND will eventually offer degree and advanced degree programs in the Asia Pacific region. It's another way we give back and share with others.

Wright

That is amazing, Michael. So it is not a one-off boot camp?

Podolinsky

No it's not. Though a weekend might be fine for elementary exploration of the topic, you need an ongoing program to really learn the business. You cannot teach somebody to do what we do in a weekend. We are taking them and really developing them to either be great speakers and trainers at the certificate level and if the continue, how to actually develop sustainable businesses in this most amazing profession. It is the first of its kind in the world.

Wright

Good for you. Along the way, you must have learned a great many lessons. What have you found that Asian businesses do that their North American counterparts are not doing?

Podolinsky

There are a number of things that Asian businesses are doing North American businesses have not been doing. For one thing, a lot of them are looking more long term and planning long term. It is much more traditional in Asia to look long term for your planning.

We have worked with some MNCs (Multi-National Corporations), and they are trying in the month of November, for example, to work out a plan to accomplish their targets for the coming year that they have just now received, just two months before the start of the year!

Whereas, you find in Asian businesses, when you work with them, they tend to look a LOT longer term. And they are willing to listen to us and develop with us a solid five-year-plan and so forth to look longer term. That is really helpful on their part and much more productive.

I think also they are much more into inclusivity with their work force as opposed to trying to "celebrate diversity." In other words, in the U.S. and much of the West, we have a tendency to say, "We have to be sensitive to everybody's needs and we have to understand everybody completely." That kind of thinking is really an impossibility. You cannot get to know everybody and what ethnic background they come from as well as their specific family culture and so forth.

Instead, in Singapore in particular, they tend to be more inclusive in their approach. Asians tend to talk more openly about race or religion, and it's just like "Okay, that's great. And if you need two days to celebrate Depavali, Hari Raya, Lunar New Year, Good Friday (or whatever), that's fine." You know it's just part of the culture here which I find is very refreshing. They don't worry if there is going to be a lawsuit or if somebody is different from them. It is more a culture of, "We just accept everybody." So it tends to be more of a homogeneous blend which I really like. And in reality, true freedom of religion and freedom of culture

Wright
What do you see holding Asian businesses back?

Podolinsky
Some of, if not MOST Asian business, has a bit of what I would refer to as either being colonial in nature or what they call locally here as Ah-Beng mentality, which is the old autocratic style. It is a bit like my Slovak grandpa used to say, "Nem so so ba so so tesel nee." In Slovak this means, "Don't do like I do, do like I tell you to do." This approach does not exactly build great bonds, loyalty or promote productivity. There are some businesses that are really stuck in this mode and are not looking at business in a more modern "team oriented" approach. There are other businesses in Asia that are very team oriented and very team centered. So I think the old Ah Beng mentality is holding some businesses back.

Another aspect of some Asian business is creativity. Creativity does not always flow naturally from many of the Asian people because for many years, the school systems were teaching in a very colonial fashion. It was the old fashioned system where the teacher talks lecture style and the students just listen, take notes and try to memorize for exams.

As a result, many workers are looking to management to be leaders and total decision makers. Now, in Singapore's schooling system, that has done a total flip-flop here. All the polytechnic schools are in problem based learning and in Singapore, the Acting Minister of Education has gone to the SAIL program that is geared towards making students think creatively and solve problems to understand the nature of the problems. They are cutting back on the total course syllabus and letting them do more real learning and less rote memorization. This shift is going to change the way that students will learn the way workers will think and later, they way managers will have to manage.

Wright
Tell me then, what role does culture play in success?

Podolinsky

Culture plays a fascinating role when you look at global tribes. There are some global tribes that have done incredibly well, and they do it because they get together either through their religious organization, through "uncles" in their family groups or in their clans, or even as semi-governmental groups. They've been able to do incredibly well and expand into certain markets.

There are organizations built around these cultures that almost guarantee that they become a success. It's like they have built in support systems.

Think about it. If every start-up company could develop with its own built-in support system to help their people grow as entrepreneurs AND if these entrepreneurs could reach out in some way to their family, friends, and relatives to get support, it would be easier for them to make financial successes in their lives and their businesses. This is part of Asian Culture.

Wright

What about *your* background helped you make you a success in business?

Podolinsky

I think a large part of my success comes from a background where my family culture nurtured and encouraged a strong work ethic. But working hard is actually, I think, only about 10% of how successful you become.

I see people here sweeping the streets and they work hard in the hot sun all day, but they are not making any money to speak of. So I think the work ethic, though important, is only *part* of the equation.

My martial arts background for the last 33 years has been incredibly helpful. My Karate instructor used to push me harder than anybody else, and gave me a belief that you can achieve things that you never thought were even possible. You could push yourself harder than ever before. So the second thing that helped me was not only to work hard physically, but to BELIEVE in yourself and to believe that ANYTHING is possible.

Apart from the family background, my faith in God and my belief that no matter what, and no matter how much pressure I get, I can always turn it over to the Lord and say, "Please help me with this because I can't deal with this." That faith is a huge factor in success in life and being at peace.

Education is another factor. I think education is really helpful and I had the incredible fortune of having very wise mentors, some incredible teachers, and a situation where in growing up and even going to university, I could design a major and be able to take courses I really wanted to take. I could also go over to professors' homes and talk to them there. That really made a difference.

But again, education I think is only about 20% of what success is or what ultimately will make you a financial success. The world is full of educated derelicts. I knew a woman who had two Ph.D.'s and two Master's degrees...working as a receptionist at a restaurant because she could not "find herself." I wanted to tell her, "Look in the mirror, there you are!" So education by itself is not a guarantee of success or even a predictor. Just another cog in the wheel of financial success.

Another 20% is that willingness to take responsibility. The willingness to not just "accept," but to request tough projects; asking for more responsibility, being a manager, team or project leader. I believe this is an ability that grows over time. I don't think there's any substitute for the time that you put into a career or work to give you the confidence to do that. The confidence and experience you gain over time will contribute to this 20%.

The last component is the ability to take risks. Personally, I think I got a large part of this ability from the martial arts too. Coping with and taking risk, for anyone, is probably 50% of the equation to becoming a success in life. Yes, it is the ability to take risks that separates the Branson, the Trump, the Gates from the 'no-name'. Face it. Go to a shopping center anywhere in the world and a sales person will sell you a pair of socks. Go to a firm selling $1M products and a sales person will sell you the $1M product or service. Which one gets paid more? Which one takes more risk? Which one is on a small fixed salary and maybe has a very tiny spiffs, bonus or commission? The big-ticket rep has the potential to make a LOT more or to make nothing at all. The ability to handle risk: 50% of the equation.

Wright

I can see that Michael. Now I'm curious. You mentioned your martial arts training a couple of times. Do you use your martial arts training in your workshops or seminars?

Podolinsky

Oh, definitely! Initially we started off doing martial arts philosophies as applied to sales and motivation, and just had a one single motivational talk. It lasted originally 25 minutes. And now we could do a *full month* of training, full days, and not repeat any material. It all grew initially out of the martial arts and the philosophies I learned in the 1970's.

David, we use examples from the martial arts all the time. Karate captures people's attention. We bring people up on stage with us, having them do a little demonstration with me or in groups. And they get it. When you relate to them physically and kinesthetically in addition to the usual auditory and the visual means, it really makes a difference. We reach more people this way. On top of it all, it's fun!

Wright

I've been in some seminars with people who used martial arts. They're not only fun, but they're enlightening, a lot more than I would have dreamed. Who were your key influencers or motivators?

Podolinsky

Key influencers and motivators? There are so many. Spending time and working out with Steven Seagal had a profound influence on my life. An amazing martial artist. In South Africa, 5th Dan Stan Schmidt, 4th Dan Sensei Willie Zimmerman, the late 4th Dan Chris Hoffleiche. 5th Sash Jack Spizale in Southern Preying Mantis Gung Fu, Dr. Albert C. Church 8th Dan and 10th Dan, Robert Trias (who signed my blackbelt certificates). Of course, the greatest influence was my own karate instructor, 5th Dan master Fred Neff, who gave me the resiliency and tenacity to accomplish almost anything I ever wanted or needed to accomplish.

Wright

What about business influences rather than the martial arts? Who influenced you there the most?

Podolinsky

I could mention Carl Luther as one of my mentors in the early years. So many professional speakers from the National Speakers Association, in particularly the Minnesota Chapter, have helped me out and had profound influences on me.

Lee Boyan, who wrote *Successful Cold Call Selling* is one of my premier mentors. He did things for me you might never expect. He would invite me to go watch him work and I could ask him questions about his performance afterward. He came and watched me speak and critiqued my performance later on. Lee even gave me my first photocopy machine and supplies.

Leo Hauser, author of *Five Steps to Success* let me sell his books at my programs, giving me income from what would have been free talks as well as a ton of ideas and encouragement.

Another top professional, Thom Winninger, would let me sit and ask him questions. He always gave me straightforward advice.

Jerry Simmons, past president of NSA, sat in on one of my programs and later, ripped it apart. He really helped me out with his honest revelations and told me what I was doing wrong and gave me new insights.

One of my closest mentors, Janie Jasin, helped me both by example with her energy and vitality. Janie helped me in a much more direct way. I really was struggling in the early years. She put me to work in her company called Fitness Plus and had me teach some martial arts and aerobics to people with chemical dependency and / or a history of alcohol abuse. It paid me for speaking once or twice a week and you know, it was fun.

Bob Montgomery helped to get my books into Learn Incorporated, our first publisher. We've sold over 70,000 audio books through Learn and the new company who bought them out, Oasis Audio. Bob's generosity and unselfish assistance really made a huge difference in my career. Dr. Manny Steil taught me so many lessons about listening and life, and continues to be a friend and mentor today. Grand master of speaking, Mr. Bill Gove, flew 3.5 hours to spend a weekend with me and coach me one-on-one.

There are so many people who have helped me and that is why it is important for anyone reading the book to NOT, I repeat, to NOT be a lone wolf. Ask people for advice, help, and ideas. Today, you can even hire a professional coach, like I did to mentor me. The whole concept of a "self-made man / woman" as a success is a load of nonsense. You cannot make it to the top unless someone helped you along the way. Do not expect them to look for you. You must seek them out if you want to become a success.

Likewise, I think it is important for anybody who has had any kind of success to pass that legacy on to somebody else. This is one reason we started PSTI, to pass on our legacy.

Do you want me to continue David?

Wright

By all means. I never thought of the "self made man" as being a myth.

Podolinsky

It sure is. A few more examples: In Asia, David Goh taught me about acting out stories, not telling stories. Lawrence Chan gave a model for business growth and development in Asia by showing me his highly successful PDL organization.

The coach I mentioned hiring earlier was THE Grand Master of public speaking, Mr. Bill Gove. He spent an entire weekend focused on me and moved me light-years ahead in one weekend. He sat in a chair and he said, "Okay, kid, give me your talk."

I stood and talked to him like it was an audience of 600, and he said, "You know, you really got that thing down. You know it word for word."

And he said, "You know, you are already using vignettes. Normally, I have to teach people to use vignettes, but you really use vignettes well and that's wonderful!"

He then proceeded to rip the speech apart. In one weekend we restructured the whole presentation. In that one, short weekend, I jumped a full point on a 1 to 10 scale on evaluations. Investing that time and considerable amount of money with that great Grand Master was one of the *best* investments I ever made.

Wright

Did all these mentors do this for you for free?

Podolinsky

Yes, except for Bill Gove, whom I paid to be my mentor. The others all helped just for the asking. I really owe them all so much for passing on their knowledge and wisdom.

Wright

How can the people reading this book make themselves more successful?

Podolinsky

There are several things they can do immediately. In 1982, I heard Charles "Tremendous" Jones state, "It is the books you read and the people you meet that will make the difference between who you are now and who you will become in five years time."

There is SO much truth in that. So read a lot of books and get a lot of mentors. Read your industry journals to learn more about your industry.

Jim Rohn taught me in the 1970's, "Spend more time on yourself than you do on your job."

Jim Cathcart, who had experience with Buck Minster Fuller, suggests we read things that we are not always used to reading. And that is a lesson I taken to heart. I have read women's magazines, and believe me I don't normally have a big interest in some of the topics. Doing so gives me some insights into what women are thinking and what the issues are they deal with. It has made me better in my programs in being able to relate to women. So read outside of your normal sphere of influence.

I am convinced one of the things that really helped us in Asia in our business is not just having one specialty. How many times have you heard people say, "You've got to specialize in just one topic?" Well that's fine and wonderful until there is some kind of a down turn in the industry or a shift and all of a sudden that one topic is not needed anymore. Whereas having a variety of topics and being well read and versed in a variety of subjects I think has helped us.

Instead of just one topic, like time management or leadership, when business leaders know they need good training and it deals with people skills, that is when they turn to us. As Joel Weldon says, "Find out what everyone else is doing and don't do it."

I believe having a variety of *experiences* as well can be very helpful. In fact, only knowing one area of a business can be career limiting. The number one reason HR people rarely make it to the MD seat is because they know HR, but do not know Finance, Sales, IT or other departments.

If I can share one story from one of our clients to make this point. Ken Theiss hired us to work with him in his company, Shakopee Valley Printing. When we started working with them, they were a $33 million company. I found out that Ken had started as a jogger for them. Now "jogger" doesn't mean you run around the building. It means when the newspapers they printed came off the printing press, the jogger would stack them up and tap them on one side and then tap them on the other to make the bundles straight. That's called jogging.

Ken started off doing this menial labor. And then when the press would break down for one reason or another, all the other joggers went off and had a smoke. Not Ken. Instead, he said to the second pressman, "What's going on? How can I help you?" And when there was an opening for a second pressman, guess whom they hired?

Wright

It must have been Ken Theiss.

Podolinsky

Correct. Ken Theiss did the same thing whenever there was a breakdown, he would ask, "Can I help you?" to the lead pressman. Pretty soon he became the head pressman and then the head of the department and then sometimes his department was waiting for plates. So he had trained his people in how to take care and service the presses on their own, so he went out and asked the plate makers, "Hey, how can I help you in the plate department? My people need work."

Ken soon learned every single aspect of the order entry, plate making, printing, bindery, warehouse, special services, you name it – and then he got into sales. It turns out the owner of the company had an elbow problem (that is he used his elbow to tip back far too many beverages), and it turned out, he was going to lose his business. But the company's customers stayed because of Ken. The vendors stayed because of him, too.

The venders said, "Anytime you want to start up your own business, we will back you." Well, it got to the point he realized the people in the plant were hurting. He went to the boss and said, "Hey, you know you're killing this company. If you don't want to get help, I want to buy you out. And if you don't let me, I'll go out and start my own business."

Well, he cursed at him and kicked him out. Two weeks later he called him back in and they worked out a buy-out deal, and now he owns this business. We had the opportunity to work with him for eight months and they are now doing $150 million a year. I find it just amazing that this guy started off as a jogger and ended up owning the company, but he did what few people ever do. He learned every aspect of the business, not just what he was TOLD to do.

Amazingly, Ken never lost his humility. He ate his lunches with the crew and had them over to his home. Some of his managers liked to go out to restaurants for lunch and that created the separation with workers we were brought in to fix. Not Ken. He would bring a sandwich to work and a Thermos of soup and ask them about their families and their favorite sports teams. A natural born leader if I ever saw one.

Wright

I love to hear success stories like that.

Podolinsky

That is again, just part of the equation. You must also have *specialized* knowledge that nobody else knows. Earl Nightingale taught me via cassette tape, "Spend an hour a day studying one subject and in five years time, you will be a leading expert." It is just that simple. Yet most people, in five years time, will just be five years older. I really believe in this concept. What if YOU knew some valuable information that no one else at your company had or better yet, no one else in your industry knew. Would that increase the amount of money people would be willing to give to you to learn from you or benefit from employing you?

Wright

Definitely! Mike, I could talk to you all day, but our time is growing short. Looking back on your career, or your life for that matter, do you have any regrets?

Podolinsky

I've thought about that so many times. There are times I think back about something that I have done that was embarrassing or maybe something I said that hurt somebody's feelings, and I think, "Yes, there are things that I wish I could take back."

But at the same time, I don't have any regrets about a lot of the choices that I made, whether they were right or wrong, because those choices got me to where I am at today. And you cannot learn in a vacuum.

David, some people have the amazing fortune of being 24-years-of-age, have started and are now running a successful $50 million operation. But for every one of these amazing exceptions to the rule you find another 100 who are successful that did not get there until after age 50. In reality, it takes time to grow the courage, mentality, strength, finances and those very important relationships and bonds with the people and partners you need.

Also, while raising a family and making ends meet, it much harder to take risks when young, not to mention the trade-off. Build a business and lose time with your family or spend time with your family and wait to build your business. There is no free lunch.

Wright

Right.

Podolinsky

When I look at the things that I've done in my life and the mistakes that I've made, I don't have any real regrets. I'm just thankful that I made it to the point where I'm at now, and I feel very good about my life. I feel at peace with it. I love my family. I really feel that we have been blessed. I love our business and I love the career and the heading of the course we are taking.

I think anybody that's worrying about regrets is going to have a problem. For 28 years I went to this retreat center called "Christ The King Retreat Center," in Buffalo, Minnesota. It had a beautiful poster on the wall that said, "Don't look back... unless you plan to go that way." David, I have no intention of going back that way.

We have so many exciting projects in the works and things that we are doing as we are moving forward. I am just happy I have a chance to learn from those mistakes and hopefully not repeat any of them.

Wright

Any last comments for our listeners and readers, Michael?

Podolinsky

Just one thought to wrap this up. Be at peace where you are at in your life right now. No regrets; and if you have any past sins or problems plaguing your mind, ask God to forgive you. He will and you start with a clean slate. Then make a plan for where you want to be in 5 to 10 years and start working on it drawing upon all your past experiences. Savor every minute of the journey and do not be shy about asking others for help. Learn from every job you do and volunteer to learn things outside your normal duties. Love God, love your family and love your job(s). Following this formula, I believe in my heart you are ALREADY A SUCCESS!

Wright

Michael, I really appreciate this time that you've spent with us. I hope I didn't inconvenience you. I'm in Tennessee and you're in Singapore, but everything went just as we had planned. We really did need your global insights and experience in this chapter. Thank you so much for taking all this time with us.

Podolinsky

No inconvenience, David. It has indeed been my pleasure and my delight. It was a quick half hour and you've been asking some great questions. It is an honor to be asked to be part of this program on success, along with my guru Jim Rohn and colleagues in writing and speaking like John Gray and Brian Tracy.

Wright

Today we have been talking to Michael A. Podolinsky, who is Asia's leading expert in developing people and people skills. For the past 24 years, he's been a business owner. He is now living in and serving the Asia Pacific region. Podolinsky International Pte Ltd has over 500 clients in Asia and worldwide. He personally addressed over 1800 audiences across six continents and 23 countries. And today we have found out why he is so successful. Thank you so much, Michael, for being with us today on *Conversations on Success*.

Podolinsky

God bless you all. May you all be incredibly successful.

About The Author

Asia's leading expert in developing people and people skills, he knows and is a leading authority on every organizations' single largest asset... their people! Michael also wrote the book on the subject of *Mining For Gold™...Facilitation Skills to Unearth a Wealth of Ideas From Your Team*. Along with *Smart Leadership, Go For Your Goals* and *Winning At Work*, his authored works, radio shows, newspaper columns, journal articles and television appearances have influenced over 11 million people worldwide.

He sat on President George W. Bush's Small Business Advisory Council and was his State Chair and winner of the Ronald Reagan Gold Medal Award for leadership, in 2004.

Business owner himself for 24 years (in Asia Pacific since January, 1989) formerly responsible for the USA's largest martial arts school, award winning sales person and president of training and speaking societies, he possesses the real-world, practical skills and knowledge to help you transform your people.

Michael A. Podolinsky

Podolinsky International Pte Ltd,

6 Petir Road, #05-06

Singapore 678267

Phone: (65) 6764.8067

E-mail: mike@michaelpodolinsky.com

www.michaelpodolinsky.com

Chapter Six

BRIAN TRACY

THE INTERVIEW

David E. Wright (Wright)

Today we are talking to Brian Tracy. Brian is one of America's leading authorities on the development of human potential and personal effectiveness. He is a dynamic and entertaining speaker with a wonderful ability to inform and inspire audiences towards peak performance in higher levels of achievement. He addresses more than four hundred thousand men and women each on the subject of personal and professional development including the Executives and staff of IBM, Arthur Anderson, McDonnell Douglas, and The Million Dollar Round Table. His exciting talks in seminars on leadership, sales management, and personal effectiveness bring about immediate changes and long-term results. Brian has a bachelors in communication with a master's degree, and is a chairman of Brian Tracy International, a human resource company based in San Diego, California, with affiliates throughout America and in 31 countries worldwide. Brian Tracy, thank you for being with us today on *Conversations on Success.*

Brian Tracy (Tracy)

It's a pleasure, David. Thank you.

Wright

Brian, trainers have changed sales format several times down through the years. It seems that recently relationship selling is recommended as the most successful format. Do these changes represent advances in techniques?

Tracy

Well, selling has really never changed. They've done fifty-five thousand interviews with customers to find out the process that they go through to buy, and there's a specific process that the customer goes through that the salesperson must dovetail their presentation and their interaction with. First of all, the customer has to like the person and trust the person they are talking to. So on that basis, relationships are very important. If I don't like you, I won't buy what you're selling, no matter how good the price is. So therefore, you have to have some kind of a relationship because the most important word in selling, I believe, is the word "credibility," which means that your claim is believable. And since human beings are primarily emotional, if I like you, I believe you more. If I dislike you or I'm neutral toward you, I'm far more skeptical or suspicious of what you say. So relationships are essential. Just the same as dating or going out with another person, the person has to like you a little bit in order to go out with you on a date. With regard to selling, the process is always the same.

First of all, the customer decides that you're a likeable and trustworthy person. Then the customer is open to talking to you. The customers only enters the sale when they realize that they have a need, and up until the time that you ask them the right questions and uncover the problems, and suggest perhaps that they could be better off in a cost effective way, customers are usually not interested, or at least detached, distanced, skeptical, unsure, uncertain, and so on. It's only when you touch on a need that the customer has, and the customer realizes, "Aah, I have that need. I didn't realize it before." Only then do they become interested because needs are what trigger interest. In nature it would actually trigger emotions, and only then do they become interested in finding out how that need can be satisfied in a cost effect way. It's something that really never changes. It starts off with the relationship. It goes to the identification of the correct need. It goes to the presentation of your product or service as a solution to that need, and then answers the question and closes the sale.

Wright

Yeah, that sounds a lot like when I first started several years ago, the sales process was divided into three parts, or at least the training that I had. The formation gathering phase, the presentation phase, and the close. Does that format still work?

Tracy

Yeah, we sometimes say that today you have to be a doctor of selling. A doctor does three phases. First of all, they do a thorough examination. Second of all, they do a diagnosis based on the examination. And third, they offer a prescription and encourage you to take it. In our live sales seminars, where we have thousands of people, we say the three keys are to prospect, which is to find people who can buy and can benefit from what you are selling; to present and show them that what you are selling makes sense to them in a cost effective way; and then it's to follow up and close, which is to get them to take action. So it never changes. It's still the same three in order.

Wright

I've noticed that down through the years in my selling, the close has—I don't define it as I used to. Close was something where I ask for the order, and there was a closing presentation, and all like that. I find that now people buy from me without really having to close.

Tracy

The reason for that is the more thoroughly you diagnose a person's needs, and the more clearly you explain that your product or service is the best thing for him or her all things considered, the easier it is for them to buy and the amount of effort in the close is very small. If the presentation has been poor, or if the qualification process has been poor, this may not be the right client. They may not have the right money. They may not have the right need, and so on. Well, then the closing is very difficult. An old style selling focused all the emphasis on closing, but the new style or the new model of selling is focused on building trust, identifying needs accurately, presenting your product or service specifically to satisfy the needs that have been identified, and then just asking the customer to go ahead.

Wright

What do you think has been the most significant change or addition to the sales process in recent years?

Tracy

Well, one of the things we have to realize in a market society, in which we live, the customer determines everything that we do or don't do. And the biggest change is customers have become more knowledgeable, more sophisticated, more aware, and simultaneously there have been more products and services developed to satisfy them. So sales people have to be more knowledgeable, more thoughtful, and better prepared. They have to know their product or service inside and out. They have to know the alternatives that are available to them. And especially, they have to take time to find out more about the customer before they attempt to advise the customer to buy what they are selling.

Wright

I remember back in the '80s, I used to attend all kinds of sales seminars, and I kept hearing speakers and seminar leaders, workshop leaders say the same thing, that product knowledge was only about 10% of the sales process. And I kept asking myself, "Yes, but which 10." Don't you have to know it all to use the 10 that's necessary to close?

Tracy

Absolutely.

Wright

Why do two sales people with the same education, using the same sales process, selling the same product differ in their level of success?

Tracy

Well, first of all no two people are ever the same. My experience with working with more than five hundred thousand sales people is that the most successful salespeople start a little earlier. They work a little harder. They stay a little later. They invest far more time in learning and preparation. In a recent study, they found that the highest paid sales people spend vastly more time in personal professional development listening to tapes, reading books. My conclusion is that if you are in sales and you drive around listening to the radio, basically you have no future. If you drive around listening to music, you have no future because all the highest paid sales people drive around listening to educational audio programs. That's what gives them the edge. It's almost like they are in constant mental training between calls. Poor sales people start at the last possible moment. The average sales person in America starts, really starts work about 11:00 and begins to wind down about 3:30. The average sales person makes about two calls a day. The average sales person takes long coffee breaks and lunches, leaves early. You know one of the jokes that I say is if you get onto the freeway at 3:30, you find that it is jammed. How can it be jammed? All these people don't get off work until 5:00. Well, one of the reasons it's jammed is all the sales people are on the way home to watch television because they think that after 3:30 nobody wants to talk to them, and before 11:00 people are too busy. So basically, they work far less. Take a complete idiot in selling, who is really ambitious and determined, starts early and works harder, stays later, continually learns to upgrade his skills, sees more people, and so on, they are going to run circles around the genius who starts late, quits early, and only sees a couple of people a day.

Wright

I had several sales mentors when I was younger and they all must have read the same books. Each one of them told me that in a sales situation, the first person to speak loses. Of course, I didn't believe it then and don't believe it now. But how can that be?

Tracy

Well, it's simply not true. I think there may be a misunderstanding, imagine going and sitting in front of a customer and saying nothing. Well, you'd soon be back on the streets because what you've done is you have made every effort to get through to get an appointment, to get face to face with this prospect. Finally, you meet with them and speak with them, and now, basically, you're on stage. Now, sometimes they say that when you ask the closing question, the first person to speak loses.

And that's probably true. If you ask them, "Do you like what I've shown you so far?" Then just be quiet until you get an answer. "Would you like to go ahead with this?" Just be quiet until you get an answer. There's a saying in professional speaking called, "stepping on your lines." This means you may tell a funny story and people start to laugh and you immediately start on again. So you step on the line and you trip people up. They don't get a chance to laugh.

So, one of the best things you can do is to just ask the question and then wait patiently for an answer even if there is a lot of silence. We say the only pressure you're allowed to use as a professional sales person is the pressure of the silence after you have asked a closing or confirming question.

Wright

I definitely posed the wrong question to you, because actually it was in a closing situation once you give the presentation. However, what bothered me was that the customer loses. I've always thought the customer wins when he buys something if I have discovered his needs.

Tracy

It's poorly phrased. What it means is that if you start talking again, the customer stops thinking about buying and gets distracted.

That's why it's so important. Oh by the way, in life it's a very good policy when you ask a question to just wait patiently for the answer. Don't rush in and trip over the line and start talking again before the person has had a chance to respond.

Wright

I've noticed that people, when I ask them questions you know down through the years, of course I've stepped on enough lines in my life, but I've noticed that some people answer very quickly. Others take a long time before they answer. And to consider that silence anything other than thinking about it is kind of dangerous, isn't it?

Tracy

Yes.

Wright

With the entry of internet sales, how is it possible for a customer to assess his needs without a trained sales person discovering needs through examination?

Tracy

Well, I have my own internet business. I do more than a million dollars a year on the internet. It's taken several years to develop it.

So I know a little bit about internet business and sales. Here's the basic rule. The internet only works to sell a product that the prospect has already determined he or she is going to buy. In other words, it is not a place where you assess a person's needs unless you are doing something as sophisticated as purchasing a computer from Dell, and even then people who buy a Dell computer using the internet are people who are very knowledgeable about exactly what they want. They are not people who are there to have their needs assessed and to be analyzed and figured out. So the only companies that are successful on the internet are companies that are selling specific fixed products that people have gone there to buy. Amazon is the perfect example. Nobody buys a book from Amazon because Amazon sold it to them. They go to Amazon to buy a book because it's convenient, but they already know the book their going to buy. So, the role of the internet is basically to sell a product where all of the discretion has been taken out of it. It's a specific product at a specific price with specific specifications, and it has to be unconditionally guaranteed. to sell over the internet. So sales people really have little or no role in sales.

Wright

Yeah, I know. I keep forgetting one of the titles of one of your books. I have recommended it to over a thousand people. You wrote it a couple of years ago. It's the one about getting a job and making more money.

Tracy

Yes.

Wright

It's a hardback. It's only about 90 something pages, maybe a hundred pages long, but I'll tell you what, it's probably the most powerful, practical book I have ever read on the subject.

Tracy

Well, thank you.

Wright

So I tell them to go to your website and buy the book that says something about make more money and find a job.

Tracy

Actually, it is *Get Paid More And Promoted Faster.*

Wright

That's it! That's it! What a great book that was.

Tracy

Well, thank you.

Wright

You know I've read more books and heard more cassettes and CDs and attended more workshops and seminars on customer service than any other single topic. Yet, customer service seems to be at an all-time low. Am I over sensitive, or do we have a problem with customer service in this country?

Tracy

Well, the challenge there, you have to understand that it's very much like saying you know some people are polite and some people are rude. So it differs from person to person. And even within the same restaurant, it differs from person to person in the same business. So, it's very much a personal thing. What we have found, by the way, is that people treat their customers the way the manager treats them. So whenever you go into a place that has great customer service, you'll find that the manager is a good manager, and takes really good care of his people. It's a natural, logical expansion from the manager to the people in the company to the customers. Whenever there is poor customer service, it means you have a poor manager. The manager treats the people poorly, so they just take it out on the first people that they meet. So all over America, and in every single business, there are different levels of customer service. Some are fantastic, some are medium, some are poor, but what we know is that customers today are so demanding that if you do not treat them really well, they will go away and never come back. They will just continue gravitating like moths to a flame. They will continue gravitating toward the companies that treat them the best. That's why the companies that have the best service are the ones that are growing most rapidly.

Wright

I know that you've trained so many people in the last few years because I've watched your career just soar. I'm a real fan, and a lot of my friends have everything taped on TPN that you ever did. So I skipped a question I really wanted to ask you because I'm interested in your feelings about it. The question is, you know, perhaps sales as a vocation is more appealing than it has been in the past; however, it seems that a salesperson does not enjoy the respect and the admiration that a "professional" does. Why do you think that is?

Tracy

Well, there's two answers to that. Earl Nettier once said that there is no such thing as a good job. There are only good people doing that job. So every single job, the person who does it brings honor to the job. Let me give you a quick aside. I was at a California Pizza Kitchen not far from us. One of the people who works there as a porter and a busboy table care is a Mexican immigrant whose name is Manuel Salverago. This guy is hard working. He's got a problem with his back and his leg, so he walks with a limp. He's hard working. He's fast. He is pleasant. He is polite. He recognizes people. He's not even a waiter. He's just a busboy. He's just in motion all the time. You go there and you sit there, and I look for this, you say, "Geez, this is an incredible guy. Look at the way he does that. Look at the way he moves." And he comes up and we talk, and I always say hello to him. And he says hello, he recognizes me. And I said to the manager, "You know that's a remarkable guy there." He says, "Oh, huh, Manuel, he's the most dynamic person in this whole company." He is so respected. He's admired by everybody. He's well paid. Everybody likes him. Why? It's because he brings honor to his work. Now, let's come to sales. In sales, I've learned a very interesting paradox. In sales, it's easy to get in. Anybody can get a sales job. But that is where easy stops. Many people think because it's easy to get in, it's easy to rise. So they get a job, and maybe they have an interview a couple of times, but then they wonder why they are just not rising up like getting into an elevator and pushing a button. After you get the sales job, from then on everything is hard, harder, and harder still. Nothing is easy.

So therefore, everybody who starts off in sales, because it's easy to get in, starts off like a marathon runner way back in the pack, and then the work begins. And you have to work a long time. You know, in order to move to the top of the field, it takes five to seven years to be a master of your craft. Now this is the most remarkable thing, and it's shocking to people. Let's say if you want to be a tennis player, if you want to be a salesperson, if you want to be a lawyer, after you have learned the basic skills, it then takes five to seven years of hard work, continually upgrading your skills, continually practicing to master your craft to get into the top 10%. Now here's a couple of points. If you dedicate yourself to becoming excellent in selling, there's nothing that will stop you from eventually getting into the top 10%. In the top 10% of your field, I don't care what your business is, you're going to be one of the highest paid people in this country. You're going to be respected and esteemed by people around you. You're going to be a major force in your community. You're going to be looked up to and admired. You're going to be taking company sponsored trips. You're going to have a beautiful home and life for your family. But it's going to take you five to seven years of hard work to get there. Now here's the second point. The time's going to pass anyway. It's very important to understand the time is going to pass anyway. Five to seven years from now, five to seven years will have passed. The biggest mistake that people make, and the biggest regret they have, is why didn't I start earlier? Why didn't I start five to seven years ago and just put my head down because the time is going to pass anyway. The only difference is five to seven years from now, are you going to be at the top of your field enjoying a fabulous living, be one of the most respected people in your business, have a beautiful home and a car and a wonderful income, or are you going to be back in the pack struggling away with the 80 to 90% of the majority. But the time is going to pass anyway.

So therefore, it's easy to get into selling, but after that it's like easy to get into a huge marathon. You may have to qualify a little bit, some you don't even have to qualify. You just have to pay the entry fee. But then the race begins, and then it's a long race. That is really hard. It's not easy after that. It's only easy to get into the race, then you have to work. That's why some people make selling an honorable field, and they are the most respected people in their business. And some people just struggle away, and they've got holes in their shoes. They never read, and they never listen to audio programs. They never go to sales seminars. They come in late and they leave early, and they blame all their problems on the company or the competition, and they don't understand why they don't move ahead. But it's purely self-inflicted wounds.

Wright

I've heard a lot about personality profiles in the past few years. There are a lot of companies that have a lot on the market. Do you think one can predict with any accuracy a good person with a sales profile that will be more likely to be successful?

Tracy

Absolutely! We use sales profiles extensively, and we use them with major corporations. I did some work with a Fortune 500 Company recently. I brought in one of my experts who did a personality profile on their entire sales force. They had about eight teams working nationwide. With just the profiles, and there are three profiles, and the first profile is does this person have the personality of a salesperson? The second profile is can this person sell? Do they have the requisite skills? The third skill is will this person sell? Do they have the internal drive? And the third one is the value test. It's very important because there are people who have a great personality, but you put them into a sales situation, they collapse. So they did all three tests. They broke them and categorized them into teams. And then he explained to the senior executives, this is your top team. This is your middle team. This is your bottom team. This is what they do. This is what they say. These are their complaints. These are their successes. And they went back and forth and explained. He never even met these people. He just had them do the test, and they were absolutely astonished. He had absolutely picked out the top performers in every team, the top team in every area; their strengths, weaknesses, what they do, and he said this is your major problem within your sales force nationally. He explained that this is they're very strong on prospecting and getting the first appointment. They are very weak on closing. They are poor at their customer development. It goes on and on, and they were just shaking their heads because all of that stuff they had learned from years of experience. So yes, personality profiles are very, very important. We will never hire a person without doing a basic personality profile on them to find out if they have the personality that we require.

Wright

You know many people, and I would probably fall into this category, look for people as role models and search for successful people to become mentors as they travel the path of becoming better or a more successful salesperson. Is that thinking still useful? If so, who are some of the people that have shaped your business success?

Tracy

Well, I worked with Dr. Albert Schweitzer in Africa many years ago. Schweitzer is famous for having said, "You must teach men at the school of example for they will learn at no other." So role models are critically important for us because we need to see how it is done properly, which is true in every sport. It's true in music. It's true in everything. So what happens with human beings is we gravitate towards what we most admire. If we admire a person, then what we do is we gravitate toward emulating the behaviors of that person. If we admire men and women of courage and integrity, then what we do is we try to exemplify courage and integrity in our own lives. So role models are very important. Mentors are important as well as long as they are role models. A mentor who gives advice, who is also admired by the person receiving the advice, is going to have a major impact on that person's personality. Then the final question with regard to me is I have been positively influenced by hundreds, maybe thousands, of people over the years. You can have a mentor or role model who died two thousand years ago, or whose books you've read, or whose audio programs you've listened too. So you don't have to have direct one-on-one contact with them. Someone can write a fabulous article or a beautiful poem, and you can admire that and respect it and agree with the sentiments in that person. Then that person's views will have an effect on your personality.

Wright

When I first got into sales when I was a young fellow, I used to just take it so seriously, and you know I was probably a drag even to myself. Then I got enrolled, I mean there were records, there weren't any cassettes out yet, of a fellow named Bill Gove in Florida who used to work for 3M.

Tracy

I know him very well. He was one of my very dear friends.

Wright

I found out that you can have a great sense of humor and still be a successful salesperson. It's not all that serious. He probably never knew that he was one of my role models, but he certainly was.

Tracy

That's great! He's a great man. He died recently, but Bill Gove was a great man.

Wright

I hated to learn about his passing. His passing is going to have a great impact, especially on the National Association of Speakers.

Tracy

Yes.

Wright

He was really, really admired by and respected widely by that group.

Finally, what word of encouragement do you have for anyone in our reading audience that might help them become more successful as they follow their career path of sales and service?

Tracy

Well, the biggest weakness we have in America is what is called the "quick fix" mentality. Everybody wants things fast and easy, and you have to get over that if you want to be successful and happy in your field. You have to realize that success takes a long time, and that you are in a race. So you are going to have to work harder than other people who want to be successful as well. You have to invest more in yourself, in learning and growing. You have to manage your time better. Above all, you have to see more people.

The great rule for success is to spend more time with better prospects, to spend more time with better prospects. The more people you see, the better you get, and the better you get, the more effective you are. The more effective you are, the more sales you make. The more sales you make the more motivated you are to see even more people. So it's what is called a positive feedback loop in psychology. If you constantly upgrade your skills and learn new things, and then try those new things with your prospects and customers, you get feedback, and you get results which motivate you to do even more of it. I'm pretty sure you'll put yourself onto an upward spiral. You must realize that everybody who is at the top today started at the bottom. Everyone who is doing well was once doing poorly. Everybody who is at the top of your field was at one time not in your field at all. What others have done, you can do as well. What others have done, you can do as well if you just learn how and just practice it until you master it.

Wright

What are you working on right now? Are you working on a book? I do want to run people to your website. It's www.briantracy.com. A lot of my friends call me and they say, "I tried to find that Brian Tracy fellow and he doesn't have a website." I say, "Well, you're misspelling it then." But anyway I would like to suggest that people go to your website for products on several different topics that I have enjoyed down through the years. But what are you working on now?

Tracy

Well, I'm just finishing up a new book. It's called *Million Dollar Habits*, and it will be out in December. I just released my latest book which is called *Change Your Thinking: Change Your Life*, and it's shipping to the bookstores as we speak. I just signed a new contract for a book called *How to Master Your Time* which will be out in march and it's going to be the best book on time management ever written. I am just getting a new contract in the mail for a book that will be out next year called *Getting Rich In America*, which is going to be a powerful book on all the different ways people go from rags to riches.

Wright

The habits book that's coming out, what is it about? Is it a how-to book?

Tracy

Oh yes, it's very practical. It shows 95% of everything that you do in life is governed by your habits, and that successful people have success habits. The habits range from the way they think about themselves to their attitudes toward their goals, setting goals each day, to their attitude toward money, toward work, toward family, relationships, health, business growth, savings and investments, and so on. It's a series of habits that people have that when you practice these habits, which you learn by repetition, you achieve more and more, faster and faster, easier and easier.

The difference in life is that some people have these success habits because they've been taught them or they've developed them, and some people have not yet learned them. The wonderful thing is that they are all learnable. So you can learn to get up a little earlier. You can learn to set priorities on your work. You can learn to write and rewrite your goals. You can learn to save and invest part of what you earn. You can learn to continually upgrade your skills. You can learn to listen better with other people. You can learn the key habits of health, and so on. What I do is I teach this. These are all the habits that are practiced by the happiest, most successful, and best paid people in our society including all self-made millionaires.

Once you develop these habits, there's a rule that everything is hard before it's easy. So developing a habit is hard, but once you develop the habit, it's easy because it's automatic. You just do it. You breathe in, you breathe out. You just follow the habit. This method becomes easy and automatic for you to do what the successful do. You'll make more progress in a week or two or in a year or two than some people make in a lifetime.

Wright

I really appreciate the time you've spent with me. Thank you so much.

About The Author

One of the world's top success motivational speakers, Brian Tracy is the author of may books and audio tape seminars, including *The Psychology of Achievement, The Luck Factor, Breaking the Success Barrier, Thinking Big* and *Success Is a Journey.*

Brian Tracy

www.BrianTracy.com

Chapter Seven

KAREN PHELPS

THE INTERVIEW

David E. Wright (Wright)

Today we're talking to Karen Phelps. Karen is a professional speaker, trainer and consultant. She's a member of the National Speakers Association, The Direct Selling Association, and The Direct Selling Women's Alliance. She is an active member of her local Rotary Club and loves volunteering for projects to help the less fortunate. Karen believes we get what we except in life. She spent twenty-two years managing her own business in direct sales and overcame the obstacles and setbacks of the industry. She learned the extreme importance of goal setting, life balance and self-confidence. She knows the secrets of successful leadership and how to promote team work within your organization. Karen, welcome to *Conversations on Success.*

Karen Phelps (Phelps)

Thank you, David. I'm excited to be here.

Wright

Karen, everyone seems to have his or her own definition of success. How would you define success?

Phelps

I learned an easy definition for success a long time ago. I was told that success is a continued realization of any worth while goal. So, to me, success means that you're living your life with passion and are continually enjoying the benefits of realizing your dreams and reaching your goals. Success is also the journey along the way to reaching your goals.

Let's say I set a goal for myself and I know it's going to take about three years to accomplish it. I've made my plan and I have the steps I need to take along the way. So, every time I accomplish one of the steps, it takes me closer to realizing my goal and I know that I've been successful. Too often, people acquaint success with amassing a fortune. You know, you could have not a penny to your name and still be truly successful. Several years ago, I read Mother Theresa's story and thought it was absolutely incredible. Mother Theresa died the way she lived, in poverty, while donating her life to helping others. Yet, how could anyone say she wasn't successful. She was one of the most successful people who ever lived because she was continually accomplishing her dreams and goals. After one goal was finished, she'd set another and another. She lived her life to help others and that was her success story. I believe that all of us have a success story that's waiting to be written. We all have to have a personal definition of what success is going to mean to us.

Wright

In other words, amassing a fortune, in your opinion, doesn't make a person successful?

Phelps

I think that's absolutely true. I've known a lot of successful people that have chosen to live their lives in poverty and who devote their lives to helping others. Yet, because they're pursuing their dreams and realizing them, they are still very successful. To me, wealth doesn't necessarily equate success and success doesn't always lead to happiness and fulfillment. Some people are born wealthy, but they haven't done anything with their life. Then I've met some very wealthy people, who have more money than they know what to do with, and pretty much let everybody know that. I've come across people that are rude and arrogant and look down on others. They're continually giving up their life in the pursuit of more money. They have no family life, no close friends, and a lot of times they're despised by the people who work for them. Fortunately, I have found that most of the people I've met that have substantial wealth don't really fall into that category.

I worked in Direct Selling for almost twenty-five years, and it was absolutely one of the best experiences of my life. I did, though, happen to work with some very incredible people. One of those people was the owner and president of our company. I can recall when I had won a trip to Hawaii, and I was waiting in the airport with my husband and our 2 sons, whom we had taken on this trip. We were waiting in baggage for our luggage to arrive when the owner of the company, John Fredrick, came up to greet us. He strolled across the airport dressed in blue jeans and a cowboy hat, gave everybody a hug and introduced himself. It was just so friendly and he really made my sons feel at ease. I can remember my youngest son, Bryan, who was about twelve or thirteen at the time said, " Wow, that's the president of your company? He sure doesn't look like a president." It was funny because I realized that I was really lucky to work for somebody that put himself at our level. He didn't raise himself above the sales force and he never made us feel inferior. Stan Fredrick and Novice Nicholson, two other owners, were very much the same way. They always made us feel like we were equals.

Last year I had the privilege of meeting Tom Tierney, a person that I really respect and admire. I was doing some work for his company out in California. If I were to talk about Tom, I'd say that he is the person everyone wants to be, when he or she grows up. He's also the person that everybody wants to work for. Let me tell you what they did on the last evening of the event. Tom and his wife Elizabeth loaded everybody up in buses and took them to their ranch for a great big elaborate dinner. It was really incredible watching how they interacted with the sales people. As I went on a tour of the company earlier with him, I could tell from the people that they respected and admired him. They enjoyed working for the company because he treated his employees and his sales force with total respect and dignity. Tom and Elizabeth are very wealthy, yet, much of their wealth goes to doing things for their community. Both of them donate time as well as money for good causes. In fact, Tom is the first chair in Peace Studies in the University of California system, which researches ways to save humanity from itself. Together, Tom and Elizabeth are leading a capital campaign for their pet project, a $400 Million, 380 bed major hospital, which is going to be complete with a children's hospital and comprehensive cancer center. These are just a couple of the projects that they're involved with. When I visited them I was amazed at how active and involved they are in improving their community. They have been recognized by the community and have received several awards including "Philanthropists of the Year" and "Volunteers of the Year." They are the type of people that I admire and respect because they're living their lives with passion in everything they do. I choose not to be a person who isn't fulfilled by not pursuing their dreams, their passions and their goals.

Wright

You have suggested three questions you feel everyone should ask themselves and if they could answer YES to these three questions, you feel that they're reaching their "success potential." So what are these questions?

Phelps

First of all, I've got to give credit to a good friend of mine, Toni Clubb, who incidentally works with Tom Tierney, which is how I met her. We were having one of those deep discussions when she shared with me some information she had learned from a Model-Netics Program. She said to me, *"Karen, people need to ask themselves three questions and the answers to these questions will help them define their purpose in life."* The first question is," *Are you going where you want to go?"* In other words, are you living the life that you've dreamed about? The second question is, " *Are you doing what you want to do?"* Are you working to live or are you living to work? Most people work just enough "to keep up with the Jones." They get stuck in jobs that they despise but see no light at the end of the tunnel because of the debt they have accumulated. Therefore, they're not doing what they want to do. The third question is, *"Are you being who you want to be?"* Are you proud of the person that you are? I feel that if you can answer yes to those three questions then you're definitely leading a very successful life.

Wright

What do you feel stops people from reaching success?

Phelps

I believe that there are several things that contribute to a person's failure to succeed. I think one of the first obstacles is that they don't know what their passion in life is. Therefore, there's not a clearly defined goal and/or objective for where they're going. The second barrier would be that they have the goal in place, but they haven't acquired the knowledge and/or the skills that they need to reach the goal. A third challenge could be that the person could have the knowledge, but hasn't made the plan to apply the knowledge. Another obstacle that prevents people from reaching success is their fear. People often fear success because the path to success brings changes in your life. Not everybody is open to change. We find today that technology is changing the world at an incredible pace and jobs are constantly being redefined. Men and women entering the job market today, it's been said, are probably going to have several different jobs over their lifetime. Unlike their parents, who most likely started and ended their career with the same company. The person who succeeds and stays ahead is the one who embraces the changes and looks for new opportunities to further his or her career. The last thing that I really think stops people from being truly successful, is their need for approval from others. Often, these people stop themselves short because they let others define what success is.

Wright

So can you sum up those five action steps for our readers?

Phelps

Absolutely, first of all, you have to identify your passion and your purpose; know where you're going, know who you want to be. The second one is, set your goals and acquire the knowledge that you need to reach them. Next, identify your course or your plan of action. Then, face your fears and do it any way, but the most important thing is to do it for yourself. Do it because you know that you can succeed and stop worrying about what the others think. I believe that when you learn these five steps and learn to overcome the "yeah, buts," that you are definitely on the path to success.

Wright

What's a "yeah, but?"

Phelps

Well, "yeah, buts" are the excuses we give others and ourselves as to why we haven't pursued our goals, ambitions and dreams. The "BUT" is what gets in our way. For an example, someone says, "I wanted to go back to college, BUT now I'm too old." So I have an acronym that helps people to get over their "yeah, buts."

Wright

Can you share the acronym with us?

Phelps

Sure. First of all, the "B" stands for "Belief." I think we have pre-conditioned beliefs about why we can or can't achieve success that goes way back to events or conversations that we've had with others in our past. These conversations then become internal and are continually growing in our subconscious. Every time we bring up a new goal or challenge for ourselves, the "old belief" crops up with it. As individuals we need to change our belief system. The easiest way to do this is to "Understand why you believe that way and Undo the pattern." So in other words, you need to write down your belief and why you believe what you do. After you fully "Understand" it, then you need to "Undo that pattern of thinking" and change your thoughts to your "new Belief system. Then you need to "Test new theories and procedures." If you have always done the same thing because you always believed the same way, then once you change your beliefs you need to change the way you've been doing things. You can't just change your thoughts without changing your behavior. So, to sum it up, change your Beliefs, Undo the pattern and Test new theories and procedures.

Wright

So, how have you overcome the obstacles for reaching success?

Phelps

David, I think everybody has little things that get in their way of success. One of the obstacles that I had to overcome, believe it or not, was a total lack of self-confidence. I was very smart growing up, but yet I was very, very insecure. It was when I began my Direct Selling career and I attended a Zig Ziglar seminar that I bought his program *"How to Stay Motivated"* and I really began to develop my self-confidence. For over twenty years I've taken a walk almost everyday, which is when I listen to motivational tapes. Trust me, I have programs from all the masters. I have Zig Ziglar, Jim Rohn, Brian Tracy, John Maxwell, Norman Vincent Peale, Steven Covey, Tony Robbins plus many, many others. So I know that this practice of getting up every morning and continually putting these positive ideas in my head has really helped me and has encouraged the development of my self-confidence. It's also been a great way for me to start the day, because not only did I listen to the program, I actually did the assignments that came with the programs. This is where a lot of people fall short; they'll listen, but then they don't follow up with the actions that are needed in order to change. So, I started doing success journals. I discovered what my purpose and my passions in life were and I realized that I can do anything I want as long as I set the goals and I make my plan of action.

Wright

What do you feel have been some of your most important successes?

Phelps

My most important successes are basically very simple and may not seem like a lot to other people, but I haven't defined my successes by what other people think success is. I feel one of my most important successes in life was being able to be a stay at home mom, with my kids, while at the same time running an incredible Direct Selling business from my home. You see, one of my great purposes in life was to be a "great mom" and I knew that, for me, that was going to involve my being able to be with my sons, Brandon and Bryan, as much as possible. I didn't want to work the whole time they were growing up, yet it was important for me to have an income to help support the family. So I spent twenty-two very successful years in the Direct Selling industry. I built a large organization that was consistently in the top of my company. I earned free trips around the world, yet I still had time to do all the things that are important to us as a family. Another success that I'm extremely proud of is my marriage to my husband, Larry, because we met in ninth grade and we've been together ever since. We've been married for over thirty years, and we're still best friends. To me, that's one of my greatest successes. I've also had some amazing successes in my direct selling years. Through the years, I continually reached goals I set for myself, like earning trips to Hawaii, Australia, and Europe. Even being Number One leader in the company. I loved to challenge myself to be the best I could be and the times that I've been most successful in my life is when I have defined my purpose and I've followed my passion.

Wright

You had a major career change several years ago; can you share with us how it came about?

Phelps

Sure. My career change actually began, in my mind, in 1992. I had purchased the Anthony Robbins, *"Personal Power Program,"* which I'm sure a lot of people have heard of. I still have the journal that came with the program. One component of the program had us write down our goals and I wrote down two goals at that time. The first goal was to have the "Number One Personal Group Sales" for our company that year, which we accomplished three years in a row. The second goal I wrote down was to be a motivational speaker and sales trainer. So you see, the seed was planted in my head a long time ago, but I was a little afraid to make the change because I had built a very successful sales organization and to become a trainer for the industry meant that I would have to quit that business and forfeit my team. It took almost tens years for that dream to materialize.

Wright

Do you remember the defining moment that inspired you to open your company?

Phelps

Absolutely. It sounds a little crazy, David, but after September 11, 2001, I really began to question myself. One of the questions I kept asking was, if I had died today, would I have accomplished everything I wanted to accomplish? I could honestly answer "no" to that question. During that time, I read a book that I highly recommend, which is *Who Moved My Cheese,* by Spencer Johnson. The book asked the same question over and over again, "What would you do if you weren't afraid?" I knew what I would do and I realized that I wasn't doing it. I definitely would have been a speaker and an industry expert because I love to help others realize their potential. So my husband, Larry, and I sat down, had several discussions about starting a new business, and in November of 2001, I took the leap. I decided to "move with the cheese" and I was ready to "savor the adventure and enjoy the taste of new cheese." I can honestly say that I have never looked back. I realize now that my purpose in life has changed and as my family grew I fulfilled my purpose and followed my plan. Now that my sons were grown it was the right time to act. And I think that's really important because sometimes we know what our plan is, but we have to have that specific time frame that's going to be right for us. Now my purpose in life is to provide others with the hope that they too can have all the success in life they want, if they're willing to identify it and follow their heart. When I started, I began reading everything I could get my hands on about success, leadership and sales. Anything that would help me with the topics I knew I would be speaking about. Another good book that I read during my transition period was *Failing Forward*, by John Maxwell. One section of this book was about "an ordinary man, doing something extraordinary." It states "one human being can affect a lot of other people and touch their lives in a very special way." I was ready to take that challenge. I was ready to begin helping other people in any way that I could. I just love it when people write to me about how one of my programs or ideas had given them what they needed to succeed in some area of their life.

Let me tell you a little story about a guy named Mike. Mike attended a self confidence workshop that I held in May of 2003. At that time, I spoke about writing down your goals and making a plan to reach them. Well, Mike set a goal to lose weight; he broke it down into steps. He sent me a before and after picture of himself in June of 2004, which was a little over a year later. He had lost seventy pounds. He sent me a thank you note for providing him with the means to do it. You know what, knowing that I helped someone like that is just such a high for me. It was so exciting.

Wright

So who supported you the most as you started your new career?

Phelps

I'm happy to say that I have a tremendous support system with my family. My husband, Larry, was and still is my number one supporter. He travels with me when he can, he listens to my program and he lets me know if I need to make a change here or there. Early on, as I was beginning my business and was learning as much as I could and setting up speaking events, he helped keep everything going by working overtime at his job. That really meant a lot to me, to know that he believed enough in me to say, "You go for it, you go do what you need to do." He worked a little over to compensate for the money that I was not bringing in at that time. *I'm really happy to say that he only had to do that for one year, which at that point, our business became profitable.* Both Larry's and my parents and all of our brothers and sisters have been very supportive. My parents continually call to ask how things are going, and I send my articles and writings to my mom to proofread for me. My mom and dad were really proud of the first book I co-authored with Insight Publishing called, *Real World Team Building Strategies that Work.* I sent them an autographed copy of it and they just love it. My sons Brandon and Bryan are always encouraging and supportive and they pretty much grew up with this positive "can do attitude" over the years, so they're pretty used to it all. A few years ago when I first started speaking, several of my brothers and sisters attended an event that I held in our area, on *"Life Balance."* It was a lot of fun having them in the audience and knowing that they were there to support me. Every now and then when we get together for a family party, which is being held at my house, if I start losing my cool or get myself over extended, they always bring me back to reality. One of them will say, "Karen, what about that life balance seminar you were doing? And have you listened to some of those things that you were telling us to do?" We all get a chuckle and life goes on.

Wright

You've come really far in such a short time.

Phelps

It's almost unbelievable to me how fast my career has exploded. Yet, when I look at it realistically, I know that I'm doing exactly what I teach everyone else in any of my programs. Larry and I sit down every few months and write down what our goals for the business are. We then make a plan of action for all the things we need to accomplish in the next few months. This includes the development of new products, booking more speaking engagements, writing articles, everything that needs to be done to help us to reach our goals. We also decided early on that I was going to do what ever it takes to be successful, which includes spending money and taking time to learn everything I can from the industry experts. I'm continually learning new ways to build and improve my business. I believe what has helped my business the most, are referrals from other people. I offer people simple and easy solutions that they can immediately implement. People who purchase my products or attend my programs often refer me to other people. You know what David, I know that I'm great at what I do and my goal is to be the woman that people can identify with. There are a lot of excellent male motivational speakers, but I want to be the best female motivator in the whole world.

Wright

You have a program titled, *"I am the Greatest,"* which sounds intriguing. How did you come up with the title?

Phelps

This program is one of the most fun programs that I do. It began as a volunteer project for a friend of mine, who was student teacher for a high school speech class. She asked me if I would come to school to give a speech to her students, to illustrate to them how to put a speech together. We basically brained stormed and came up with the topic of self-confidence, thinking that it might be useful for a high school class. My presentation included several stories about well known people, as well as a few stories about my children. I emphasized to the students that they needed to be careful about the thoughts that they have everyday and to be conscious of whether they're positive or negative.

For instance, a student might come to school really prepared for a test, but he could be thinking to himself, "Man, I hope I don't forget everything." Instead, he or she could change their thoughts to, "You know what, I'm prepared for this test and I know I'm going to do well on it." Changing your thoughts can really change the outcome of the performance. To make a long story short, the full time teacher, before I came in to this class said, "You know what, expect some talking, expect some disruptions, these are high school kids and it's really hard to get them to pay attention." Well, David, you could have heard a pin drop during my presentation. After I was done, I asked the students to write down what they had learned and to turn it in before they left class. It was one of the most incredible things I've ever been a part of. The feedback was absolutely amazing! I knew that for that one hour I had really touched their lives, had given them some confidence and inspired them to look at things from a different perspective. The title evolved when I was asked to speak to a group of senior citizens, who were members of a service organization. The person who asked me to speak had been looking though my list of topics and asked me to do a program on self-confidence. I just laughed and said, "Ok, what am I suppose to tell senior citizens about self-confidence that they don't already know?" I was really nervous about how to relate to the seniors, but I used stories about one of my favorite "self-confident" people, Mohammad Ali. I tied in various self-confidence principles along with stories and I used a quote that was made famous by Cassius Clay, who later became known as Muhammad Ali and the quote is, "I AM THE GREATEST!" I instructed the group to shout it really loud and everyone was laughing and having a good time and so that's kind of how the title of that program was born. You see, we can be GREAT at a variety of things. We can be a great spouse, a great student, a great teacher, a great engineer, a great sales person. If we accentuate our greatness in a particular area, we will be forced to continually improve in that area! And we will always be looking for new, different and better ways to become GREAT at what we do.

Wright

So what are some of the other programs you offer?

Phelps

I offer a variety of programs on subjects that I feel I'm an expert on. Having spent twenty-two years in Direct Selling helped me to learn and practice a variety of things that companies hire speakers for. "*Legendary Leadership©*" helps to define the skills needed to be a successful leader in any industry. In "*Life is a Balancing Act*," I help people identify what's most important in their life. I help them find ways to do want they want to do rather than continually doing the things they have to do. "*There's No Way But Up From Here*," teaches us to learn from life's ups and downs. My program "*Live Your Dreams*," challenges people in the audience to live the life that they dream about. I also have several programs that are specifically geared for the Direct Selling industry.

Wright

How do your programs differ from those of other speakers and what types of things can your audiences expect to learn from you?

Phelps

I know that the people in my audience will be able to identify with me as a person. My goal is to bring hope to the people in my audiences. They will learn that it's ok to fail but it's not ok to quit trying! My programs are fun, entertaining and interactive. They're going to learn simple and easy action steps that they can use immediately when they get home.

Wright

I've been told that you have a plaque that you have had hanging in your home for years that epitomizes what success means to you. Could you share it with our readers?

Phelps

I love this plaque. It was actually given to me as a gift over twenty years ago and is still something that I take the time to read almost every day. It was written by Barbara J. Burrow and is entitled, *That Woman is a Success*. It reads, "That woman is a success....who loves life and lives it to the fullest; who has discovered and shared the strengths and talents that are uniquely her own; who puts her best into each task and leaves each situation better than she found it; who seeks and finds that which is beautiful in all people...and all things; whose heart is full of compassion; who has found joy in living and peace within herself." When I read this, I ask myself, "Is this how I'm living my life?" If I can answer yes, then I know I'm on the right course. Then I can leave this world knowing that I've done everything within my power to use the talents that God has given me and I've lived my life with passion and fulfilled my purpose in life.

Wright

Well, you certainly motivated me. I've been taking notes here as we talked. I plan to follow up on these things. I really do appreciate you taking this amount of time with me here this morning to talk about success and I know our readers will enjoy your thoughts.

Phelps

Thank you so much, David. It's been my privilege to be here today.

Wright

Today we've been talking to Karen Phelps, who is a professional speaker, trainer and consultant. She believes that we get what we expect in life and I think that we have found out today that she knows what she is talking about. Thank you so much, Karen, for being with us on *Conversations on Success*.

About The Author

Karen Phelps, an international speaker, author and Direct Selling expert is the President of Phelps Positive Performance Inc., a company dedicated to helping others reach their "Peak Performance." She is an active member of the National Speaker Association, Direct Selling Association and Rotary International. Karen expects the best from herself and helps and encourages others to do the same. With 25 successful years in the Direct Selling industry she is someone who has "walked the talk," having been recognized for her outstanding personal and group sales achievements year after year. Karen's topics include positive attitude, self-confidence, teamwork, leadership, direct selling skills, and life balance and her real life experiences prove she's an expert on these subjects. She continually earns rave reviews for her high content, fun and energetic presentations. You can sign up for a free monthly motivational electronic newsletter on her website, www.Karenphelps.com.

Karen Phelps

Phelps Positive Performance Inc.

4041 Baybrook

Waterford, MI 48329

Phone/Fax: 248.673.3465

Email: Karen@Karenphelps.com

Chapter Eight

ROSA BATTLE   TIFFANEY BEVERLY   LOLITA HARRISON

THE INTERVIEW

David E. Wright (Wright)

Rosa Battle is a recognized leader, motivational speaker and sought after trainer in the network distribution industry, specifically known for her candied insight and her committee and devotion toward, practical solutions to the unique challenges women face in this industry. She is the Co-founded of a national women's empowerment organization, with an outreach base of thousands of women. Most recently held a *"Women With Vizion...Building Wealth"* empowerment seminar in Las Vegas, Nevada, which focused on helping women to create physical, spiritual, financial, and mental balance necessary for success. Currently, has an organization (along with her husband) that is quickly approaching 15,000 associates and generates over $5 million dollars in compensation, organizationally. She has reached the top executive position in several companies, most notably becoming the first female to do so in a predominately male dominated company. She was awarded *"Black Female Entrepreneur of the Year for Technology and Innovation, in 2001*, in Chicago, Illinois, awarded and currently wears the prestigious *"Six Figure Ring"* award to independent associates that earn $100,000. plus, in her home-based business, with Pre-Paid Legal Services, Inc.

Tiffaney Beverly has been in network distribution for five years. Despite her short tenure in the industry, she has reached a pinnacle commission level in Pre Paid Legal Services, Inc. She wears PrePaid Legal's prestigious 6-Figure Ring, which means she earns over $100,000/year in a 12-month period. She also holds the highest corporate field position: Regional Vice President. Having built a nationwide organization of thousands, she was recognized as one of Pre Paid Legal's *Rookies of the Year* for 2001. Despite her limited experience in the networking industry and humble beginnings as a manager in food manufacturing, she quickly has become a highly sought after speaker and trainer. She is known for her humor, candor, and from-the-heart speaking style.

Lolita Harrison is a sought after trainer, motivational speaker and personal development coach. She is the co-founder of Women With Vizion with an outreach base currently in the thousands. She has hosted several women's conferences nationwide. She has a passion for helping people and in the last six years, changed career paths from a 17-year background in the healthcare industry to embark upon the network distribution industry with an emphasis on legal services and economic empowerment. In a short period of time, she is earning a six figure income from home and wear the coveted *"Six Figure Ring"* awarded to independent associates that earn a minimum of $100,000 in their home-based businesses. She is one of the top executive directors with her company, and has been instrumental in helping many others reach the top levels of the company, where some earn six figures as well from home. She is a member of the National Black Chamber of Commerce. Mrs. Harrison is a happily married mother of two teenage children and currently resides in the Maryland area.

Rosa, Tiffany and Lolita, welcome to *Conversations on Success.*

Rosa Battle, Tiffaney Beverly, Lolita Harrison
(Battle, Beverly, Harrison)

Thank you, David. We're happy to be here.

Wright

Tell me, Rosa, what is WWV? Give me your definition of a Woman With Vizion.

Battle

David, WWV are letters that stand for Women With Vizions. It is an organization that was created for women by women. Originally, the women leaders of our home-based business started women share & care group meetings, if I recall correctly, by my partner, Mrs. Harrison. The women's share & care group meetings were started because of a crying out from women in our company to be able to understand clearly how to build a successful business, while still taking on life's day to day challenges. Later, when I came on board with our home-based business, I could see a huge need for women to bond and become a part of something that through unity would ignite a synergy that could help propel all women to higher heights, which were willing to explore the possibilities. So, understanding their need, but having a much broader vision, we organized and created "Women With Vizion." The broader vision includes all women from all walks of life. It includes women that are willing to take a close look at herself, regardless of her life's circumstances, her background, or current environment. This concept is supported by the fact that my partners and I truly believe that your past doesn't have to dictate your future. WWV is an organization that focuses on the empowerment, enlightenment, and uplifting of women. Now, to answer the second part of your question; How do I define a Woman With Vizion? A WWV is the women that feels she has a higher calling, a significant role to play in life. Additionally, a WWV woman wears proudly a giant size "S" on her chest, which stands for Superwomen, Significant, Strong, Synergistic, and Survivor. The WWV women may or may not clearly know what their role is, at first, but realizes that one reason for her existence on earth is to find it. In the book, *A Sole's Code*, the author explains your life's work is finding your life's role, and then to exercise the discipline, tenacity, and hard work it takes to purse it. David, we invite all women to join us on this bold mission, to take a look at where you want to go in life and to become fearless in the search to get there.

Wright

Tiffaney, do you define it any further?

Beverly

I think a Woman With Vizion, if I can expound on that a little, would be a woman who is willing to go beyond the status quo. A Woman With Vizion wants more out of life; and if she is content with her life, she is working diligently to help women who aren't content with theirs. Women With Vizion don't just sit back and watch; we act. In WWV, we just want to be the catalyst for a positive life change; to help women realize that they can make difference for themselves and others. WWV gives them the right road map and the courage to get there. I agree; I just think that it's a woman who knows that they deserve more and is willing to step out there to get it; and our organization helps them to do that.

Wright

Do you define it any differently, Lolita?

Harrison

Not really. David, echoing the same sentiments as my partners, and along those same lines, defining a Women With Vizion is an organization of women with purpose. We originated from a currently 90,000 + organization, known as NuVision Inc., which encompasses thousands of powerful like-minded men and women with a common vision and goal. Women With Vizion depicts John 20:29: *"Blessed are those that have not seen, and yet have believed."*

Wright

Rosa, what is you mission?

Battle

David, actually, we have a mission statement for Women With Vizion that I would like to share with you. Women With Vizion's mission is to create an organization of women that represent women from all walks of life, which are willing to take a close look at herself, regardless of circumstance, background, ethnicity or financial status; women with a purpose in mind of being a part of a sisterhood, which focuses on empowerment, enlight, and uplifting of women. The establishment of Women With Vizion will enable this diverse, creative sisterhood to utilize this kinship, to support women's unique challenges in family, business, and community. This unity will enable women to explore and ignite the true glory within her and allow the possibilities to become reality. Together, we can make a difference in our spiritual, financial, mental, and physical well being, that will enable us to continue to grow, guide and give. That's our mission statement, David.

Wright

Tiffaney, could you tell me something tangible that one of your members would do to make this mission statement true?

Beverly

What we do to make this mission statement tangible is put on extremely dynamic events that educate and train on philosophies that will build a better life. We know that good philosophies lead to good attitudes. Good attitudes lead to good actions. Good actions give good results. Good results will then give the desired lifestyle. We train on the proper mindset and attitudes in the areas of physical, mental, spiritual and financial. We actually put on trainings about three times a year where women will come and learn from those of us who have become mentors and role models for them because we have applied the proper philosophies in our lives. An exciting part of putting on these events is watching women grow from a member of the audience to a trainer; women who started in the seats are now joining us on stage giving back to other women. The women receive gifts at these events to constantly remind them that they are Women With Vizion. They also grow from the inside out, which makes their income grow as well.

Wright

So, as I understand it, you're treating the holistic view, the mind, body and spirit, is that right?

Beverly

Yes, that's exactly right. We get that philosophy from our mentor, billionaire, Mr. Paul J. Meyer, who teaches every aspect of your life must be balanced and in order for you to be a true success. Balance is something that women in society struggle with, and that's something a lot of women have come to us and asked us to help them with. One of the things we focus on in every event is not to just teach how to be successful in our business, but how to be a better overall individual. We teach how to focus on these different areas of their lives and how we have been able to achieve balance so they can be better overall.

Wright

Paul J. Meyer is a thirty-five year friend of mine. I have known that man forever. He has helped me do a lot of things. Lolita, do you have anything to add to that?

Harrison

David, Tiffany has hit it right on the head. I would like to add, along with the big events that she shared, we will also soon be launching smaller events. This will be called "Girl Talk." The goal is to continue to educate, empower and inspire our older and younger generations through personal development, fellowship and shared faith in our local markets in a more intimate setting.

Wright

Let's talk about success for a second; every time I ask someone to define success I get a different definition, depending on whom I am talking. Rosa, how would you define success and how is it measured?

Battle

Well, David, I couldn't agree with you more. There are so many different ways you can define success. I tend to agree with how Zig Ziegler defines it; success is involved in every facet in life, your relationships, your business, your health, your happiness, you financial security, and your peace of mind of knowing that you are respected, loved, trusted, and supported by others. Success is as simple as how you feel when you wake up each morning. If you feel good about the day before, you've had success in the feelings that you are now being rewarded. As simply as when you lay down at night, there is a smile, there is the thought that it doesn't getting any better then this, and believing in your heart you must be dreaming already before you go to sleep because life is so grand. Success can be as complex as having a five-year financial plan and reaching your financial goals in four years. I believe success is measured in all different types of facets as well, but more importantly, I feel test, scales, standards, grades, or comparisons do not measure success. But subsequently, by you everyday waking up thriving to be at a better place than the day before. When you feel like you are there. I think that answer of how success is measured lies within the individual, the perimeters, the goals, the feeling that you want to feel. David, the ultimate measure of success for me is when a person walks up and states, "Mrs. Battle, you just don't know how much you've impacted my life." When my husband smiles, and I know I put it there, when my prayer is concluded by, "Thank you, Lord." These are ways I measure success, David.

Wright

What do you think, Tiffaney?

Beverly

Well, when you asked that question I had to smile because I have never come up with my own definition of success. John Wooten has an incredible definition of success that I have adopted as my own: "Success is peace of mind, which is a direct result of self satisfaction in knowing you did your best to become the best that you are capable of becoming." I've learned in this business that the joy is truly in the journey. So to me, it's not having the nicest cars, the most money or the best clothes. Before I got involved in this industry, I thought that was success. Your success was how much jewelry you had or how much was in your bank account; but now I know that there are a lot of people who have all of those trappings of success but don't really have true success because they don't have the self-satisfaction and the peace of mind of knowing that they did their very best, and basically are happy with that. I now know that success is truly being satisfied in knowing you did your very best at being your very best. That is in your spiritual walk, your business, your family life, etc. To me, success is not what I have; it's who I have become. As long as I know that I have done my very best at becoming my very best; that is success to me. Now, I try to instill that in others so they don't get wrapped up in all of those non-important things, those tangible assets that really don't mean anything, because we can't take them with us.

Wright

Could you add anything to that, Lolita?

Harrison

Yes, absolutely. Often I reflect on that because there are so many different meanings for success for so many different people for what they deem as success is in their lives. For me, success is when you are fulfilling your purpose. That's what puts a smile on my face. Living life in your purpose gives you a sense of fulfillment. We were placed on this earth for a purpose. I do realize that many people are not walking in their God given talents, their abilities and their purposes in life because of their circumstances, situations and lack of finances. However, when you understand who you are and the reason why you are here and you are operating in that, to me, only then can you have true success.

Wright

Paul J. Meyer says that success is a progressive realization of your own personal worthwhile pre-determined goals. I think all three of you have hit right into that. Rosa, let me ask you, what are some of the unique challenges that women face in your industry?

Battle

David, we're involved in an industry that is predominately male dominated. It is the industry of network distribution. However, I would be remised not to mention, although male dominated today, women are quickly reaching higher levels in a lot of companies across the country. When you think about it, women really should dominate this industry. The reason I've made such a bold statement is because most network distribution companies are home based and most women, if given a choice, would prefer to work from home. I feel that being home based is a perfect fit for many women, specifically women with school age children, husbands that work away from home, and women that take overall responsibility for the day to day running of a household. Now, back to your question. One challenge is that of getting the respect level from our male counterparts, specifically not being taken seriously about our business and authority. Of course, this challenge is not isolated to our industry, it across the board. It is in corporate America, in our community, church, even in our homes. It's all around us. The respect level is definitely a big challenge that we face. Another challenge is juggling of work-life and family. Women are, in most cases, the caregivers for their children and spouse. I like to describe women as the COO, Chief Operating Office, of the household. Generally, women are responsible for the day to day operations of the home...getting the children ready for school, preparing meals, cleaning the home, and if married, supporting the spouse. Not to exclude single women, for many they have these responsibilities as well as juggling a social life, or significant other. Prioritizing these huge responsibilities and running a business, working a job, or pursuing your passion can be a major dilemma. Recognizing these unique challenges and focusing on solutions is our goal for Women With Vizion. We do this when we put on our training and empowerment seminars. We help women to see how they can overcome these challenges. Additionally, we stress to them how we can't allow these challenges to become obstacles for us in our journeys towards success. I feel that gaining respect and juggling work-life and family are big challenges. But, would like to quickly point out that these can never be barriers to us our success.

Wright

Tiffaney, what do you think are some of the unique challenges faced in your industry.

Beverly

I 'm just going to speak for myself. I am not a wife or a mother; it's just me. So my challenge was being a new entrepreneur and having to do it alone. I had to stay focused on accomplishing my goals in Pre-Paid Legal so I could get the other things I wanted in life, like a spouse and children. Sometimes I feel we put the cart before the horse. For some of us women, our journey is to be a successful businessperson first, then wife, then mother. Also, like Ms. Battle pointed out, we are in a male dominated industry. I have dealt with the challenge of learning to become a strong leader, but still remaining a respected woman. There's a fine line for a lot of us where once we become a strong leader, or a strong businessperson, people tend to stop treating us as a woman. I've had to deal with still being a strong woman, remaining feminine, and not losing my identity as a woman in this industry, but still earning the respect of male leadership or male subordinates and letting them know that I am here and I am a force in this business. I'm not here because I'm cute, I'm not here because I'm a woman, I'm here because I'm just as strong and just as good in this business as my male counterparts. One of our challenges is just surviving in a world that still depicts women as frivolous. As if we are to be looked at, and not necessarily respected or heard. Even though there are countless successful women in the world, in every arena, even though we are well into the new millennium, we still have to be cognizant that there are people out there who still do not treat us as equals until we demand it. So I think that it is a huge challenge in our industry that we are helping women remain strong, beautiful women, but still be great entrepreneurs and leaders.

Wright

Someone has said that a strong male leader is aggressive and a strong female leader is pushy. Actually they use the "B" word, but I didn't want to embarrass anybody.

Beverly

I was thinking the same thing, David. I didn't know if it would be appropriate; but the truth is always appropriate.

Wright

Lolita, what do you think some of the unique challenges are?

Harrison

I am in agreement with my partners. Definitely, respect is the main thing. As women we are seen as the weaker vessel. Most men, not all men, have a lack of understanding as to the word weak. As women, we may be weak in physical strength compared to our male counterparts. However, when it comes to intellect, creativity, endurance etc., we can rank right up there with the best of them. We can certainly hold our own. David, there used to be a saying, "Behind every successful man is a strong woman." I believe that things are evolving a bit. There are a lot of women who are just as successful. Some making as much, and in some instances more money than their male counterparts. I am just so blessed to have a husband who is strong enough to let me be the woman that I am pre-destined to be and that is not taking anything away from him. I appreciate my leadership within my industry (all males), who have allowed my strength to illuminate where we complete each other and not just compete with each other. In addition, another challenge is managing our emotions. As women, we are emotional beings. As a result, our emotions can hold us back from our goals and visions in life, but we have to learn that life is 10% of what happens and 90% of how we respond to it. Lastly, we are constantly being challenged with being heard and not just seen. My partners and I, being attractive women are very cognizant of our dress, posture and our language; basically, the overall way we carry ourselves is very important to be taken seriously. Also, David, if I could expand on that "B" word, I've actually given it a different definition for those who have used that word. For me, it now stands for a "babe in total control of herself." It's from my experience that people only use this specific adjective as a defense mechanism. Sadly, they are intimidated by women who know what they want and threatened by women who know how to get what they want. However, I just helped them to turn a negative word into a positive one.

Wright

Rosa, how do you handle some of these unique challenges? What do you do to make them come alive and help these ladies?

Battle

David, I feel they become alive by the fact that we identify with women and their circumstances. Knowing first hand that the unique challenges are real for women. I can't help but to share with you an experience that I had with one of my male business partners. We were having a conversation and he shared with me that he felt that women did not have any more challenges in business than men. Of course, we are all entitle to our opinions, but the fact of the matter is that if I've experience occasions where our challenges where in questioned, so have other women. So it's important to women to acknowledge that these challenges are real. We definitely focus on how to handle these unique challenges in our seminars with action-oriented solutions. During our seminars, when we address gaining respect, we train on creative and appropriate ways to communicate with others to achieve positive results. We re-enact real life situations in the form of skits and provide scripts with the appropriate dialogue to be used in these situations. Additionally, we have Q&A sessions in order to address the specific needs of the women in attendance at the seminars. In my opinion, communication is key, and how well we as women do this has an overall impact on the results we get. We train women how to be very, very clear when establishing goals and work expectations with our male counter parts. Professionalism and knowledge of our business are critical success factors we must display. I feel having these characteristics will not only warrant respect, but also demand it from our male counterparts. David, when we address the challenges of creating a work/ life/family balance, we focus on how critical organizational skills are. We provide women easy strategies to get organized where it's a win/win for both business and home. On the other hand, we are quick to point out in our trainings that we can't use challenges as excuses for our failures. David, bottom line, one thing I know for sure is that men and women wake up each day with one thing in common, both have 24-hours to work with, and it's simply a matter of what you do within those 24-hours that move you forward in life. Our purpose is to help women to jump out of bed with a head start.

Wright

Tiffaney, what advice would you give to an aspiring female entrepreneur?

Beverly

First, I would say jump in headfirst. Don't make the mistake of listening to a lot of unsuccessful people and end up doing what unsuccessful people do, and that is listening to their friends, family members and neighbors. I say that first and foremost, because it was my friends and family members that almost kept me from taking this step into PrePaid Legal Services. My life would not have been changed for the better if I had listened to them. In the book, *Think and Grow Rich*, the number one reason for failure is that people listen to their friends and family members. Believe that you can do it and just go for it; that's the first thing. I feel we have a tendency to value a little too much what others say we can do with our lives, instead of what we feel we can do with our lives. In a nutshell, the first advice I would give is: don't listen to anyone else, just listen to your heart, listen to your Creator and go for it. The second bit of advice that I would give is: be willing to fail. Laugh at your failure; learn from it and keep on going. I have literally failed my way to $100,000.00 per year in PrePaid Legal, and I will fail my way to $250,000.00 per year and beyond. Don't be afraid to fail, realize that all successful people have failed. Watson, the founder of IBM, said, "The way to succeed is to double your rate of failure." I think, as women, we think that we have to be perfect and if we do something wrong everyone is going to see and think badly of us. I have embraced my failure. Every failure that I have had has led to my success. It has given me courage and wisdom to help others. I would also say watch your associations! Ask yourself: "What are they (my associations) doing to me? And is it okay? Get away from people who have your problems and get around those that have your solutions. Associate with good people; be willing to limit your associations and disassociate with people that will keep you from success. Women are great with relationships and keeping relationships going. Even if the relationship/friendship is going nowhere, it's a hindrance instead of a help, we keep putting work into it and we keep trying to salvage it. We have to learn that it's good to burn the bridge; but it's great to blow it up! Get away from those people that are keeping you down. I could go on and on, but I think that just going head first into your dreams, not listening to other people, and watching your associations is key. Also, be a continuous student, a perpetual learner. Remember, there is no such thing as a full-grown tree. Constantly feed yourself with personal development.

Wright

What advice would you give to an aspiring female entrepreneur, Lolita?

Harrison

I would encourage them to have a plan and vision. Without a clear plan it is like embarking into an unfamiliar city or town looking for a specific place with no roadmap or directions, and we already know that without vision, people will perish. Secondly, work the plan consistently with great passion, a burning desire and strong work ethic. It's amazing the type of success and people that you attract when they can really feel your heart and not just see your hand. Thirdly, Tiffaney touched on this, but I know it is worth mentioning again, that is personal development. You've got to personally develop daily. In order for your success to grow on the outside, you have to grow on the inside. You have to become someone different in order to attract something different. There are so many incredible books out there that can continue to feed us in a way where one of my mentors always says; "You have to feed your mind in order for your pockets to be fed." There are books such as, *Think and Grow Rich, Rich Dad, Poor Dad, Thinking For a Change, Who Moved my Cheese,* and *The Bible,* just to name a few, that can give you what you need to have the success that you deserve. Again, personal development daily can help you to become better every day. And lastly, taking action. As Ms. Beverly talked about, head first, just take action and be unstoppable with it. We know that the race is not given to the swift, nor the sword to the strong, but the one that endureth to the end. Perseverance is so necessary. With so many success stories of those who have gone before us such as Oprah Winfrey, Maya Angelou, Madame CJ Walker, Helen Keller, just to name a few, persevered through their trials and still triumphed. These are just a few things, David, which I would share with an aspiring entrepreneur.

Wright

Tell me, Rosa, to what do you contribute to your success?

Battle

David, I can contribute my success to many factors; however, I feel one of the major reason is that I've always believed in God and myself. I felt I could accomplish anything with God in my life, and if I set my mind to it. I really have no limits or bounders. If my mind thought it to be so, it was possible for it to happen for me. I contribute my current business success to the fact that I have a friend, business partner, lover, and husband, Jorrick, that believed more in me than I did myself when I started in the network distribution industry. Additionally, to him for having the knowledge of this industry, which gave him the insight to align us with our incredible team—Team Nu-Visions, under the impeccable leadership of Darnell and Traci Self. My philosophy in life is to always look beyond the oblivious, to look at the possibilities and how to change those into realty. I've always had a burning desire to live life to the fullest and felt it was ok to do this. I read one biblical passage almost everyday that reads: *"He came so that we might have life and have it more abundantly."* A very wise and respected gentlemen that heads PrePaid Legal Services, Inc., Harlen Stonecepher, the company that we are all executives with, read this passage at one of our national convention. He then went on to say that people can put whatever spin they want on this scripture, but he believes it to mean that it's OK to enjoy the finer things in life; it's OK to have the nice house and drive the nice car; it's OK to be rich and not poor. I agree and believe it to mean that we have the green light to have no limits as to the abundance we experience in life. It is our birthright to do so. Failure has never been an option for me. Average and ordinary have not been options for me; coming in last was taken out of my available options as well. Understanding that life is about choices, after I used the process of elimination, my only option in life is to succeed. So knowing that, David, I wake up every morning with the determination to thrive for greatness. My father told me when I was a child to always aim for the stars, and if you end up on the moon, you're still above everyone else on earth. I have always had that attitude. Additionally, I definitely contribute having the right attitude and not allowing my circumstances or environment to dictate my success. I recognize and utilize the beauty, talent, and greatness that I know I have within myself. David, I also know that every single woman out there has their own beauty, talent, and a form of greatness and it is one of my goals in life to share with women that it is within all of us (if she is willing to just reach down and pull it out); it can and will dictate our success.

Wright

Tiffaney, to what do you contribute your success?

Beverly

All my life I always had a very, very high bar set for me. I became very competitive. But over time, I understood that it was not about competing, it was more about completing. I needed to complete myself, then I could help complete others. The success that I have now is all because of this opportunity that I am involved with today, PrePaid Legal Services, Inc. Before this opportunity, I had been in corporate America, the Air force, and other organizations and sports in college and high school. I was always good and way above average in everything I did, but I still wasn't content; I wasn't at peace with me. I was always chasing the next brass ring to make myself feel fulfilled. But it never worked. Then I got involved with this opportunity and I got surrounded with all of these people who believed in me, more than I believed in myself. They saw more in me than "the next level." When they said, "You will be at the top," I believed them. With their belief and my newly found true belief in myself, I achieved more than I ever imagined. I also attribute my success to some simple words in *The Power of Positive Thinking,* by Norman Vincent Peale. He said, "You have to picturize, prayerize, and actualize." I learned to do just that. I learned to visualize myself at the top of our compensation plan. I could see my income being at a certain level. I could see my organization growing all over the country. I could see myself in front of thousands of people speaking and training. I would affirm these things every single day. I picturized, then I prayerized. God is the reason that I am here today and have the success that I have. I have prayed my way to where I am today. I have asked Him to use me to His glory. Then I actualized. I just went to work, sunup to sundown. I didn't have a lot of balance in the beginning, because I knew that the hard work that I put into my business at the start would give me the lifestyle that I wanted later. I picturized—I saw it. I prayerized—I put God first in everything that I did. I actualized—I worked extremely hard to get here and I absolutely refused to believe that the contrary would happen and I would not achieve my success. Even now, there are levels that I still have yet to achieve and I am doing the exact same thing to get there.

Wright

Lolita, to what do you contribute to your success?

Harrison

It's so many things, David. First and foremost, to God be the glory, for all the wonderful things He has done. In thinking on success, I'm reminded of a success law I read by Brian Tracey that says, "Your life only gets better when you get better and since there is no limit to how much better you can become, then there is not limit to how much better you can make your life." So, in meditating on that I just went to work on myself. I contribute my success to personal development for starters, consistently working on me and applying it to my everyday life. Secondly, having faith. We know that faith is the substance of things hope for and the evidence of things not seen. I continued to walk by faith and not by sight, seeing those things that were not as though they were coupled with a great work ethic knowing faith without works is dead and during the journey with prayer things started to manifest. Thirdly, it is my associations. I humbled myself to those who had my answer and got away from those who had my problems. It's a true blessing to associate with a Darnell and Traci Self, who are my friends and mentors in business. They are former mall workers in the Maryland area, who were recently awarded entrepreneurs of the year for 2004 by the National Black Chamber of Commerce and are millionaires today. Mr. Antonio Adair and Mr. Michael Humes, also friends and mentors, two former postal workers in our nation's capital and self-made millionaires. Minister Allan Gray, friend and co-founder of NuVision Ministries Inc. Last, but certainly not least are my pastors, Drs. Mike and Dee Dee Freeman of Spirit of Faith Christian Center in Temple Hills, Maryland, who are such a great man and woman of GOD, and through their teaching and leading by example, helped me to live my best life now.

Wright

Rosa, as co-founder, the three of you just recently put on an empowerment seminar focusing on creating balance. How important for women is creating balance in the overall success?

Battle

David, I think that creating balance is very important, but I feel how you measure that balance is even more important. What I mean by this statement is that oftentimes women are in search for that perfect balance. During our search of that perfect balance, procrastination sets in and we fail to accomplish anything. So that is why we just take creating the balances head on. Yes, we know, we need to have that spiritual aspect in your life. Yes, you need to have that mental and physical balance in your life, and definitely, we need structure and financial stability. Perfect balance may not be the answer for everyone. Everyone must make the determination of how much or less they need for their overall well-being. Women With Vizion shares ways to help women keep it all in sync. So yes, I believe that it is a critical success factor for women to have balances; however, helping women to understand how to measure balance and to recognize when they have reached the balance for them and their families.

Wright

What do you think, Tiffaney?

Beverly

I agree with Ms. Battle one hundred percent. Like I said earlier, I didn't have a perfect balance, but I knew my ultimate goal. I think I have a great balance in my life now because of the sacrifice that I was willing to make in the beginning. What we do in our empowerment seminars is teach women that everyone's balance is going to be different; its just like a fingerprint, its not going to be the same for everyone, so you have to identify what you need to be successful. Spiritual, physical, mental, and financial all are important, but you have to identify the areas you need to work on to achieve that overall balance that you want. The three of our lives are so different. When Mrs. Harrison got involved with PrePaid Legal, she was a mother, a wife, and a business owner. Mrs. Battle recently became married, so she had to deal with the balance of being a newlywed, as well as a business owner. I was single, so I just focused on being an entrepreneur. So we have all dealt with the balance challenge, if you will, in different ways. All women are going to deal with them differently. We help them with good philosophies. Our personal experience and personal development find the correct balance for each individual life so that they can have their own individual success stories.

Wright

Lolita, you don't define as balancing as home and career, you just define balance as balance?

Harrison

Absolutely. Webster says balance is a state of equilibrium. Now, with that understanding, identify those areas of importance and find that equilibrium for you. For example, when you take a closer look at spiritual; if you do not have some kind of spirituality where is your guidance. Let's take mental; without the right balance in this particular area where is your focus. You will have the potential for many distractions. Think about physical. If you are health challenged there is no strength to endure what you have to go through in order to get to the level of success you desire and deserve. So definitely, the physical is very important. Finally, there is financial. With all the success and wealth that you will obtain, if you are not a good steward of money and not educated in that area, you will lose it just as fast as you obtained it. To me, having some state of equilibrium in all areas defines balance.

Wright

What an interesting conversation. The three of you really seem to have it together. As I sit here, the only downside I can see is that I am not a woman, so I can't join your organization. I am sure I could get a lot out of it. Maybe some men will start the same thing. Today we have been talking to Rosa Battle, Tiffany Beverly and Lolita Harrison, who are leaders in Women With Vizion, with a membership base in the thousands. We have found out today, all three of these ladies know exactly what they want and exactly where they are going. Many could do well to participate in this worthwhile organization. Rosa, Tiffany, Lolita, thank you so much for being with us today on *Conversations On Success,*

Battle, Beverly, Harrison

Thank you, David. It has been our pleasure.

About The Authors

Rosa Battle is the Co-Founder of "Women With Vizion," a national women's empowerment organization, with a current out-reach base of thousands of women. She is a leader, speaker, and sought after trainer in her and her spouses (Jorrick) home base legal/identity theft services marketing company. Currently, Rosa (along with spouse) has over 14,000 associates on board in their successful business, which has distributed over 52.000 legal/identity theft plans, generating over $5 Million dollars in compensation. Rosa has reached the top executive position in several companies, becoming the first female to do so in one company, with predominately male leadership. Additionally, Rosa is a successful entrepreneur with art distribution and real estate businesses. Rosa completed her undergraduate studies at the University of North Texas, her graduate work at Northwood University, and began her doctorial studies at the University of Michigan.

Rosa Battle
P.O. Box 2805
DeSoto, TX. 75123-2805
Phone: 866.215.6560
Email: rosabattle@yahoo.com

Tiffaney Beverly has been in network distribution for five years. Despite her short tenure in the industry, she has reached a pinnacle commission level in Pre Paid Legal Services, Inc. She wears PrePaid Legal's prestigious 6-Figure Ring, which means she earns over $100,000/year in a 12-month period. She also holds the highest corporate field position: Regional Vice President. Having built a nationwide organization of thousands, she was recognized as one of Pre Paid Legal's *Rookies of the Year* for 2001. Despite her limited experience in the networking industry and humble beginnings as a manager in food manufacturing, she quickly has become a highly sought after speaker and trainer. She is known for her humor, candor, and from-the-heart speaking style.

Tiffaney Beverly
9242 W. National Ave. Ste. #3
West Allis, WI 53227
Phone: 866.457.6422

Lolita Harrison is a sought after leader, motivational speaker and personal development coach. She is the co-founder of Women With Vizion with an outreach base currently in the thousands. She has hosted several women's conferences nationwide. She has a passion for helping people and in the last six years, changed career paths from a 17-year background in the healthcare industry to embark upon the network distribution industry with an emphasis on legal services and economic empowerment. In a short period of time, she is earning a six figure income from home and wear the coveted "*Six Figure Ring*" awarded to independent associates that earn a minimum of $100,000 in their home-based businesses. She is one of the top executive directors with her company, and has been instrumental in helping many others reach the top levels of the company, where some earn six figures as well from home. She is a member of the National Black Chamber of Commerce. Mrs. Harrison is a happily married mother of two teenage children and currently resides in the Maryland area.

Lolita Harrison

P.O. Box 295

Accokeek, MD. 20607

Phone: 877.560.7815

Chapter Nine

JOHN LAZAR

THE INTERVIEW

David E. Wright (Wright)

Today we're talking to John Lazar, M.A., M.C.C. John has been a performance consultant and coach for over twenty years, including ten years as an executive coach. The International Coach Federation has certified him as a master coach and he works with individuals, groups and organizations, catalyzing their perspective, motivation and performance to produce emotionally intelligent leadership, breakthrough results and business success. John is co-founder of and Co-Executive Editor of the *International Journal of Coaching in Organizations.* He is completing a chapter, "Coaching for Performance," that will appear in the third edition of the *Handbook of Human Performance Technology,* due for publication in the fall of 2005. John, welcome to *Conversations on Success.*

John Lazar (Lazar)

David, thank you very much. It's a pleasure to be here.

Wright

You can ask people their definition of success and you'll get as many definitions as you have people. What is your definition of success in life?

Lazar

David, I think that my definition is a "work in progress." As I was preparing for our conversation I gave a fair amount of thought to this and did some reading on the subject as well. Because the coaching I do addresses the whole person, not just the "part" of them that goes to work, I'm curious about success in a broader context. I noticed that I didn't have a definition I live by but I do have some things I've borrowed from other, thoughtful people.

For example, Deepak Chopra, in his book *The Seven Spiritual Laws of Success*, talks about success as "the continued expansion of happiness and the progressive realization of worthy goals." So for him, it's growing your capacity to enjoy life and accomplish important things. Relative to that, I believe this points at and values both the quality of our internal experience and our impact in the world. What I also focus on is that you as an individual have a major say, in the sense of influence or control, about what's important to you and how you experience and assess yourself. You have the chance to declare for yourself what success is, rather than consciously accepting or obliviously drifting along with whatever society says it is. You have the chance to be the author.

I'm also reading a book right now called *Just Enough*, written by Laura Nash and Howard Stevenson. It's tools for creating success in your work and your life. And it presents a model that I'm just beginning to understand. I like what it distinguishes and how it can contribute to defining success, applicable for me and others as well. The authors define and talk about four different dimensions: happiness, achievement, significance and legacy. And each of those dimensions can be applied in four different directions: to oneself, to one's family, to one's community and to the world. The authors studied successful people in business and other contexts. Their model reflects their understanding of the themes drawn from the data they collected. Nash and Stevenson talk about taking a "kaleidoscope approach," in other words, not putting too much emphasis on any one thing. Thus the title *Just Enough*.

So it's a matter of having variety. It's about putting your attention on different things; knowing yourself well enough to be able to engage in a particular area; knowing what success looks like in that area; getting enough of that to be able to say "That's cool, I'm done." and moving on to another area; and being able to dance back and forth. That notion of dancing, by the way, and one's ability to move back and forth in a fluent way across areas of human concern appeals to me. So while I'm discovering more about what this is, I'd say it was a direction I'm taking as a way to understand "What is my success in the areas of happiness, achievement, significance, and legacy? And how is that showing up?" As I say, I've got many more questions than I have answers right now.

Wright

What's helped you see that and live it?

Lazar

I draw on four different things: my experiences, a subset of those experiences I consider to be defining moments, role models, and certain questions that I return to. For example, when I think about formative experiences that had an impact on me about success, I recall a decision and declaration to myself I made when I was about nine: "I won't be like my father." I loved my father. He was a good dad, he was successful in his business, he did a great job taking care of his family. And he wasn't around all that much because he was out doing what fathers do, making a living. But for me as a nine year old, I'm saying to myself, "I really miss him, I don't like not having him around, feeling close. I don't want to be like that. I don't want to be like him." What that meant for me then was "I don't want to be successful (like him)," which is ironic in the context of our conversation. It also meant "I won't be competitive and I won't be emotionally unavailable." So I have lived inside of the world given by that perspective for many years. In the last ten to fifteen years, however, I've started to make new choices. Now I'm playing a different, bigger game and defining success on my terms, not as an emotional reaction of a nine year old. Out of this experience, I'm a stand for authentic connection with others and bring that intention and emotional availability to how I am with people.

Another set of experiences was my mother's unflagging, unconditional emotional support for and acceptance of me for who I was and what dreams I could realize in my life. Those interactions occurred regularly. We also used to talk about philosophical issues, asking questions about why people turn out the way they do, what factors contribute to one's success. I remember that we concluded that a positive attitude and persistence around achieving one's goals and dreams were very important.

I seem to take roundabout routes to achieve my goals. As an example, I flunked out of college, did a tour in the Navy, then returned to the same school to complete my undergraduate degree in psych. I went to graduate school to get an advanced degree in clinical and developmental psychology. But before I defended my thesis, I stepped away from school and took a job working with severely and profoundly handicapped kids and their families for over seven years. I then made the decision to go back and complete my master's degree. Making that decision and acting on it reflected my conclusion that it was very important for me to complete this, important for me to persevere around what I was committed to, and to lay a solid foundation for moving ahead in my life.

In terms of defining moments, there are several that revolve around what I learned about myself while pursuing love. Here's one: I've been married and divorced twice. The first time I was engaged, just weeks before the wedding, I realized that there were some serious communications issues between me and my fiancée, ones I wanted to address before we moved ahead. This would mean postponing our wedding. When I discussed this with her, she said that if I didn't want to have the wedding as and when we had planned, then the wedding would never happen. I was so concerned with pleasing my parents about this that I didn't listen to my heart and head. I acquiesced, we got married as planned and were divorced within a year. It was a very large, painful lesson about knowing oneself and respecting the power of one's own truth.

Here's another. When I was in the Navy in the late sixties, I was stationed in Key West, Florida. I was befriended by a civilian, an elderly gentleman by the name of Lyle Weaver. It happened at a time in my life when I was not my own best friend. So it struck me profoundly that this total stranger would take an interest in me and not have any ulterior motive as far as I could tell, other than wanting to be connected. We became and remained friends for many years. As a matter of fact, David, that had such an impact that when I got out of the service I used that as a reason to return to complete my undergraduate degree, in psychology. Because I saw what Lyle did with me and I wanted to have that kind of positive impact on other people. I wanted others to be able to reconnect with themselves, to accept and love themselves, to get out of their own way, and to be in action to live the life they aspired to. That perspective continues to be alive and well for me thirty years later.

Another was when I attended the Landmark Education Corporation Forum in late 1993. Landmark provides transformational educational experiences. From the Forum, I learned two things. First, I distinguished at a deeper level than ever before that personal responsibility could occur as a freedom rather than as a burden. What worlds of opportunity that opened up! Second, I learned about how to produce results while still maintaining strong relationships. In other words, often when we are goal-directed, we put our attention on producing the desired results at the expense of relationships. So we get the results we want, then look around at all the bodies strewn along the way. What Landmark offered through the Forum was distinctions and a structure to enable you to have both, not sacrifice one on the alter of the other.

More recently, I had heart surgery. I found on an annual physical that I had a heart condition called mitral valve prolapse. Over a period of four months, the circumstance deteriorated from "This is no big deal" to "This is something we can handle with drugs and if you need surgery, it's years away" to "How soon can you get yourself scheduled for surgery?" What occurred was I took the chance to choose having faith that it would all work out. Once I took that step, I also put my trust in my family and community, and shared with them what was going on. I put myself inside their love, good wishes and prayers, and trusted that whatever happened would be for the highest good. The surgery went well and with no ill effects. For me, it was an acknowledgement of the power of the love, trust and faith.

Regarding role models, I guess that I have a number of them, people whose ways of being, intellect and/or achievements inspired me over the years and touched me personally. In addition to my mother, I appreciate and honor David Krantz, my undergraduate advisor, for his intellectual curiosity and rigor; Judy Hale, a friend and colleague, for her commitment to excellence in the field of human performance and her insistence on the importance of perceiving patterns; and Julio Olalla, my teacher of over twenty years, for his heart and soul and modeling how to be a masterful coach.

Finally, there are several questions I find myself asking that foster inquiry and open up new worlds to explore: What game are you playing such that this is what winning looks like? What are the limiting factors in your world? Is that fact or opinion? What's another interpretation that could be an equally likely story? What does your heart say? How much is enough? And what does success look like so you can recognize it?

Wright

Tell our readers what your coaching approach is.

Lazar

When I coach, there are several affirmative assumptions I make that influence my perspective and approach. One is that I view coaching as giving the coachee the chance to regain an authorship and voice about who they are and to express that through their work and in their life in general. Another assumption I make is that the presenting problem or symptom isn't necessarily the problem that we ultimately will address. So it may morph in its formulation to what we work on and accomplish. A third assumption is that whatever the person does makes sense within their world and within their logic. Part of my job as a coach is to use my listening skills and my toolkit to understand their world as they know it, then show them the parts that limit their choice and effectiveness. Their new awareness of former blind spots enables them to put together the pieces of their world differently, see avenues of possibility and ways to act where before there were only cul-de-sacs. They have choice. Put those three pieces together, add a respectful yet challenging, and trustworthy working relationship, have clear agreements for how we work together, and clear, measurable outcomes for what's to be accomplished. Then plan the work and work the plan. With an elevated perspective of where you want to go, still you must be able to get back to ground level. Here's where the coachee will work issues "locally," getting traction and making incremental progress, adjusting as needed, learning at every point, keeping in mind the results to produce that will satisfy both the coachee and their organization.

Wright

In researching for this conversation, I read some of your materials. In some of them, you write that you worked to produce "emotionally intelligent leadership, breakthrough results and business success." So could you tell me what "emotionally intelligent leadership" is?

Lazar

Daniel Goleman and other researchers over the past twenty years have identified an area of personal and professional development that is called "emotional intelligence." This is a label for our competences at knowing ourselves, being motivated and capable of self-management, being interpersonally sensitive, and being able to use all that to establish healthy working relationships. In organizations, emotionally intelligent leaders are those who can create resonance and relatedness with their followers. In other words, they are able to drive the collective emotions of the people in the organization in a positive direction. They are empathetic, able to create an emotionally supportive environment so that organizational associates feel "in sync" with the leader. The positive climate supports the willingness to give extra effort that enhances productivity and business results. Goleman talks about this in his book *Primal Leadership.*

There are specific competencies that tend to be associated with being an emotionally intelligent leader. David, it starts with the foundation of accurate self–awareness. You've heard the adage "know thyself" that's a thousand years old. It is incredibly important to have the grounding to know what's needed to manage yourself wisely and to operate with integrity with others. In addition to that, you need to have empathy, being able to sense and appreciate other people's emotions and understand their perspective. Then finally, this translates to how the person is able to interact with others, building and maintaining good working relationships. How do they inspire? How do they guide and motivate others through a compelling vision? How do they influence others? How are they able to develop others? How can they foster open dialogue and use conflicts constructively? And how are they able to be the captain of their "ship of business" that must adjust course and redefine itself regularly? Because as a leader, you're constantly dealing with the dilemma of what stays the same and what needs to change in order for the business, the organization, to be successful.

I was talking with a researcher a year or two ago. And I asked her, "If you were to estimate what percentage of business leadership in American business is emotionally intelligent, what would that percentage be?" She said between fifteen and twenty percent, operationally defined. What that suggests to me is that there is a lot of opportunity for development, a lot of opportunity for leadership to be grown to the next level and the next level, such that workplaces become not only productive and profitable places to work but good places to work as well.

Wright

I understand that you co-founded and are Co-Executive Editor of a coaching journal that just completed its second year of publication. With all that you've got going now, why did you take on that challenge?

Lazar

It's partly by design and partly by default. The design part is that I met a gentleman several years ago at an executive coaching summit, a conference of very senior executive coaches, held here in Chicago. He proposed to the people in attendance the idea of publishing a journal. At that time, there was only lukewarm interest expressed. I had dinner with him. His name is Bill Bergquist and we had a chance to connect and talk over good food. I hardly knew him but he seemed like a rather interesting guy. From that conversation, we decided to co-author an article and during that process, we again picked up the question he had posed earlier. "John, does publishing a journal interest you at all?" "Hey Bill, are you still interested in doing a journal?" and we decided to make it happen.

Bill became not only the co-author of our article, but also the co-founder, co-owner and Co-Executive Editor with me of the *International Journal of Coaching and Organizations.* We saw a need in this emerging field of coaching to provide a disciplined, convenient and respected forum where important conversations could be held. These conversations were designed to forward the field, moving it towards becoming a profession. It's been an extraordinary ride! I continue to learn and grow, gaining expertise. David, it's been great for me to connect with people, bringing them into the conversation as players in different ways. Whether as editorial board members, as issue co-editors, as sponsors and subscribers, as strategic partners, but especially as authors able to contribute to the field of coaching and coaching in organizations.

Wright

Values seem to be important to you. Through this conversation I kind of picked that up. So what values guide you in your life?

Lazar

There are a couple: personal responsibility and social responsibility. Social responsibility, like how does what we do locally have an impact in the world beyond ourselves? And how do we modify our behavior and our thinking accordingly? As you may have noticed, contribution is also important to me. And integrity, being my word and operating consistent with my standards. Generous listening. Unconditional love, appreciating people for the unique people they are and whatever they have to contribute. Courage. It takes courage to actively take part in your own development and cause your own transformation, even to get up each day and do whatever needs to be done, to the best of your ability. Especially when everything inside of you is saying, "No, no, don't go there." Lifelong learning. Finally, I would say wisdom, both developing it and sharing it as best as I can.

Wright

In addition to your work, where do you find expression for your creative side?

Lazar

There are a couple of things, David. I love to cook, whether for myself or for family and friends. In fact, at one time, I thought about becoming a chef. I had the application ready, then decided I just wasn't ready to sacrifice the other things that also were important to me. I won't call myself a connoisseur but I'm certainly a wine buff. So I enjoy wine tasting, wine collecting, and pairing wine with food and people that I care about. I love to golf. Golf to me is so much more than simply getting the ball in the hole. It's a mental game as well as a physical game, so there are opportunities moment by moment by moment to be creative and resourceful about using one's self-awareness and self management in the service of executing each shot well and enjoying the round. Finally, I enjoy volunteer work. I have a couple of not-for-profit organizations that I regularly work with in different kinds of ways. Often, there's a chance to exercise and model leadership or another way to contribute. I appreciate being able to contribute to a cause larger than myself, being able to give back in that way.

Wright

What an interesting conversation. It sounds like you have a fulfilling life going there, John.

Lazar

Thanks. As I said before, David, it's a work in progress. I just find myself grateful to be here, to be alive, enjoying my circumstances and making opportunities to contribute in ways, large and small. It tickles me greatly.

Wright

Today we have been talking to John Lazar. He is a performance consultant and has been coaching now for over twenty years. He is the co-founder and Co-Executive Editor of *The International Journal of Coaches and Organizations*. His by-line is "Building workplaces that work," which I really like. There are so many workplaces, John, that simply do not work. I really do appreciate you taking all of this time with me this afternoon to talk about success and I really do appreciate you being with us on *Conversations on Success*.

Lazar

David, thank you again for this opportunity. I certainly look forward to whatever is next.

About The Author

John Lazar, MA, MCC has been a performance consultant and coach for over 20 years, including ten years as an executive coach. He is certified as a Master Coach by the International Coach Federation (ICF). He works with individuals, teams and organizations, catalyzing their perspective, motivation and performance to produce emotionally intelligent leadership, breakthrough results and business success. John is co-founder and Co-Executive Editor of the *International Journal of Coaching in Organizations*.

John Lazar

Phone: 708.771.9176

Emails: jblcoach@lazarconsulting.com

john@ijco.info

Websites: www.lazarconsulting.com

www.ijco.info

Chapter Ten

JERRY CLARK

THE INTERVIEW

David E. Wright (Wright)

Today we're talking to Jerry Clark. Jerry became a self-made millionaire while still in his 20's. Today through his company, ClubRhino.com he conducts personal and professional development seminars around the world. The topics covered range from peak performance training, effective communication strategies and how to increase your productivity and profitability in your chosen career. Jerry is the producer of over 100 of the most empowering audio programs available in the self empowerment industry, many of which he is also the author such as, *The Magic of Colors, Creating Magic, The Magic of Influence.* Jerry's training products are currently being used by dozens of companies in over 35 countries worldwide. Jerry recognizes that change occurs at the individual level and he's committed to training others how to improve themselves by teaching peak performance strategies that get results. Jerry has shared the stage industry leaders such as Tony Robbins, Jim Rohn, Charlie Tremendous Jones, Les Brown, Brian Tracy, Denis Waitley, Florence Littauer, Robert Allen, Mark Victor Hansen, Robert Kiyosaki, and many others. He also has interviewed some of the world's giants of motivation, wealth building, sales, marketing, humanities, spirituality and more. Jerry specializes in training and coaching commissioned based and home based sales people and entrepreneurs. His articles appear in many major publications such as *Success Magazine, Working at Home Magazine, Wealth Building Magazine, Money Makers Monthly* and many others. Jerry is the CEO and president of ClubRhino.com and the founder of AMG Business Group. Jerry welcome to *Conversations on Success*.

Jerry Clark (Clark)

David, it's my pleasure to be here.

Wright

Your name is Jerry DRhino Clark. The name of your company is Club Rhino Inc. Several of your automobiles have Rhino on the license plate. And you have an entire wing of your home in which you call The Rhinos Lair. Can you tell us what is significant about the Rhino?

Clark

The Rhino signifies what is necessary for commissioned based individuals to make it through the entrepreneurial jungle so they can reach the land of paradise. It requires thick skin. So, the Rhino symbolizes the thick skin that is going to be necessary sometimes brutal conditions of the entrepreneurial jungle. The land of paradise simply means being able to do what they want, when they want, with whom they want. It means having the financial and time freedom that most people seek. The only way to make it as a commissioned sales person is to produce results. No results, no money. That's the name of this game. In the entrepreneurial commissioned based jungle, you're going to get people telling you no, you're going to get lots of so-called rejection, you're going to get all that. If you don't have the type of skin necessary to keep charging, whenever the going is maybe not so great, then you might just quit. And you'll never make it to your land of paradise. So that's why the Rhino is so significant within what I'm doing, my company Club Rhino, my web site Club Rhino.com, all my web sites have something to do with rhino. I own about 300 different web sites that have something to do with rhino, RhinoBooks.com, RhinoPublishing.com, RhinoPress.com, RhinoPowerTips.com; I could keep going on and on. The Rhino is Significant to me because the thoughts generated around this magnificent creature called the Rhino assisted me in becoming a

Millionaire. So, I just thought it would be great for other people to know about it and learn about it.

Wright

One of your fundamental trainings is what you call the Success Triangle. What is the Success Triangle and what kind of results have people reported from using it?

Clark

Wow, David, that's a great question. The Success Triangle is my fundamental teachings. No matter where I go throughout the world, Malaysia, Singapore, Japan, Indonesia, Sweden, Norway, Denmark, England, Paris, Holland, Australia, New Zealand, Germany, Austria, Switzerland, Africa, Canada, the Bahamas, Panama, I'm talking all over the world where I go and train, I make sure that everyone is indoctrinated with the fundamentals of what it's going to take to set themselves up to be able to create the results that they say they desire to create. To me those fundamentals are something called the Success Triangle. At the base of the triangle is what I call internal communication. Internal communication has to do with how we communicate with ourselves. So it has to do with our thinking patterns, our belief systems, our philosophies, our attitudes, our ideologies, that's all part of our internal communication. On the left hand side of the triangle is what we call external communication. External communication is critical for us to master as well, and that has to do with how we communicate with others. External communication simply says that the more you understand the people you are communicating with, the more likely you're able to decrease the tension level that may exist between two parties when they start to communicate. When we decrease the tension, we increase the cooperation level and that's what we all want to do in business, and in life in general. We want to decrease the tension so that we can increase cooperation so we can increase the results that we accomplish. That's why it's important to understand the external communication. And then you have the technical know how. Now that's the last angle in the success triangle on the right hand side. The technical know how, which simply is the how-to's. This is going to depend on what particular business a person is operating in. For example David, you a rein the publishing industry. Since you're in the publishing industry your technical know how would be understanding the publishing business, understanding the intricacies of how that works. Someone who's in sales, they want to understand sales, they want to understand their products, and they want to understand whatever they've got going on with the company that they're in. So that's what the technical know how is. Now what I've noticed is that all three of these go together. I've also noticed something that's very interesting: A person can learn how to do whatever it is they're doing, but if they don't master the internal communication, they're not going to be as effective at doing the how to's. They're not going to be as effective because they might not get themselves to consistently perform at the higher levels that's required of them to create magical results. And people will find out that if they don't master the external communication, even when they're performing the technical know how and performing it on a consistent bases, they won't maximize the results that they could achieve if they maximizing their ability to understand people. So that's the reason why I have a program that's called *the Success Triangle*. I've even written a Free Report that people can check out which is available at my www.clubrhino.com website. At the base, the internal communication, I have a program called *Creating Magic*. *Creating Magic* goes over how to be more specific and more effective in dealing with your belief systems and attitudes and so forth. The external communication program, I have one called *The Magic of Colors* that goes over the different behavioral styles, the personality styles of the different people that you're going to be coming in contact with in business and in life in general. On the technical know how side, since my specialty is commissioned based individuals, people who are in direct sales and network marketing, I have a program called *High Achievement Network Marketing* that assists people in that area. That's just a little overview of the success triangle and of course anyone of those particular areas we can touch on a little bit more, if you desire, later on.

Wright

You mentioned your program called *The Magic of Colors*. Last July you spoke at the Jim Rohn weekend event in Anaheim. You talked about the colors and it was very fascinating. Can you give us a better understanding of it here and let us know how it made a difference in your life?

Clark

Once again, the Colors have to do with the external communication part of the Success Triangle. It has to do with the fact that any time two people get together there's going to be cooperation or tension. If the tension level is high the cooperation is going to below and vice versa. So what the Magic of Colors has done for me is completely revolutionized my life, once I understood it. Because I originally learned this information from a lady named Florence Littauer, she didn't use colors, she used the same names that the Greek Physician Hippocrates used over 2,400 years ago: choleric, melancholy, sanguine and phlegmatic. Those are the words that she used. Well since I was born in the garage and raised in the ghetto, I couldn't even pronounce those words so I eventually ignored the information. But a few years later in 1991 I ran across a 21 year old lady who was earning over 40,000 dollars a month and I was shocked. What in the world are you doing to make that much money? More importantly, how did you do it? I asked her these questions and she told me that one of her secrets was that she understands people and she started to master the understanding of people. She explained that a Multi-Millionaire had taught her. I paid $300 to attend a seminar she was conducting where she started explaining these four different behavior styles or personality styles in detail and how she used colors to explain it. I got excited because I realized that the information was pretty much the same that I had already learned from Florence Littauer. However, the twist was that this young lady was using colors to explain the information. For me, Colors was much more easier to pronounce. Thus, I got excited about it. In a nutshell, the four colors are yellow, blues, greens and reds. A tour www.clubrhino.com website, The Magic of Colors is currently our best selling audio program.

Here's a very quick overview of the colors. Yellows are the people that are very relationship oriented, so they want to develop a relationship first, they want to get to know you, they don't want to go straight to business, you've got to take your time with them, you've got to slow down a little bit and they want to work together, they want to help people, they're team players, they're very loyal and dedicated individuals and these are people who don't want any conflict, they don't want any fights or confrontations or disharmony. It's critical that we all learn how to work more effectively with these people because about 35% of our population is composed of the yellows. While we're on this topic, it's important to understand that each color has it's unique strengths and weaknesses. We don't have time to go into all the details of the strength and weaknesses here. What I can say about the yellow is that they have a tendency to be overly sensitive, sometimes. They take rejection very personal a lot of times. That's something they'll want to understand, they want to work on. Another thing that's important before we even get into just a quick synopsis of the other colors is that we all have a little bit of all these colors in us. So we all have a little bit of yellow, blue, green and red in us, but we tend be dominant in one of. What we want to do is understand what our dominant Color or Behavioral system is so we'll be able to understand a lot more about ourselves. But also we'll be able to understand a lot more about others, our prospects, our co workers, the people that we're working with, the people that we're living with, our family. We can learn a lot more about them by understanding this information. So back to the yellows. Another thing I will say about them is that they are some of the best listeners on the planet. They love to listen, because they really want to see what they can do to help people. So that's what they are, they're about tranquility, stability, harmony, and they really don't care for sudden changes, they like peace and love and happiness and so forth. Now let's move on to the blues. These people are also relationship oriented just like the yellows. But the difference is that, the blues, they are faster paced and they are more engaged in talking instead of listening. So these are the talkers of society. They're very enthusiastic people, they're optimistic, they're persuasive, they're playful, they're creative, but what happens is that they're constantly talking. A lot of times they don't take the time to stop and allow someone else to really talk. That's going to be one important thing for them to understand, learn, and get better at.

The Blues are typically not afraid to go out and prospect, they're not afraid to tell people about their products, they're not afraid to tell people about what they have to offer. All of this of course assists them greatly in the business of sales. It also provides them with the raw material to be great promoters. But the blues deserve to work on their follow up skills. I understand that I'm only giving you a quick little overview because I just want you to know that there are strengths and there are weaknesses with each color, and each color can be very successful in their own right. The blues overall they make up about 15% of the population. Ok, let's now briefly discuss the greens. These are some of the most analytical people on the planet. They're very slow and systematic. Also, instead of being interested in relationships, they're more interested in the tasks. They want to know what the facts are, let's take care of what we got to take care of and let's make sure we get all the details necessary in order to make a highly informed decision. Now, one of the weaknesses of that approach is that sometimes the green shave a tendency to over analyze, so they become paralyzed by overanalyzing. A lot of times they're too critical and they're also too cautious at times because they have a tendency to be perfectionist. Of course, this perfectionist mindset can have a tendency to cause a delay in making important decisions due to the constant analyzing and re-analyzing. They make up about 35% of the population.

Last but not least (especially according to them), we have the reds. The reds are the final color here that we'll overview. The reds are task oriented just like the greens. In other words, they want to take care of business, get to the point but the difference is that instead of taking the amount of time that greens take as far as analyzing everything to the detail that greens analyze, the reds simply want to take care of business immediately. They're much quicker in their decisions. They want to get to the point, stick to the point, get off the point, and get to the next point. Let's get down to business is their preference. Their motto is my way or the highway. The reds make up about 15% of the population. They're dynamic people, they exude what appears to be natural born leadership qualities. They are very goal oriented, they don't have much sympathy for other people, and a lot of times they come across as pushy brats. So we want to understand that each color—once again—have their strengths and they have their weaknesses, and once we understand this in business, it will be very empowering but also once we understand this in our own personal lives it's going to be very important for us because opposites tend to attract. This means that the reds tend to marry the yellows, and they're two opposite personality styles and if they don't understand each other it's going to be a challenge. The greens tend to marry the blues. And if they don't understand this they're going to have a big challenge as well. Of course all colors marry all colors, but it's important for everyone to understand each other because that's how we're going to increase our effectiveness in external communication, which is going to increase our effectiveness in being able to master that part of the success triangle—which, in turn, will increase our effectiveness in being able to live life on our terms.

Wright

So why do you feel some people succeed while others fail in entrepreneurial endeavors that require them to be independent?

Clark

I believe that some people succeed and some people fail simply because some people really don't take the time to master the success triangle. I think it really boils down to that. A lot of people don't take the time to master their internal communication; in other words, they're not really concerned with what goes into their mind. And the only thing that can come out is what goes in. So a lot of people don't take the time to deliberately take control of their internal communication to see what is going into their consciousness. Instead they stay up all night watching the news. That's a lot of negativity going in right there. There's also a lot more negativity going in from all of the negative people they talk to. Of course, there's the newspapers, radio, and a host of other sources to get negative input from. Since negativity is what is going into most people's consciousness, I believe that a lot of people don't succeed because they are not success oriented. They don't have a success consciousness. I believe a lot of people fail because they have a failure consciousness and that's what they're focusing on. People also do not succeed because they don't take the time to Master the External communication and Technical Know-How as well. So the bottom line in regards to success and failure, I believe, is a person either chooses to master the success triangle or they don't. The people who choose to master the Success Triangle will have the best probability of creating some magical results in their life. The ones that choose not to or just don't by default; I believe will have the higher probability of not having magical results occur in their life.

Wright

Could you share a couple of philosophies with our readers that you have learned throughout your life that has made the biggest impact on you?

Clark

Earlier, you mentioned that I spoke at one of the Jim Rohn events and one of the things I learned from Jim Rohn about 15 or 20 years ago was a philosophy that transformed the quality of my life. The philosophy was this, every day, in every way, us human beings are either performing simple disciplines or simple errors in judgment. Simple disciplines are simply doing the things that are going to be necessary to move us towards our desired reality. Simple errors in judgment are simply doing things that are not going to move us towards our desired reality. Here's a quick example. Let's say we have a desired reality to be healthy, to be able to live a life full of vim, vigor, and vitality. But let's say that on a daily basis we're smoking cigarettes, on a daily basis we weren't doing any exercise, on a daily basis we're not eating properly or any of those things that we know that's necessary in order to be healthy, vibrant, and fit. The first day that a person smokes a cigarette or the first day they don't eat properly they might not notice a difference. But what happens is that's a simple error in judgment. And if that simple error in judgment is repeated over and over and over, eventually what happens is something called the compounded effect will kick in and all of a sudden their health is destroyed. But it wasn't destroyed overnight. It was destroyed by the constant perpetual little actions that were performed on a daily basis. Now this is the same way a person is going to be healthy or successful. If they perform simple disciplines, the simple act of eating that apple a day that we've all heard about, the simple act of taking nutritional supplements, the simple act of doing some type of exercise even if it's just walking around the block or something. The simple act of doing these simple disciplines, nothing big, real simple things that everyone can do, can literally (over time) alter a person's entire Health and Well-Being.

So the key to realize is that, yes, the next day after performing a simple discipline, we might not be healthy, we might not be fit, but if we do that over and over and over again, eventually the compounded effect will kick in and all of a sudden we'll be vibrant, we'll be healthy, we'll be fit. That was a major philosophy right there that really transformed the quality of my life. Another philosophy that I'll mention that really transformed the quality of my life is that no matter what you do you're not going to please everyone. That philosophy really took a lot of pressure off me because there was a point in my life where I was really trying to please everyone. The challenge with this was when someone wasn't pleased I couldn't understand it, why come they don't like me, why come they're not pleased, I'm doing everything I can to please them. This all changed for me one night about 15 or so years ago when I was up one night watching an interview of Bill Cosby. One of the questions they asked him was this "What is the secret of success?" And Mr. Cosby said, "Well I really don't know what the secret of success is, but I can tell you that the secret of failure is to try to please everybody." And that just changed me right there. From there I started focusing on doing things that were fulfilling and joyful to me instead of worrying about what other people thought about it. At this point in my life, I really don't concern myself with worrying about whether or not everyone is going to be pleased with what I'm doing. The key for me is to do my best to create and articulate value to the marketplace, and do my best to make a positive contribution to mankind. Not everyone is going to enjoy or like or agree with the way I choose to add value or with the particular value I bring to the marketplace. The same goes for you as well as each and every last one of those who are reading this information right now. (Yes, that would be you)…

Wright

What are some of the biggest -- for lack of a better word – traps that you have noticed that many people fall into and how can they go forward avoiding them?

Clark

That's a really good question. I'll give you a quick one right here. It's one of the major traps that a lot of people, especially people who is in entrepreneurial endeavors, fall into: The trap of feeling like they are entitled to success just because they are in a business for a period of time. I call it the entitlement trap. Once a person falls into the entitlement trap it's a really sad situation because most of the time people who are in this trap do not even realize that they are in it. I see this frequently, especially with some of the direct sales and network marketing distributors that I work with. Once they have been in the business for two, three years, four, or whatever number of years, they really believe they should be earning X amount of money and if they're not earning X amount of money—whatever that amount is for them, they all of a sudden feel as if something's wrong. It can also apply for people who are in the corporate arena. They get in the corporate world and they're told of the promise of moving up the corporate ladder—and if you work hard, you're loyal, you're industrious—all of a sudden you'll be able to set yourself up for some financial success. Well sure enough they dedicate themselves to the company, they go in early, they stay late, and they psychologically divorce their family almost because they're married to their job. And then what happens is they don't get that promotion, they don't continue moving up that Corporate ladder like they were told and they feel like they were entitled a certain degree of success just because they've been around for a period of time. And so the point to understand is you're not going to get promoted or earn more money just because you've been around for X period of time. You're going to earn more money based on the value that you bring and effectively articulate to the marketplace. And if you don't bring and effectively articulate much value to the marketplace, then there's only so much you're going to actually end up earning .You're going to keep earning the same thing. The entitlement trap is really a huge trap that I really feel people fall into.

Wright

Jerry, you became a millionaire while you were still in your 20's and now you're in your 30's and you're a multi-millionaire, the question is relating to one about money and happiness, money and solving problems. In your opinion does money make you happy and does money solve all your problems?

Clark

That's definitely a good question, in fact, that's one that I get quite a bit. Many people really think or believe that money is going to bring along with it nothing but happiness or it's going solve all their problems; however, I can share with you one of the most important realizations of my life. It's simply this: Happiness is a state of mind. It's important for a person to understand that regardless of what kind of money they have, they can choose to be happy right now. It took me until I was 27 or 28 years old to realize this. Because by that time I had already become a millionaire, I had a million dollar house. I had bought multiple Mercedes Benz's because it was my favorite car. I bought all kinds of other stuff. I had a gorgeous super model as a girlfriend who was featured on the Cover of many Magazines and was quite popular. And so I had all this stuff that I thought was going to make me happy and what happened is right at that point I remember I was walking through that million dollar house that I had and as I was walking through that house all of a sudden something hit me and it kind of like stopped me in my tracks and it was almost like a communication took place with me, not of words, I didn't hear voices or anything, but it was a weird feeling that kind of told me that none of this stuff is going to bring you happiness, happiness is already in you right now. It had already been with you the whole time, even when you didn't have any money. And then all of a sudden I got this feeling of peace that I had never had before, I'd never experienced anything like it before. And it was that point, at the age of 27 or 28, that's when I never had to worry about chasing happiness because I knew happiness wasn't something to chase. Happiness was something to be. And so I just decided to be happy. The peace of mind that I've had since that point I think also allowed me to attract even more money in my life because I was just so peaceful about it. So that was one thing.

Now as far as the problems, does money solve problems? Well, money will solve some of the problems that you have now but it will also create other problems that you don't have now and that you didn't even realize were possible to have. I think this is important for people to realize. They think that money is going to solve all their problems. If you've got a problem of not paying your mortgage payment then yea, money will solve that problem. But once you get lots of money, you will inherent a host of other problems that you currently do not have. All of the sudden when you get it, now all of a sudden you've got relatives coming from all over the place that you didn't even know existed. They really expect you to give them some of your money. If you don't then they tell everyone that you're greedy, stingy, and evil or something like that. So it's important for everyone to understand once you get all the money, now you've got to figure out what to do with it. You've got to decide where to invest it and I'm telling you, there are so many options out there in this area alone that it can certainly be mind-boggling. So don't worry about money solving all of your problems because with money you'll simply get a different set of problems. I was born in a garage and I was raised in the ghetto and I've been able to transform my life. But I'll tell you this, I've been with a Net worth of negative zero, and I've been with a Net worth of Multi-Millions. I prefer the multiple millions. The key is to Focus on Solutions, not Problems. Solution oriented people can donate more to charity, they can give more to their church or to wherever they see fit to do so. But understand this. Money is not going to solve all your problems and it's not necessarily going to make you happy. But don't let that be an excuse to not get it.

Wright

One of your most popular training programs is your two-day Rhino Boot Camps, what exactly do you teach in those courses and why have people been raving about it for years?

Clark

I believe people rave about the Rhino Boot Camps because those are the trainings that I get a chance to go in depth about transformational strategies. At this point, we have three different types of Rhino Boot Camps and each of them are two days in length. Number one is called Prosperity-Mastery Rhino Boot Camp. And it's where we go into depth about how to master your ability to have more abundance and wealth attracted to your life, how to bring it into your life. So that's the Prosperity-Mastery Boot Camp. People love that because of the exercises we do and the realizations they get from being able to become aware of their preferred "Money Map" and how to enhance it's power to create more riches for themselves and their loved ones. Everyone operates from a particular money map and they have a method to utilizing their money in a way that most of the times they are unconscious about. And so people get a chance to discovery some really neat insights and they are able to break through many of them that may have been limiting their overall growth and success. And then I have another Boot Camp called Persuasion-Mastery Rhino Boot Camp. The Persuasion-Mastery Rhino Boot Camp is the one that goes into how to be more effective with people, how to utilize influencing skills with integrity and so forth. These are critical skills for anyone desiring to have a great impact and make a more empowering difference in the lives of others. Our third Rhino Boot Camp is called the Self-Mastery Rhino Boot Camp. And that's the most popular one actually, that's the one that has been around the longest and has impacted the most people up to this point. It's a Self Mastery Rhino Boot Camp because that's where people get a chance to really examine the inner workings of themselves, how their mind really works, what kind of beliefs may have been holding them back, etc. They really get a chance to get a different relationship with their beliefs; they get a chance to start transforming some of their beliefs to be able to allow them to more effectively and automatically take the actions necessary to create the results that they desire. So these are just some of the reasons I believe people have been raving about the boot camps. They produce results when they come out of the boot camp; they produce more results than what they produced before they went to the boot camp. It's only a two-day boot camp. But the first day goes for 12 hours. Yes, we literally go from 10 A.M. until 10 P.M. and the second day go from 10 to 5 P.M. Most people say that the 12 hours from the first day seems like only three hours have passed. That's because of the nature of it and what we're doing. The time kind of suspends itself and kind of just passes by without us being consciously aware of it.

Wright

Most people desire to increase their productivity and profitability, what pointers can you give our readers to provide or assist them in doing so?

Clark

There are three things I'm going to suggest that I noticed has really increased my personal effectiveness. My personal productivity increased by over 300%, just by following these three simple things right here. Number one, before I even start anything, I make sure I've finished it already. This is another concept I learned from Jim Rohn. He said you shouldn't really start anything until you've finished it. What that means is you always want to begin with the end in mind. Before I start anything, I see the whole result that I'm seeking to accomplish in my mind. Then I get it very clear, it's very specific. So the first tip for people increasing their productivity is having what I call clarity of outcome. You want to be very clear and specific about the outcome you desire to produce before you start anything. That's number one. The second part of the whole equation for increasing productivity is in understanding the 80 20 rule. It's called a Perrato Principle, what that basically says is 80% of your activities will produce only 20 % of your results. Another way of saying it is 20% of your activities will produce 80% of your results. Unfortunately most people focus on the 80% of their activities that produce only 20% of their results. So in other words, they major in minors. What you want to do is major in the majors. And that's focusing on the 20% that will produce 80%. The 20% activities is what we call the high payoff activities. So that's the second step. It's what I call consolidation of power. You consolidate all of your power into 20% of activities that's going to produce 80% of the results. And that will increase your productivity tremendously. And the third thing really goes back to what we talked about earlier, which is to stay committed to simple disciplines. These are those 20% activities that you know are important, that produces the biggest pay off, then if you do that over and over and over again, then your productivity will increase exponentially. It will really go through the roof. These are very powerful steps to increasing your productivity.

Wright

You've created hundreds of audio training programs, and other well known speakers even come to you for advice. What drives you to pour out the tremendous output of material into the marketplace that you do?

Clark

What drives me is really my philosophy of life. My philosophy of life is this: Human Beings are all energy, and from what I understand about energy is that it never dies. What that basically means is before we even showed up on this planet we were somewhere else as energy. And it also says to me that after we're gone in physical form from this planet, then we are going to be somewhere else as energy. The whole point about this is that since we have been somewhere else for a long period of time before we showed up and since we're going to be somewhere else for a long period of time after we're gone in physical form from this planet, then we're here in general for a short period of time. And anytime you go somewhere for a short period of time to me it's called a vacation, it's a holiday. So I believe that all of us humans are on vacation right now, we're on holiday. And if you are on holiday I believe you are supposed to maximize it. I think a lot of people do their best to plan their holidays to really get the most out of it. And that's what I'm doing. I'm doing everything I can to plan my holiday here to get the most out of it. And one of the things that allows me to get the most out of it is to really feel that I've contributed to the other human beings on this planet. The way that I feel that I'm contributing to the other human beings is to come out with empowering programs, like the 100 Plus audio programs that I've come out with and many are available at ourClubRhino.com website. I also get joy from getting the opportunity to work with and assist other trainers bring their powerful information out to the Marketplace. This excitement and inner passion for what I do is why I can work on creating programs for 12 to 15 hours at a time in a day without even realizing that 12 to 15 hours have passed by. It's also really neat to see the stories of people who have attended some of my trainings, listen to my audio programs, attended my seminars, watched my DVD's, read my books, joined my membership program at ClubRhino.com, etc., and to see what has happened in their life. I have several people who've become millionaires now as a result of following some of the principles, strategies, and insights I teach. They simply decided to master some of the teachings I have presented over the years and it has paid off very well for them. I've got to give them credit of course; just because you buy my Cd, Dvd, or go to my seminars doesn't mean you're going to become a millionaire. You have to actually choose to apply the information and master it in your own life. So when I see that taking place it excites me. It really gets me motivated and it really makes me feel like I made some kind of contribution. So that's one of the reasons I do what I do and why I'm excited about what I do, and why I was excited about sharing this information with you via this interview for others to learn and benefit from.

Wright

Well, this has been a great conversation for me Jerry. Today we've been talking to Jerry Clark, who is the founder and CEO of his own company ClubRhino.com where he conducts personal and professional development seminars around the world. He recognizes that change occurs at the individual level and he's committed to training other show to improve themselves by teaching peak performance strategies that get results. Jerry, thank you so much for being with us today on *Conversations on Success*.

Clark

David, it's my pleasure. I look forward to reading all the other *Conversations on Success* that you've had from the resources you all make available, via your interviews, with other empowering authors. Go, Go, Go!!!

About The Author

Jerry Clark became a self-made millionaire while still in his 20's. Today, through his company Club Rhino, Inc., he conducts personal and professional development seminars around the World. The topics covered range from peak performance training, effective communication strategies, and how to increase your productivity and profitability in your chosen career. Jerry is the producer of over 100 of the most empowering audio programs available in the Self Empowerment industry, many of which he is also the author, such as The Magic of Colors, Creating Magic, and The Magic of Influence. Jerry's training products are currently being used by dozens of companies in over 35 countries worldwide. Jerry recognizes that change occurs at the individual level, and he's committed to training others how to improve themselves by teaching peak performance strategies that get results. Jerry has shared the stage with industry leaders such as Tony Robbins, Jim Rohn, Charlie "Tremendous" Jones, Les Brown, Brian Tracy, Denis Waitley, Florence Littauer, Robert Allen, Mark Victor Hansen, Robert Kiyosaki, and many others. He has also interviewed some of the World's Giants of Motivation, Wealth-Building, Sales, Marketing, Humanities, Science, and more... Jerry specializes in training and coaching Commission Based and Home Based Sales people and Entrepreneurs... His articles appear in many major publications such as *Success Magazine, Working At Home Magazine, Wealth Building Magazine, Money Maker's Monthly*, and many others. Jerry is the CEO & President of Club Rhino, Inc., and the founder of AMG Business Group.

Jerry Clark

Club Rhino, Inc.

3020 Legacy, Suite 100-373

Plano, TX 75023

Phone: 972.747.9769

Phone: 800.405.3302(24 Hour Message Center)

Fax: 972.747.7159

E-mail: jerry@clubrhino.com

www.clubrhino.com

Chapter Eleven

ANDREW PALOMO

David E. Wright (Wright)

Today we are talking to Andrew G. Palomo who was born in 1970 in the south side of Chicago, a White Sox fan. Andrew is the co-founder of Pillar Financial, LLC. He also is a managing partner of three other companies involving commercial and residential real estate. As a certified mortgage consultant and a certified residential mortgage specialist, Andrew has helped thousands realize the dream of home ownership. Andrew is known for his straightforward analytical approach in helping his clients. After receiving a B.B.A. from Loyola University Chicago he entered the world of real estate finance and has counseled thousands regarding the benefits of home ownership. Andrew, thank you for being with us today on *Conversations on Success.*

Andrew Palomo (Palomo)

Thank you, sir, for having me. It is a pleasure to be here.

Wright

What would you say would be the biggest contribution to your professional success?

Palomo

Pretty simple. The basics would be hard work, delivering what you promised to clients, employees and vendors. Basically it amounts to honesty and ethics and giving people what you promised them.

Wright

Aside from personal role models, who are the people who have served as your role models for success?

Palomo

Abraham Lincoln and General George Patton.

Wright

Why?

Palomo

I find them to be similar individuals. Abraham Lincoln did what he thought was right at the time in the face of what you could only call great pressure. He changed the nation. He was not a popular man. Not a lot of people were on his side but he did what he thought was right and saw it through to the end, eventually paying the highest possible price that you can. In terms of a role model, anytime there is a difficult decision to make you think, my God, this guy changed an entire country just by his sheer will and doing what he believed was right. George Patton is an individual, who again, was not very well liked, even by the troops that he led. He is historically the most successful General ever with an extremely simple philosophy. His philosophy is to do what you have to do, do it right away, and don't sit around and hem and haw about it. Get it done right the first time so you don't have to redo it! And as a result, his men didn't like him. But everyone wanted to be in his unit because he had the fewest casualties of any unit active in World War II. General Patton was an incredible man. He took more land, more square miles, captured more prisoners and captured more cities. No one has even come close to his record, which also had the fastest time frame and fewest casualties.

Wright

What do you think are the biggest obstacles people face in trying to become successful?

Palomo

Themselves. People generally decide how they can't do something, or not to do something, more often than they determine how something can be done. They get in their own way. People will come up with five reasons off the top of their head on why something cannot be done, but they won't sit down and write out a plan as how to get something done and make a plan. Maybe its human nature, people are a bit lazy. It's easier to fail than to succeed, so I think people get in their own way.

Wright

So I take it you're a goal setter.

Palomo

Yes, punch and list all day long, it's all I do.

Wright

So what makes your perspective unique?

Palomo

I grew up with an unusual family background without a lot of money. I had the influence of different cultures and religions. My parents are not only different ethnicities but also have different religious beliefs. Growing up without fitting in makes you humble and independent. I was always able to stay grounded, but I challenge anyone to tell me that I can't do something, because I have literally come from nothing. So I don't believe that argument for an instant. That is a hard sell, if you can sell me on that one, then I think that you are the greatest salesman on earth.

Wright

You've been successful at starting businesses. What is your fundamental business strategy?

Palomo

Basically apply the golden rule. Treat others as you would like to be treated. Communicate with them honestly. Look out for the client's best interest. When you are doing that you are coming from a good place. Everything else just seems to take care of itself. The foundation for building a long lasting relationship with someone is when they know that you are in it for them as much as you are in it for yourself.

Even if that means referring a client somewhere else because you can't help them the best, clients come back to me. It also helps me get a good night's sleep.

Wright

So what is the root cause of why organizations don't focus on customers? It sounds like a simple philosophy.

Palomo

I think most organizations are too engrossed in their day-to-day operations. To make something completely focused on the customer, I think a lot of places feel that it is too risky and expensive. They don't see an immediate return, and they can't calculate it. So it's just easier to do what they do and then wonder why something is not going the way they wished it would. It's easier to stay doing what your doing everyday (status quo) than to make a change that can be painful for some folks, I guess.

Wright

So can customer focus boost employee productivity?

Palomo

Absolutely, customer focus makes everyone's experience a pleasant one. Once you get an employee to understand that: A. They are not there without the client, and B. If they are focused completely on that client's needs, the whole transaction is easier. They are honest and coming from a good place. People just sense when you are on their side. Bad news, good news, or whatever the news is when you are working with your customers, it's a team effort and it actually makes an employee's job easier. They don't have call reluctance because the phone does not weight a thousand pounds when you have to call someone with bad news if you already have a relationship with them. You're calling to discuss a mutual plan to figure something out and people end up enjoying their jobs and coming to work happier and actually liking their jobs, because it's easier to do.

Wright

Could you tell our readers a little bit about what drives you to be successful?

Palomo

Security for my family's future drives me. I don't want my children to go through what I did. Maybe I'm taking a little bit away from them, but I'm going to take that chance. But I get up every day more for them than for me. I want to leave a lasting impression on their lives and I would like nothing more than for them to be proud of me. And on the day that I pass on I hope my children say, "well, he was a good man and helped a lot of people and helped our lives and we're grateful and thankful."

Wright

What is the message that you want people to hear so they can learn from your success?

Palomo

Don't let fear control you. Get out of your own way and think about things that can be done and why things can be done and don't focus on the negative. Like children with their imagination; somewhere along the line, something comes into all of our lives and squashes that childlike imagination and I think that's the difference between people who are successful and determined, and those who are not. Some people aren't going to let that childlike "I can do it" spirit get squashed. You just have to find it if you've lost it, rebuild it if it's been destroyed and let it be. Focus on the positive.

Wright

So the bottom line is that as far as you're concerned, people get in their own way to success more than others or circumstances get in the way?

Palomo

Absolutely. You can pick up the newspaper any day and there is an article about somebody that has done something under the worst circumstances. Somebody sent me an article about a young man that lost both of his arms and proceeded to be a novelist. At first glance you wouldn't think that could be done. But this person with a stick in his mouth types more than I can with two hands. More words per minute and with his face basically than I can with two hands, because that is what he is focusing on—what he wants to accomplish. There is another story of a young man born with no arms and no legs and he is a championship wrestler. Tell that guy he can't be a wrestler, and he is beating people up on a competitive level in high school and then on to college with no arms and no legs. He is out wrestling people and tying them into knots. So it is definitely people telling themselves what they can do rather than someone else or circumstances.

Wright

So why do you think there are more people not in tune with their passion if it's something that all people possess?

Palomo

They listen to the "nay sayers." They listen to the negative and worse yet they start to believe themselves that it can't be done. I think if you believe somebody that says you can't do it, and it's something that your are passionate about, then you've lost and they have beaten you down. They think we have a passion to do something and do it well and as long as there is no one telling you that you can't; your fine and you just have to learn to tune them out.

Wright

So share with me a little bit about what you plan to do for the next few years.

Palomo

The next few years for me entails, in large part, focusing on Pillar Financial with the primary goal of educating people to the fact that our company is absolutely the best choice for their mortgage needs. We want to communicate to people the fact that a mortgage is the largest debt that they have and that it needs to be managed the same way as 401K or any stock investment. And they can basically become wealthier or financially independent by paying attention to this part of their portfolio as well. Also, I will be focusing on building Pillar into a national mortgage banker. We are in two states and growing and we want to take it to a level where we're probably about in ten states.

Wright

Well the most important question for the day, what are the chances of the White Sox next year?

Palomo

Not very good if you have been looking at the sports page today, they let their perennial all star go.

Wright

I saw that.

Palomo

There are a lot of us scratching our heads, saying, "I hope that they are smarter than us, I hope that they are going to use that money for a fifth pitcher or I hope they know something that I don't, because it doesn't look good." But at a certain level, all kidding aside, I respect the attitude of the ownership and the manager, because they quite simply don't like dealing with the person who represents the three biggest free agents. They feel that the person negotiates in bad faith and they feel like that person sets things up the wrong way and they quite frankly passed on people. They won't work with anybody represented. This particular agent, the management feels he brings negativity into the organization.

Wright

Well at least they are staying true to their heart.

Palomo

It's got to count for something, right?

Wright

Absolutely. Well, if you had a platform Andrew, and you could tell the public anything that you wanted to, that might help them, that might make them become more successful or happier, more well adjusted, what would you say to them?

Palomo

I would say they should literally write down what it is that they want out of life. What do they want to be, financially, spiritually, family-wise, business-wise, and what they are doing for a living, whatever it is, write down what their ideal day, or ideal life would look like. Then just sit down and analyze that and figure out how to get from where they are to that place; like a personal road map. Sometimes I think people might find out that they are doing exactly what they want to be doing and they do it very well and they think that they are unhappy because other people tell them that they should be doing something else, or they should be making more money. I think if people would just sit down and have a quiet conversation with themselves then write it down, and enact a plan, it would be great. The plan doesn't even have to be perfect. George Patton said "I would rather enact a good plan today than a perfect plan next week."

Wright

Right, I remember that. Well Andrew, I really appreciate all of this time that you have taken with us to talk to us about this important topic, success. I know that you are busy today, but I really do want to thank you for taking all of this time with me.

Palomo

I appreciate it. Thank you.

Wright

Today we have been talking to Andrew G. Palomo. Andrew is the co-founder of Pillar Financial, LLC. He is a certified mortgage consultant, a certified residential mortgage specialist and as we have found out today, cares a whole lot about success through helping people buy real property and manage it as well as any other investment that they may have. Thank you so much, Andrew, for being with us today on *Conversations on Success*.

About The Author

Andrew G. Palomo is co-founder of Pillar Financial, LLC. Pillar Financial, LLC. is a full service mortgage broker serving the greater Chicago area. Through his dedication to service and professionalism, Pillar has grown from a one-room operation to a company that closes nearly a quarter of a billion dollars of home loans annually. Andrew is currently one of five individuals in the state of Illinois to hold both the CRMS and CMC designation. Through close working relationships with attorneys, accountants, financial planners, and real estate professionals, Andrew brings a wealth of knowledge and financial strategies to the mortgage planning industry.

Andrew G. Palomo

Pillar Financial, LLC.

415 Creekside Dr. #130

Palatine, IL. 60074

Phone: 847.359.1700

Email: Andrew@pillarhomeloan.com

Chapter Twelve

LASHAUN BROWN-GLENN

David E. Wright (Wright)

LaShaun is the president and owner of Nails Naturally, Inc., a hand and foot spa located in Downtown Chicago. An Illinois nail technician, she has operated her full service nail spa for over sixteen years. After attending Jackson State University, where she majored in Computer Science and Accounting, LaShaun received her nail technician certificate from Onyx Vocational and certificates in English Writing and Persuasive Speaking from the Feltre School.

Because continuing education is her top priority, LaShaun not only attends frequent classes and trade shows for her personal enhancement, but she also shares her extensive knowledge and experience with others. Since 1996, she has been an educator for major nail care manufacturers including Backscratchers and Creative Nail Design. In 1999, Creative Nail Design designated her as an "Award Winning Educator" and inducted her as a member of The International Training Team. In addition, she is featured as a lead nail tech in the newly released educational videos for Milady Publishing Company.

LaShaun has also competed in numerous industry events over the years, most recently being honored as NAILS magazine, "1999-2000 Nail Technician of the Year.

LaShaun's dynamic personality, personal drive and professional affiliations with some of the most exciting and prestigious societies in the industry has led to her visibility in the media. Brown-Glenn is a member of the Chicago Cosmetologist Association, the International Nail Technicians Association and the National Speakers Association. During the past five years, LaShaun has served as an Advisory Board Member and Educational Committee Co-Chairperson for the Nail Care Association and on the Education Committee for the Global Nail Exchange. She is a Registered C. E. Sponsor with State of Illinois.

In an effort to help business owners and their staff become more successful, LaShaun started "Speaking On Point," a company designed to promote and provide education and consulting on business development, teambuilding and customer service. LaShaun, welcome to *Conversations on Success*.

LaShaun Brown-Glenn (Brown-Glenn)
Thank you, David.

Wright
LaShaun, you had some interesting experiences that add to your point of view. Can you tell us a little bit about how your childhood began to shape your enthusiasm for speaking and helping others?

Brown-Glenn
Please allow me to share a story with you. This is story about a little girl who was in an environment that sometimes society did not deem ideal for a ten-year-old girl. It was an atmosphere of comfort and welcoming. It was like another family that welcomed you with opened arms. It was a place where people went to be heard. Lights were dimmed just right, colors were soothing and smoke filled the air. This young girl would find herself at this place everyday Monday through Friday after school from about 3-8 p.m.

The little girl would sometimes find herself sitting on the jukebox as she watched the patrons being poured their feel good of choice and as the bartenders would lean in as their guest spoke. You heard in the background soft sounds of music. Some of the tunes that you heard were June Christy, Etta James, Nat King Cole, The Dells and The Temptations. She sat there humming a few notes and seeing the look on people's faces when they heard something that took them back down memory lane or lifted their spirits. She watched the subtle eye contact and nod from across the room for acknowledgement and the remembering of names and favorite things. While she could not hear what they were saying, she was able to understand the body language. Sometimes she would watch as the bartenders would rest their hand upon the shoulder of a guest, pat them on the back, offer a tissue or give a celebratory hug.

As she sat there she began to take in what was happening around her. There are those that may take exception to a child being exposed to this kind of place and then there are those that might recognize that some of her earliest lessons on language and what worked and didn't, were gifted in that very same cocktail lounge.

That little girl was me. Looking back, I now realize that there were some very profound business lessons for me in that lounge. My mother's business is one that depends strongly on communication to flourish. Looking back, there was tremendous value in those years.

I have now realized the significance of those early experiences and I don't believe that it was luck. We all have experiences to draw upon. Experiences alone don't seem that impactful, but combined with thought and exploration it gives insight that previously went unseen. These are lessons that were learned before we knew we had reasons to learn them.

What most of us don't take the time to accept is that listening is a skill that is first watched then developed. Then…honed a little, before being sharpened even further. We all listen for different reasons: to get the information we need, because we have to, because it's expected, it's a part of our job or because it gives us pleasure. But, how often do we listen when we want to be heard? How often do we take the time to recognize the unique experience in others, before offering our take on things? How often do we finish someone else's sentences? Or cut someone off mid sentence because we just had a thought. It might be intriguing at first, but soon you long to have a singular personal thought on your own.

Wright

What other lessons did you learn from your mother's business that you feel is important to the success of business?

Brown-Glenn

The strength of character that was exhibited by my mother and the respect that she earned from patrons, vendors, the community and city officials helped me to understand at a young age the importance of community involvement and networking. I remember when my mother discovered that her property had been sitting on two lots and she had been paying taxes for one. It was noteworthy to me how the Alderman stood by her side and rallied for assistance so that she would not lose her property. It's funny, I had seen that Alderman and other officials on countless days and evenings convene in my mother's establishment to meet and have food provided for them, but it was at that time that the respect that they had for a woman who was a single mother and in business became most apparent.

Something else that stands out for me, learned from my mother and applied to my business, is consistency. Consistency is the foundation for success in a business that depends on returning customers. My mother taught me how to be self-organized. Consistency is critical to client relationships. We are creatures of habit. Change is hard for us, we will resist it. We like to go to our favorite restaurant and order the same thing every time. We want it brought out to our table in the exact same way it was the last time we ordered it. One of the lessons that Ray Kroc and the Howard Schultz has taught us is that no matter where you go, whether in Chicago or Texas, the food and the coffee is going to be the same. Consistency in any relationship, whether it's personal or professional, is born out of self organization.

Clients need to know what to expect from you. Even if the client is not consistent, it is important from a business perspective that you as a business owner bring consistency to the partnership. Most people have support systems incorporated into business and life. As a business owner, if you are fortunate enough to be a respected member of the team, many benefits come from being respectful of that trust. However, you cannot respect that trust if you do not respect yourself. Find what works and the do it consistently!

Children are yet another perfect example of the payoff that you can get from being consistent. When we create clear cut boundaries, there is less room for miscommunication or misunderstandings. To build consistency you have to work at being the best. You must do what you do well and do it again and again.

Wright

How has that worked out for you in the beauty industry over the past sixteen years?

Brown-Glenn

David, when people come in to see me for a service it is not just about grooming their hands and feet. No, it's much more. It is part of the total experience. You are sitting about six or twelve inches across from your guest for an hour or two. During that time together, people want to be heard. It's about being a sounding board. People pour out their hearts and their life experiences. Everyone wants validation that their personal experiences are important. And, after all, we can learn from each other. It also gives me an opportunity to reflect on my own life and be reminded of my many blessings. I have walked down the aisle with some of my guests as they got married and been to divorce court with them (mentally, that is). I've gone through their job interviews and celebrated with them, as well as cried with them when they didn't get or lost a job. David, you can really connect with people and become like a part of their family. I've been through their good and bad, ups and downs.

As a business owner, I have been able to create a culture where people are happy to come to everyday. It has been my goal to create an environment that is inspirational and supportive. It is important for me to have people around me that want to be there, not because they have to. I have an open door policy where employees are free to express themselves and seek support if they need it. We have a common goal and vision for the business and everyone has to support one another. If someone is out late at night and has had too much to drink they know that they can call me for a ride and a cup of coffee. If you need me to provide you with a wake-up call, say so and it's done. Whatever the need is, just convey it and if it is within my power, consider it done. I know someone reading this is thinking, "I'm not babysitting grown people." However, I look at it as, I am supporting you to become the best that you can be. It is a way of nurturing them to bring out the good that is in us all. How many movies have we watched where there is a person that shows up and shows that they care just a little and turn a negative situation completely around?

When I work with others in my capacity as a facilitator, I offer a few suggestions to get them started in creating such an environment.

- Be willing to listen to clients and employees-even if you don't like what you're hearing. Allow them to have their say.
- Reserve judgment. When possible let the speaker lead themselves to the answer. Usually, they already have a solution or an expectation.
- Be aware that it is okay to have certain feelings. It's how we react to those feelings that create change-negative or positive.
- It is important to have an "It doesn't leave this room policy" when discussing personal challenges and don't break that trust.
- Be willing to put yourself in their shoes and see things from their point of view.
- Tell them what they are doing well. Everyone likes to be affirmed for their efforts.

I am there to bring their challenges to the table. I am also there to help mediate and create a direction for the company to move in for the good and betterment of everyone involved. Whether it is the employer, employee or the customer on the phone, how do we get everyone what it is that they need?

Communication is the key to your business being successful and not just from a financial stand point. Communication allows you to build trust and respect and these two elements can create good working relationships, less turnover and client loyalty.

Being in and around my mother's business and experiencing that culture has been a blessing. I learned not to just listen to what a person is saying, but to hear what a person is saying. The other value that came out of that environment is knowing that they don't want you to advise them or tell them what you would do...just LISTEN!

Wright

I can see how that might sharpen your listening skills.

Brown-Glenn

Yes, it does. What I understand is that it doesn't matter whether you are a housewife, politician, CEO or janitor, people just want to be heard. I never forget this lesson and I make it a point to use in my daily communication with my husband, daughter, extended family and my clients.

I have just another little story to share. This past Christmas eve I was dropping off my daughter, Taylor, who is now four-years-old at a close family friend's home because there was no school and my husband and I both had to work. Now, this friend is the same friend that keeps Taylor for us when we travel for work or pleasure. As we were headed there, Taylor ask if she was coming back home that evening because she was really concerned about being left over night. So, of course, as a parent, I want to check to make sure that she was happy spending time with this friend. She answered yes...then she said, "But I miss you, mommy, when I'm not home with you, and I love you this much," as she stretched her arms out as far and as wide as she could get them. I reassured her that she would be back at home with mommy and daddy and sort of laid out how the day was going to go. After going over the agenda, she then said, "You promise mommy," in a sweet, loving and whiney voice. I said, "Yes, I promise," and I told her that I loved her.

Of course, this was a little difficult for me to hear because I travel on a regular basis and have done so even before she was born. When I got to work I shared the story with one of my guest who has been coming to me for well over twelve years. She is like another mother to me. Upon her suggestion to teach Taylor to count sleeps, I went to an Office Depot and spent about seventy-dollars and purchased stickers(metallic stars, hearts, and smiley faces) and then just a variety of other stick-on and scrapbook like stuff to include flowers, airplanes, luggage, letters and a planner. Now the goal was to teach Taylor to count sleeps until my return home, as I was leaving in just a short couple of weeks.

Together we decorated the cover of the planner with flowers and smiley faces and spelled out her name. Then on the inside we noted the dates that I would be gone and the day that I would return. For the days that I would be away I drew hearts on the dates and then placed a smiley face and heart sticker on the day that I would return. I instructed Taylor to place a heart sticker where I had drawn them, one each morning when she awakened. I told her that when her hearts met my smiley face and heart that I would be back home; after just four sleeps.

Needless to say, the first trip of this year was very difficult for me, but because I heard her, I found a solution. This way, it was not too difficult for either of us. It made it a little more fun for her and gave her something to look forward to.

Wright

This seems like an appropriate time to ask this next question. You're juggling a lot of balls into mid air, you have marriage, motherhood, you're an entrepreneur, you're a teacher, you're a mentor, and you're a professional trainer, so how do you keep it all together?

Brown-Glenn

I try very hard to practice what I preach, so it's a combination of things. For one, I'm in a business where I pamper people and make them feel good, so I make sure that I personally take time out to use the products and services that I talk about. I go out of my environment and experience the pampering first hand.

I have my husband, James, come into the salon and get regular pedicures and manicures and that's great because he gets a little grooming and it brings him into my world. But it also allows us time together and it gives him a chance to take care of himself.

My husband and I decided to have a family day. That designated day is every Tuesday. On our family day, we spend it doing things together, as a family. An example of how the day might go is that we drop Taylor, our daughter, off at school. James and I will go out for breakfast, catch a movie and then out for lunch or a walk along the lakefront holding hands. We will then pick our daughter up from school and go to the aquarium, see Disney on Ice or do something of interest to her, followed by dinner out or enjoy something at home that we have prepared together.

This was important because we did not want to get caught up in the rat race and the demands and scope of our perspective businesses. My husband has a successful property management firm, so it is important to us that we did not sacrifice what we felt was sacred to us. Family should always be at the top of your list. What good is success if you don't have anyone to truly share it with? Someone who knows the struggles and challenges that you have gone through to get where you are. Someone that has been there to support you and keep late nights with you during difficult times.

It is important to be organized when juggling so many different balls in the air. For me, everything has a place. There are days that I work in the office and take care of payroll, banking, marketing, meetings, etc. Then there is the time put aside to provide guest with services at the salon. I have guest that have been with me for more than fifteen years, and no matter what, they only want me to provide their services. Most weekends are spent speaking, teaching or training.

When I travel, if I am going some place where there are activities available for my family, I have them travel with me. So, David, the key to doing it all and having it all is being organized and prioritizing each part of your life.

Wright

It's strange that you said you have your husband come in. I've been married for twenty-six years and about a month and a half ago my wife decided that I needed a pedicure and manicure. I said, "Not me." She said, "Yes," and a made an appointment. I will be going again tomorrow, which will be my third time around.

Brown-Glenn

That's great, David! I have seen a growth in my business where men are concerned. More and more men are getting into taking care of themselves and are stepping away from the stereotypes that was once associated with having a manicure or pedicure. It is good grooming and I too went down that road with my husband, but once he experienced it for himself he was hooked. Now, I'm trying to work on getting him a massage and a facial...then he will be complete.

Wright

I warned her that I might marry the girl who does the pedicure.

Brown-Glenn

Well, David, I would have to say that the nail technician who is providing you your service is giving you a very good and complete experience. She is obviously appealing to your senses. I would expect that she uses products that are gender friendly, provides your service in a clean environment, listens to you and hears your needs. And she connected with you from the beginning when you were apprehensive about receiving the pedicure and manicure. Most importantly, she welcomed you into her space and made you feel comfortable being there. However, I don't think your wife has anything to worry about...(laughs).

Wright

Among the many topics that you speak on, to which would be team building and customer service, do you address any female or male audience on the subject of balance and career balance of life? It seems like your life kind of worked out, you're a mother, entrepreneur and you own your own business. Owning a business within itself is very difficult, I know about that, but being a mother, a business owner and a wife, that's tough to balance. Have you ever thought about speaking on that subject?

Brown-Glenn

Absolutely, David. I offer a workshop perfectly named "Balancing Act." What happens in a Balancing Act workshop is people have a chance to really take time to look at every area of the lives. I help them see that they have two different lives, a personal one and a professional one. I also use this time to get people to understand the difference in who they are versus what they do. Oftentimes people tie them together and there is a difference. I am LaShaun, a speaker, entrepreneur, wife, mother, etc., but that is not who I am, that is what I do.

I also have them to look at their daily schedules. So I'll say write down what your day looks like from the moment you get up to the moment you go to bed and I ask them to share. Someone might say the following...

- At 5am the alarm goes off and I hit the snooze.
- At 5:15 the alarms goes off again and I get up and shower.
- By 5:45 I'm out of the shower and getting dressed and putting on makeup.
- At 6:15 I wake up my five year old, give him a bath, get him dressed and brush his hair.
- At 6:45 I'm getting my eighteen month old up and repeat what I've just done.
- By 7:15 We are headed out the door and I drop off both kids at two different locations.
- By 8:05 I'm on my way to work and I work from 9-5 on a good day.
- At 5:15 I've made it to the car and I pick up the kids and head home, prepare dinner, do homework and get ready to do it all over again.

And when the weekend is here there is Spanish class, martial arts, dance recitals, bill paying, grocery shopping and only God knows what else.

I then have them to look at what's missing from their lives. Things like date night, family day, most importantly some *me* time and so on. David, it is important that you look at your life as a whole and rate the following areas. On a scale of one to ten, with one lacking and ten being great, rate your spiritual life, health and well being, family life and on and on. How do you rate? Consequently, it is important to be honest with yourself. It is the only way to get true results. If you are low in an area or two, choose one, set a goal to make the necessary change and give yourself a time-line. So, your plan would look something like this: Let's say you gave yourself a four rating in the area of health and well being. Determine how that is working for you (in the words of Dr. Phil) and how can you make it better. You want flat abs, lose ten pounds and eat more nutritious foods. The plan then becomes to incorporate a three-times-a-week work out schedule into your week, do some grocery shopping so you can eliminate fast food from your diet and you are going to start the plan in about two weeks on January fifteenth. Share this plan with someone who will encourage you and hold you accountable because it only benefits you. Reward yourself when your mission is complete. As mentioned before, I think that it is very important that we all have some *"me time."* What is meant by me time? This is time that you are away from the daily hum drum of life as you know it. It is so easy to become a sacrificial mother, father, employer, employee, etc. You have to schedule time that is all about you and only you. An example of what I do for myself to get the *me* time is, first, at the beginning of every year for the past fourteen years, I take what is a called a mental health week. That is time that I take alone to meditate and be prayerful. It is a time that I take to reflect over my life, my goals and accomplishments from the previous year. Did I do as planned or not and why? If not, do I want to move it forward in the New Year? Then let's say about every three months, I either plan an overnight stay at a hotel or a day of pampering. And that day of pampering might look something like this. I drop Taylor off at school by 9:00 am and head to spa for a massage, pedicure, sea salt glow body treatment and some steam, but not without first stopping by Starbucks for a tall White Chocolate Mocha in a Grande cup filled with extra whip. When the pampering is over, I head out and treat myself to a nice lunch with a glass of wine, and on a good day I manage to buy myself a pair of shoes in between shopping for Taylor.

I believe that time alone helps you to release some negative energy and prevents burnout. You feel renewed and it's sort of freeing. It allows you time to think clearly and just have the world be all about you. That time will only make you a better parent, spouse, employee and/or friend.

Wright

I can only imagine your mom being a single parent, having lots a lot of challenges, balancing a career and family with no help at all. At least you have your husband, who is a successful business owner in his own right. So balancing a home and a career are really tough. It seems like you would be a perfect one for that.

Brown-Glenn

Thank you, David, and I would have to agree with you. I have had a chance to learn and experience balance from both sides of the coin. First, through my mother's experience as a single parent and in my own life with a help mate, as my mother would refer to my husband. I believe that one common denominator is not being afraid to ask for help. So often we feel that we don't want to impose on anyone, but I say impose, it is for the good of everyone involved. When someone offers to help you, take them up on it. You have to build a support system that is built of family and friends that you can trust when there are children involved. Whether single or married with a child(ren) ask you friends in similar situations if you all could trade off some time. One weekend the kids stay with you and give that parent(s) a break for some alone and together time and vice versa. Get together with your spouse and plan the time that you need for yourselves and get it scheduled into your Outlooks, PDA's, and planners. Don't allow for excuses; keep the commitment to yourself just as you would a dental appointment, doctor's appointment, business lunch or dinner. Just commit to making yourself a priority and know that it is ok.

Wright

"I Feel Good All Over." What an interesting topic title. Please tell me more about it.

Brown-Glenn

David, I believe that in business our focus has become more about the mighty dollar and less about the clients, customers, patients (or however you refer to them). It is so important that we realize that people come to us for the complete experience not just the purchase or service. You may be a great doctor, dentist, stylist or salesperson, but if you are not able to deliver a well rounded experience eventually it will result in a lower bottom line.

When you feel good all over it shows in the way you present your personal self to the world. You're well groomed; your hair, nails and clothes are immaculate. You're smiling brightly and you are comfortable and excited about the journey ahead. It is a total package. That package consists of all your senses. Yes, that's right, your senses; see, hear, touch, smell and taste. You have to be able to reach your clients on all levels. Ask yourself, are you relating to your customer in this way? How can I create this total experience for my client every time? Make a list of things that you would expect from another business. What would your expectations be and are you meeting those very needs for your client. Start a list and the write down at least one way to accomplish the experience. If you are selling carpet your list might look like: good lighting, staff listens to how I use areas to choose the right carpet material or good selection of colors. In the salon industry a list would include: Friendly reception staff, privacy, well trained nail technicians who are personable. Basically, think of it as if you were writing the perfect want ad for the services you provide. How would it read? Is it the statement that your business makes currently? This is your list. Now take action to put it into play, but remember you must be totally honest with yourself.

Wright

This is good stuff, tell me more.

Brown-Glenn

One of the most difficult challenges for any human being is to leave their personal life outside of work. What I try to explain to people first is that you have to leave your world outside once you cross the threshold of work. It must always be about the person that you are servicing / selling. They must feel your goodness when first greeted by you in person or on the phone. Yes, it is true; people can tell if you have a smile in your voice. You also have to be willing to put yourself in that persons shoes and ask yourself what you would want from the situation at hand. Think of the experience that you would give someone in your home. Treat them as though they were a guest in your home. How would that role play out? What does that look like to you? For me, it would go something like this. I would greet you at the door with a smile, invite you in, take your coat and offer you a seat. Once comfy, I would offer you a drink or something to eat and then tell you to make yourself at home.

I do realize that sometimes the outside world can bring us detrimental situations and we all handle those things differently. For myself, when there is something negative in front of me I prefer to be with people because the time alone can sometimes make it very difficult. I actually have the ability to sit and provide a service or stand and speak in front of hundreds and no one would ever sense that I was facing a challenge. Now, for others that might mean calling into work and taking a vacation day. Maybe you want to try going into your work environment and seeing if you could find some comfort there.

Wright

Are there people who inspire you?

Brown-Glenn

Without question, it would have to be my mother. My mother has successfully kept the doors of her business open now for twenty-nine years. She did that all while being a single parent. She made sure that she instilled in me unwavering and personal guidance throughout my life. She is a very strong woman, and she passed that on to me.

I am a mother now, I have a husband who is very much hands-on, and I still have to go to mom every now and then and ask her how she did it.

The next person who inspires me would be my husband. James is truly a gift from God. He has an incredible heart and never complains. He just wants to help everyone and make the world a better place for all. He finds a way to transition from business owner, to father to husband to Board President with such ease and grace. When I am trying to take care of him, he is trying to take care of me.

People who have a passion for life move and inspire me. Anyone who lives life to the fullest and who lives as though it is his or her last day inspires me. It is all about the happy people for me with the always-present smile upon their face.

Who can't find some inspiration from Oprah Winfrey? Oprah has a way of lifting you up and showing you how you can make a difference in your life and the lives of others. She makes you look at your life and see how you can use it for the good and betterment of others. Whether you are hearing her speak or watching her show, you can take something totally not related to your situation and see the similarities and begin to take action and change your situation. Oprah will have you thinking about what your legacy will be when you make your life to death transition. Is it what you want it to be? Then you had better start to make a difference with the time you have left.

Wright

Do you have a favorite quote?

Brown-Glenn

Yes, I have a few but the one that always comes to mind and has been a favorite for years is that of Les Brown...no relation, laughs. "Shoot for the moon, even if you miss you will land among the stars."

Wright

I think that's great.

Brown-Glenn

I believe that quote speaks to me because it is right in accord with one of my mother's constant messages. Always be the best that I can be. She said, "Spread your wings and soar: that the sky is the limit." I learned to believe that with prayer and focus, I could do all things.

Wright

So what do you believe is the secret to your continued success and career growth?

Brown-Glenn

I would have to say that it is my commitment to being a life-long learner. I am always looking for ways to improve on what I do whether it is as a mother, wife, facilitator or whatever capacity that I am functioning in at any given time. It is important for me to get to the next level. I have to know what it takes to get through the closed doors. I don't allow myself to think I can't. My daughter is not allowed to say can't. Can not is not allowed in the vocabulary of anyone in our home. We believe that you may meet with some stumbling blocks, but if you fall down just get back up and try it again.

Wright

When you started out was success a goal for you? In other words, did you plan on being successful? Did you plan on being the best?

Brown-Glenn

No, I did not start off with a goal to be successful per se, but I did plan on being the best that I could be no matter what my endeavor. Therefore, that meant being the best nail tech, salon owner, speaker and trainer that I could be.

I think that success is inherent for you if you are pursuing your passion. I believe that success comes when you are doing something that makes you feel satisfied and it is what gets you up in the morning or makes you stay up all night. There are many people that have achieved their goals and are successful, but they are not fulfilled.

Wright

If you had a platform in front of people who were interested in growing and being better, what would you say that would help them to become better people; more satisfied, more knowledgeable.

Brown-Glenn

I think first and foremost their faith is very important, whomever that faith is in. Truly, my faith and constant prayers have been at the forefront for me. I don't make a decision without going into prayer first.

It is important to have a great support system in place. That should be built of close family and friends. You want to have people around you that are going in the same direction as you. Keep people in your life that are positive, but who will also be true to you and help you in your development.

Wright

Down through your life you have made important decisions having to do with your job, career and your family. Has faith played an important role in the decisions you've made?

Brown-Glenn

Absolutely! Whenever I need to make a decision or I am faced with a challenge and need direction and guidance, it is truly my faith and prayers that get me through. I allow myself to be quiet and listen to that tiny but still voice inside of me. The biggest challenge for me is patience because I don't always want to wait. But one of my clients put it best and she said, "If you are going to worry why pray and why pray if you're going to worry?" When she shared that I thought, "Wow." I hold onto that and when I'm struggling , I go right back to it.

Wright

If you could have our readers take away one thing with them today, what would it be?

Brown-Glenn

I would want to share with them that respect is a fundamental of business. It is a reciprocal relationship. You must first give respect before you can get it. Successful business people respect other people's time by being prompt. Respect is letting the speaker finish his or her sentence before interjecting your own thoughts. Respect is honoring confidence. Respect is accepting that every human being has a past and a set of experiences that have set the basis for his or her current view. All parties involved keep their word and deliver on their promise. They respect themselves first and act in a trustworthy manner.

Trust has to be earned. In the board games of business, if you fail to deliver, you lose points in the trust account and must start over. People trust you when you have a history of consistently delivering what is needed.

Consistency, respect and trust helped my mother be successful in business and they have helped me to carry on a family tradition. With every opportunity, I pass on this tradition to others through personal contact and workshops. I help others identify the needs of their clients and employees so that they can start to reap the rewards of increased business, client retention and employee satisfaction.

I have one final thought and that is to remember that listening is the first step to being heard.

Wright

What an interesting conversation. I've learned a lot today. I know how busy you are and I really appreciate all of your time

Brown-Glenn

Thank you. I'm so honored to have had this privilege and opportunity to be able to speak with you.

Wright

Today we've been talking to LaShaun Brown-Glenn. LaShaun is the president and owner of Nails Naturally, Inc., a hand and foot spa located in Downtown Chicago. LaShaun founded Speaking On Point, a speaking and consulting firm that focuses on helping businesses build client and employee loyalty. Her topics includes customer service, work/life balance and team building. She's sought out for her expertise in the beauty industry and other business as well; her writings have been featured in several trade magazines. LaShaun, thank you so much for being with us today on *Conversations on Success*.

About The Author

With over fifteen years of entrepreneurial experience LaShaun Brown-Glenn shares a message on teambuilding, customer service and business development. Brown-Glenn is an Award Winning International Speaker, consultant and author. In addition to being a successful entrepreneur, she serves as a product and marketing consultant and seminar facilitator for various businesses. LaShaun is a member of the National Speakers Association.

LaShaun Brown-Glenn

Speaking On Point

55 E. Washington Street

Suite 421

Chicago, IL 60602-2893

Phone: 773.531.7991

www.speakingonpoint.com

Chapter Thirteen

RON CANHAM

THE INTERVIEW

David E. Wright (Wright)

Today we're speaking with Ron Canham. Ron is an accomplished keynote speaker and seminar leader with over 25 years of experience in the areas of leadership, customer service, and self-motivation. Ron has served organizations in the private sector, guided nonprofits in educational groups, and worked extensively with government offices. From giants such as Block Bluster Video and Make a Wish Foundation, California State University, the city of Scottsdale, Arizona, and hundreds of groups in between, Ron brings an enthusiastic participative approach to his programs focusing on practical ideas that attendees can take away and implement immediately. Whether you're trying to lead and develop others or more effective manage yourself, Ron's programs deliver strategies to help insure both you and your organization grow successfully. Ron, welcome to *Conversations on Success*.

Ron Canham (Canham)

Thank you, David. I'm happy to spend some time with you today.

Wright

We hear so much about the importance of attitude today. What is attitude in your opinion?

Canham

That's a harder question than it sounds like. I have a couple of different definitions that I will share with you. The one I like the best is that it is a HABIT OF THOUGHTS and emotions, which tells me that, like any habit, it can be developed and improved upon. You can change your attitude if you choose to do so. This "internal habit" is like the lens of a camera through which people look at and approach their world. I've also heard attitude defined as your "mental approach" to life or simply your "point-of-view" towards the world. But the key thing about attitude is how easily we see it in people's behavior. Take the example of going to a nice restaurant to have dinner. The food may be great and the waiter may do all the right "waitering" tasks, but I can certainly see his attitude in his comments, facial expressions, and other non-verbal behavior when I want to change my order or ask for something out of the ordinary. You can SEE the "habit" of a poor attitude and that can literally ruin the whole experience, regardless of how good the food or other aspects of the meal were.

Wright

I've got a great friend in Houston, Texas. He has a t-shirt that states his tag line, which is, "The only difference between a good day and a bad day is your attitude."

Canham

And he's exactly right! We have a choice every day about how we're going to face what each day brings us. And it all depends on your attitude, how you choose to look at the many events that impact us every day. You mentioned Texas, and in my talks I often use Southwest Airlines and their founder, Herb Kelleher, as an example of the importance of developing a positive attitude. I would say Herb was "humorously blunt." He use to say about hiring people, "You know, flight attendants and people who handle baggage and people who sell tickets are a dime a dozen, but those same flight attendants and baggage handlers and ticket sellers who have a good attitude, those people are priceless!"

Wright

So what do you think? Is a person's attitude more a product of genetic factors or environmental factors?

Canham

I think even the best psychiatrists and psychologists tend to disagree about that. Is genetics a factor? Yes, but I would tend to believe that the majority of a person's attitude comes from the environment. If I believe that attitude is primarily a result of genetics, then I'm acknowledging that it is predetermined, that it can't be changed. We'd all become that person who justifies his or her behavior and beliefs by saying, "Well, that's just the way I am." We know everyone isn't like that. People change, they learn and grow. And the same environmental factors that influence change and growth—other people, events, self-knowledge—are the things that also shape and change our attitudes.

Wright

President Ronald Reagan said, "When you're waste deep in manure, just look around. There's got to be a pony there somewhere."

Canham

That's a great example of what we've been talking about. People who have a positive attitude help us feel better about ourselves. We enjoy being around them and they serve as a great role model for what our best selves can be.

Wright

You were talking about the chairman of Southwest Airlines. When it comes to hiring people in the workplace, assembling a team to or recruiting volunteers for that matter, what do you think is the most important, skills or attitude?

Canham

At Southwest, one of the tenets of their Human Resource Department is "Hire for Attitude." A colleague of mine, Steve Gilliland, says it best: "If you hire people for WHAT they know, you will fire them for WHO they are." Simply translated, that implies that when the technical skill levels of job candidates are fairly equal (and sometimes when they're not), select people who have a good attitude.

When I'm teaching a leadership seminar I always ask the attendees this question: "When you have to discipline or terminate a difficult employee, is the reason because he/she can't do the job (a performance issue), or because of behavior problems related to the job (a conduct problem). Ninety-five percent of the time the responses focus on conduct issues, not performance problems. Job conduct— your ability to get along with others, to provide great service, to do whatever needs to be done—is simply a choice that is driven by a person's attitude. So all things being equal, I would choose a positive attitude over experience or skill nearly every time. People can get training to learn the technical "how to's" of most jobs. It's much more challenging to change or re-direct a person's attitude. But "hiring for attitude" leads to the difficult question of, "How do you interview for attitude?" There are questions you can ask job candidates, but attitude is still a difficult concept to quantify or assess. Some questions I've used in the past include: "Tell me about a time you were disappointed at work or a project was failing. How did you maintain your sense of well-being and enthusiasm for the job?" "Tell me about a time that a customer was rude and treated you poorly. How did you handle it and get ready for the next customer?" "What do you do on those days when you get up and you've just got the blues but need to be enthusiastic at work?"

What you are looking for in the candidate's answers to questions like these is the knowledge and use of coping skills to help maintain and regain a positive, enthusiastic attitude. The other important thing to remember is that people who have developed positive attitudes aren't that way all the time. They have bad days. Difficult times and unpleasant events happen to them. But having a positive, optimistic outlook allows people to recover much more quickly when the tough times come.

Wright

Well, I don't know about that genetic thing. I had a mother who was under every stress there was when I was growing up. I would define her life now as horrible. But, I'll tell you what. She came through everything and everyone loved her and appreciated her. There were truck loads of people at her funeral when she passed away.

Canham

That's a great example. A positive attitude is a choice and can be developed in anyone. It's not just those who have a minimum of bad things happen to them. The phrase I use to describe people like your mom is, "They believe the world is out to do them good!" That's not an easy philosophy of life to live by—desirable, but not easily adopted.

Wright

Some of her approach to life rubbed off on me, my brother, and my sister.

Canham

David, your comment leads directly into the question of how does attitude develop, and more importantly, if you don't like your attitude, how do you change it?

Wright

Well, that was going to be my next question. It seems as if many factors that influence attitude occur early in ones life.

Canham

That's true. The basic foundation for a person's attitude forms fairly young in life, simply because when we're young, we're like sponges—always soaking up knowledge and ways of behaving. But in general, there are three major ways we develop or change our attitudes. One is PEOPLE. As you indicated, at a young age family and relatives play a key role. As we age, teachers and peers become key in influencing how positive our approach to life is. And once we're adults, our friends, both socially and at work, further shape our attitude. The key thing about these people who influence us is—are they positive? They can contribute to either a positive or negative attitude by the support, love, and encouragement they show us. A great "attitude exercise" involves thinking back on who influenced you most in your life. One of the people in my life was my 4th grade teacher, Ms Preece. She was the first teacher to really publicly acknowledge me in school and encourage me to do my best. And while I had always gotten decent grades (my performance was OK), I was also a behavioral problem (my conduct wasn't). I believe her impact on my life was not about learning nearly as much as it was about being a better, happier person. That impacted my attitude and my approach to other people and situations to this day. One other aspect of the impact of people who help shape our attitude when we are growing up—when the impact is positive, we're much more willing to hear criticism and feedback that is less than positive. When managing a staff I would have to occasionally counsel or discipline an employee. I always made it a point to say, literally, "Your behavior in this instance is not OK, but you as a person are OK." That distinction, when communicating with others, helps preserve a person's self-esteem and positive mental approach to life.

Another big thing that influences a developing attitude are the EVENTS that impact us. Most of those events are personal—death of a loved one, getting a driver's license, having to switch schools at a young age. The list is endless. But events that occur on a broader scale— war, the tragedy of 9-11, etc., can certainly influence our attitudes. But again, the key thing, whether it's good or bad, is our attitude. And that is what determines how we respond to the events of our lives. Just because bad things happen to us, doesn't mean our "Attitude" about it has to be negative. I was very close to my grandfather and his passing away 15 years ago was very sad. But after the initial sadness I began to focus on the great memories, on how my personality was so much like his, and how we resembled one another physically. My attitude helped me find the good in a very sad situation.

The third factor that shapes attitude is SELF-KNOWLEDGE or SELF-DETERMINATION. That is simply my own decision to do something about improving my attitude. We're a country of self-help, pop psychology people, yet this personal decision to improve my mental approach to life, while often talked and written about, is much more difficult to put into practice. Most often, it requires the realization that my life isn't working very well and I need to make some changes.

Wright

One of the things that I appreciate so much, you mentioned his name a few minutes ago, Steve Gilliland. Steve has attended several conferences and workshops where I have been training speakers. A lot of guys that have reached his plateau sit around and you can read their body language. It's like, "Well, I know this stuff" or worse still "I tried that back in '02." One of those kind of deals.

Canham

You hear the "we tried that" and "I know that" a lot. But circumstances change. The people involved change. And no matter how well you "know" something, you can always learn new approaches to the same information. I've probably attended 15 conferences and read 20 books about "attitude," but I've learned something from every one of them. Part of having a good attitude is being open to new ideas and new ways of thinking about things we all know.

Wright

That's right. But Steve sits and participates at the highest level of anyone in the room. By his participation he literally teaches from the audience because everyone listens to him.

Canham

He's providing a great role model for how we can all learn and grow from one another. People with poor attitudes seem to take the approach that "that's the way I am," I can't change." And so they don't.

Wright

Yes, he has a great attitude.

Canham

Yes he does.

Wright

I kept my judicial robes on until I was in my mid 40s. I would get up every morning and judge myself, beat myself with a toothbrush and then get on to work.

Canham

I like your phrase "judicial robes." I would call those robes our "self talk," that internal voice that's always on, always commenting on what's going on around us. It's often one of the greatest barriers to having a positive attitude. Psychologists estimate that as much as 75% of our "self talk" (which reflects and impacts our attitude) is negative. What a challenge it is to overcome that. I'll use the example of dieting—one of this country's most popular pastimes. "Why do most diets fail even when people see positive physical results?" I would tie it to self-talk, that internal voice / attitude that still hasn't changed. A voice that says, "Dieting is too hard," or "I miss my Krispy Kreme donuts." Changing that internal voice is hard work and sometimes even when we see positive external changes we fall back. That tells me that true change, to be successful, is driven much more by my attitude, which is internally driven, than by external changes that I may see in behavior or appearance. A great example is Roger Bannister, the first person to break the 4-minute mile. No one had ever done it. The belief at that time (1954) was that it couldn't be done. But Roger Bannister did a very unique thing to change his own self-talk. He took a stop-watch and clicked off one second, which was the time needed to run a mile in under four minutes. Every time he doubted that he could, or when he encountered people who told him he couldn't run a mile in less than four minutes, he clicked off that one second. He would say to those people (and to himself), "One second is an instant. You can't tell me that I can't improve my time by that small amount." And by repeatedly giving himself that message, he changed his internal message to one of what was possible, not what wasn't.

Wright

The key question that I would have for you since we all do things basically for what's good for us is how does having a good attitude impact an individual's life?

Canham

That is a great question. I'll suggest three or four major ways. First of all, since your attitude is a habit of thought, it determines HOW YOU VIEW AND THINK ABOUT THE WORLD. I think the author F. Scott Peck describes it best. He talks about seeing the world as a place of abundance or a place of scarcity. People who have been developing a good attitude see abundance. If they lose their job, they believe there are more good jobs out there. If they want a new home, they believe they can find their dream home. That's an entirely different way of looking at the world than people who see the world as a place of scarcity. Those people worry about getting the things that they want in life, about competing for limited resources, about people taking advantage of them. It's not a fun way to live, but it is a direct outgrowth of a less-than-positive attitude about life.

Another way attitude impacts our lives is what author John Maxwell calls the "SELF BECOMING SELFLESS." People with great attitudes are much more willing to share success, to let other people take the glory, to let other people stand out. Their attitude allows them to feel secure enough help others, to put other's needs ahead of their own. Maxwell used gymnast Kerri Strug as an example. In the 2000 summer Olympics, she severely injured her ankle on one of her vaults. People didn't realize it at the time, and she never said anything, but she knew right then if she vaulted one more time she would lose the opportunity to compete in her strongest event, the floor exercise. But she went ahead and performed the final vault. The team won the gold medal and Kerri Strug was out of the Olympics because of the injury. She was selfless in that she put her teammates quest for a gold medal ahead of her individual quest.

Third, your attitude, maybe more than anything else, DETERMINES YOUR SUCCESS OR YOUR FAILURE. People with good attitudes expect good things to happen. They do, in fact, get what they expect. It sounds trite, but Jesse Jackson said it very well when he said, "Your Attitude Determines Your Altitude." Any great athlete, teacher, or politician is successful in part because of believing they can succeed. Any defeat or failure is merely a temporary setback from which they can learn how to become more effective and successful. Positive people see a defeat or set-back as a one-time, almost random event. Negative people see a defeat or set-back as a long-term, permanent event caused totally by their own lack of knowledge and ability.

The fourth thing that I would suggest in terms of how attitude impacts a person's life is it MAKES YOU A PERSON OTHERS WANT TO BE AROUND. You're unique. Your own enthusiasm and upbeat perspective on most situations draws people, resources and opportunities to you. People want to be like you and they feel better about themselves when they're around you. That is a very powerful, very desirable situation or lifestyle to be living.

Wright

One of the deciding factors is do people rejoice when you walk into a room or do they rejoice when you walk out?

Canham

Exactly. Or as my family minister once joked, when people saw him they said either, "God, it's good to see you again" OR "God, it's you again." For people with great attitudes, it's always the former.

Wright

If a good attitude can have that significant an impact on individual behavior and success, why in the world do we hear so much about attitude problems today, especially in the workplace?

Canham

I think there are four things that contribute to the issue of "less than great attitudes at work." FIRST, THE WAY WE HIRE PEOPLE. We always look primarily for skills, not attitude and for performance factors vs conduct factors in the interview process. The truth is, for most jobs, it is much easier to teach job skills than it is to teach an appropriate, positive attitude. So oftentimes it must seem like that "great performer" we hired on Friday must have sent his or her evil twin to work the following Monday. I believe one of a manager's biggest challenges is employees who can do the job but who no one wants to work with or be around. To quote Steve Gilliland again, "If you hire people for <u>what</u> they know, you will fire them for <u>who</u> they are."

A SECOND factor in creating difficult or poor attitudes, is the UNBELIEVABLY HIGH EXPECTATIONS found in much of today's workforce, especially people 50 and younger. The irony is these high expectations came quite innocently, starting with post WWII parents who told their children, "My kid's gonna have it better than I did." They basically spoiled an entire generation, leading us to believe we could "have it all." I bet you remember those messages yourself, David.

Wright

Right.

Canham

We all grew up with these unbelievable expectations, not only for our jobs, but for our relationships, our incomes, for almost every aspect of our life. High expectations, unfulfilled, create a lot of frustration and attitude issues.

The THIRD area would have to do with EDUCATION. Specifically, the need to teach young people skills in developing positive self-esteem, a sense of self worth, and a positive attitude towards life in general. Those type programs have only become more common in our schools in the past 10-12 years.

And last, poor attitudes can result from people simply NOT GETTING ENOUGH POSITIVE FEEDBACK about themselves and /or their behavior. We all know that positive feedback reinforces desired behavior. Yet, every seminar I lead, be it 20 people or 200, at some point I will ask the group, "How many of you, by a show of hands, feel you get enough recognition for the good work you do?" It is seldom more than 10% of the group. So even though we know that we need to nurture one another, we often don't. Nurturing feedback, especially if it starts at an early age, is one of the key determinants in developing a positive attitude.

Wright

It seems to me that we shouldn't have to learn those lessons. I remember finding myself standing over a toilet bowl applauding vigorously when my son finally pottied by himself. It was the positive reinforcement. He had a big smile on his face and we were all dancing around. But, then somewhere after that I stopped applauding at the toilet with my employees, and that should have been enough lesson for me.

Canham

Well, you give a great example. In my seminars I use the example of teaching a child to walk. When you come home from work and you have a small child about to start walking, what does any good parent do? We get down on your hands and knees, don't we? We put out your hands and say something like, "Come on. You can do it. Take a step. Walk to daddy." We never give that kind of encouragement to employees and then we wonder why they seem aloof and lack commitment. We quickly label them as having a "bad attitude" even though much of what was needed to develop a positive attitude was not present.

Wright

Yes, it's a real shame. In the world of business, can you give our readers a few examples of how we see the impact of attitude?

Canham

Sure. Two examples stand out. The first involves leadership. I'm continually amazed at how many companies I work with still are led by the traditional top-down, "my way or the highway" type leaders. You can see the frustration in the employees throughout the organization. What I hear when I talk to these leaders is an attitude of fear. It's an unspoken fear caused by the realization that so many people are depending on you—employees, stockholders, families. For a leader with a poor attitude, that fear manifests itself as mistrust, or micromanaging, or needing to be involved in or make even the most minor of decisions. Whereas the leader who has a good attitude channels that fear into more positive behaviors—involving people in decisions, delegating authority, building trust, recognizing accomplishments. To put it another way: "Leaders who have a good attitude believe people WANT to make a difference, while leaders with a poor attitude believe people DON'T make a difference."

The other area where examples abound are Customer Service. I'm convinced that great service is an attitude. More specifically, it's a good attitude and positive self-esteem that allows front line people to do a great job despite irate and demanding customers, restrictive policies, and limited authority to actually DO SOMETHING. Let's be honest. Customer Service is about common sense and courtesy. A positive attitude makes good service great because the person is willing to go the extra mile, doesn't take complaints personally or acts in the best interests of the customer and the organization, even when they may not have the necessary authority to do so. I recently had a cashier at a McDonald's restaurant introduce herself to me and hand me my order as I approached the counter. How did she do that? She had seen me come in several times and remembered what I always ordered. Now that's great service and I'm sure she wasn't taught that at Hamburger U. The simple truth is "A Great Attitude Creates Great Service."

Wright

What strategies would you suggest for people who want to develop a more positive attitude or even fine tune an already good attitude?

Canham

I'll mention a few key ideas. What's interesting is most of these ideas come from clients that I and my associates have interviewed because they were singled out as having great attitudes. We wanted to find out what it was that causes some people to make the choice every day to make the best of whatever that day brings.

We were most surprised by the number of people who mentioned learning things from their children. One person called it NAÏVE

HONESTY. That's how kids face the world isn't it...a kind of positive optimism that believes "the world is out to do them good."

They say or do what's on their mind. For example, if you take a small child, up to a year or two years old, and pick them up and toss them above your head, what do they do? They giggle. They know you are going to catch them. It's like having "reverse paranoia" where we believe someone is out to help me, not hurt me. Adults who have developed good attitudes believe the world is out to do them good.

Another strategy people mentioned was the ability to be PERSISTENTLY PROACTIVE. Taking action has two great benefits. First, many people we talked to said that when they took action, they were often permitted to continue acting, regardless of supposed constraints on their authority. Call it deciding to empower yourself. The other benefit was that by taking action, people's beliefs about their ability and authority to make a difference also improved. Most of us want, in many aspects of our lives, to make a difference. I've also found that people who are proactive tend to be much more creative. The flight attendant at Southwest who looked at the airsick bags and asked, "Why do we have Southwest printed on these bags?" saved the company hundreds of thousands of dollars by switching to plain paper bags. People with positive attitudes seek a better, more effective way.

A third strategy is to become more aware of your SELF-TALK (that little voice in your head that's always commenting on everything that goes on). As we mentioned earlier, nearly 75% of most people's self-talk is negative. Pay attention to it for a few days. You'll find yourself thinking things like, "Another boring meeting," "Ugh, it's Monday," "The weather stinks," "I'm no good at interviewing," "Smoking is the hardest addiction to overcome." It goes on and on. The self-fulfilling prophesy tells us our thoughts cause us to act in ways that results in much of what we were thinking about actually happening. People with good attitudes are very aware of their self-talk and the impact it can have, either positive or negative. My own personal example is computers. After my initial experiences were negative, my self-talk was terrible: "I don't like computers," "I'm not logical enough to get them," "I don't like high tech people anyway," and on and on. It wasn't until business necessity literally forced me to learn how to use one that my self-talk changed. But it was a difficult process. It's only been in the past few years that I've gotten somewhat comfortable using a computer. I had to change my self-talk, which then began changing my attitude toward using the dreaded machine (see, I STILL can lapse easily back into negative talk about computers!).Our self-talk might be the most powerful tool for changing our attitudes.

Attitude can also be modified by WHO YOU HANG AROUND WITH. What are your friend's attitudes? Your co-workers? I believe we do become more like those people we most closely associate and identify with. I try to make sure most of my contacts, both professionally and personally, are people who see life as being pretty good. The unexpected advantage from associating with positive people is the feedback they give you. You would expect recognition and positive reinforcement and people with good attitudes do acknowledge others much more frequently. But they are also comfortable giving feedback that we all need but may not want to hear. And that usually involves us needing to change some aspect of our own behavior and/or attitude. I call them "Propellers." They propel us to re-think what we are doing and then change our behavior. Giving honest feedback seems easier for people with good attitudes because they feel good about themselves and are not fearful of the other person getting angry or being upset. That might be your true friend's greatest gift of all. The Beatles said it well, *"I Get by With A Little Help from My Friends."*

The last strategy that many people identified for maintaining or developing a more positive attitude was FINDING THE GOOD IN ANY BAD SITUATION. A common misperception is that people with great attitudes never have bad things happen to them. That's not true. But what they do have is an ability to recover more quickly when things go wrong and find something good in bad situations. Three techniques were mentioned most frequently. 1) Some people take the rational approach and ask, "What have I learned from this experience and what / how will I behave differently next time?" Think of all the people who keep repeating mistakes—choosing poor partners, choosing jobs that are a poor fit. The old saying, "You can't keep doing the same thing and expecting different results" is true. And people with good attitudes often think very logically about what they need to do differently in the future to reduce the likelihood of the same unpleasant events occurring again. 2) Many people also mentioned humor. A person with a great attitude can usually see the humor in difficult situations, especially if their behavior has created or contributed to the situation. That doesn't mean they don't take the situation seriously. But they understand that most bad things that happen are temporary and can be corrected or overcome and seldom have long-term, debilitating consequences. Think of all the humor that centers on ex-spouses, or poor bosses, or something embarrassing a child did. I'm sure these situations were serious, even painful at the time, but a great attitude helps us see the humor in many of the events that shape our lives. Southwest Airlines is a great example of a company that uses humor because they understand that much of flying today is a hassle. So they sing songs and tell jokes and try to re-define the often tedious task of flying. I think I mentioned it earlier, their motto of "Hire for Attitude" allows them to do things that are still unheard of at other airlines. What is really significant, though, is the fact that this emphasis on fun and hiring people with positive attitudes has resulted in Southwest being the safest airline to fly, consistently being at or near the top in on-time arrivals and your baggage getting there with you, still continuing to make money despite all the difficulties the airline industry has faced, and consistently being ranked number one in customer satisfaction. That proves to me that "attitude" is a pretty powerful tool in creating and maintaining a successful business.

Wright

I was flying on Southwest one time from Dallas to Waco. I was going to visit Paul Myer, and this was a 13 seater. I was sitting in the first seat. The only thing separating me from the pilot was a curtain, and he opened the curtain and we talked the whole time it took to get there. But when he approached the airport, he closed the curtain. And I thought, "Well, that's probably just something that he has to do." But in a few seconds he said, "Ladies and Gentlemen, we are now circling over Waco, Texas, getting ready for our final approach. Would you please set your watches back 100 years." And I'm thinking, "This is a great airline."

Canham

That's a great line. I love that. And it's so typical of what happens at Southwest.

Wright

In 50 words or less, could you sum up the importance of attitude in influencing or determining personal growth and success?

Canham

Sure, David. I see attitude as part of a process that moves from internal thoughts and ideas to external behavior in all of us. It goes like this: Your internal habits of thought (your attitude)determines how and what you think. What you think determines what you do. What you do determines who you are. And who you are, ultimately, determines your character. If this process is true, then your attitude is a primary determinant, not only of your success in life, but also your reputation as a person and at some level, the integrity and enthusiasm with which you live your life.

Wright

Well, today we have been talking to Ron Canham. He is an accomplished keynote speaker, and as we have found out today, this man knows a lot about attitude. I just wonder where you were when I was growing up.

Canham

I was like most of us, David, trying to figure out how my attitude could help me become the enthusiastic, successful person that I knew I wanted to be. And to that extent, I've had a very enjoyable and very blessed life.

Wright

Ron, I really do appreciate the time you spent with me here this morning, and I really appreciate you participating in our book, *Conversations on Success*.

Canham

Thanks, David. I enjoyed it and you made it very easy.

About The Author

Ron Canham is an accomplished keynote speaker and seminar leader with over 25 years experience in the areas of leadership, customer service and self-motivation. Ron has served organizations in the private sector, guided non-profits and education groups, and worked extensively with government offices. From giants like Blockbuster Video and the Make-A-Wish Foundation, California State University, the City of Scottsdale, AZ and hundreds of groups in between, Ron brings an enthusiastic, participative approach to his programs, focusing on practical ideas that attendees can take away and implement immediately. Whether you are trying to lead and develop others or more effectively manage yourself, Ron's programs deliver strategies to help ensure both you and your organization grow successfully.

Ron Canham

Performance Plus

P.O. Box 4182

Pittsburg, PA 15202

Phone: 412.766-0806

Fax: 412.766-8998

www.roncanham.com

www.performanceplus1.com

Chapter Fourteen

THE INTERVIEW

David E. Wright (Wright)

Today we're talking to Glenn Green, born in Dallas and educated at East Texas State University. Glenn Green spent the first 25 years of his professional life building two Fortune 500 companies that serve the major motion picture and music industry. After his success in Hollywood Glenn's eye for business trends spotted the Internet wave, and for the past ten years he's been developing cutting-edge marketing tools and technologies to help others ride that wave. His client list includes names such as, MasterCard International, Ford Motor Company, Lincoln Division, Jaguar Motor Cars, Lexus, The National Football League, General Electric Medical Systems, and Gulfstream. Glenn lives with his wife Starla in The Woodlands, in Texas. Glenn, welcome to *Conversations on Success*.

Glenn Green (Green)

Thank you David.

Wright

You started out in the production business in Hollywood. How did you evolve from there to technology development and where are you now?

Green

I think, David, we always evolve no matter what industry we're in. With the birth of the Internet we started to see the change and shift in our industry. It became pretty apparent that things would eventually evolve towards strictly Internet interactions, so I started thinking of things we could do to develop in and around the Internet itself.

Wright

So you've been marketing or in marketing for most of your life. In that time, how do you think it's changed and where do you see it going?

Green

The landscape of all business has changed, again, due to the Internet. What worked even five years ago doesn't seem to work as well, or even work at all now. If you look at any industry, the change is dramatic because of the information systems that are now available to us.

Wright

How do technologies like the Internet and wireless telecommunications contribute to these changes?

Green

I was in a seminar last month and we were talking about how different things are because of "availability." One of the best things about the Internet is that we have information at our fingertips *right now*. One of the worst things about the Internet is exactly the same thing—we have information at our fingertips *right now*. What has happened to all of us is that we've moved to a world where we expect everything *right now*, and we don't want to wait. We've gotten used to that "availability," and thus, as consumers, we've changed the nature of business.

When we were growing up, we didn't have all this information at our fingertips. We had the traditional types of information available, and the traditional technologies to find it; we had to search for it and it took a long time. But, that was ok because we had different expectations. Not lower, just different. Now what has happened, and what *is* happening, is that depending on the type of business you are in, you have to start to restructure and figure out how to move *your* business in the direction of "availability" in order to keep up with new expectations that consumers have developed because of the Internet and wireless technologies. Now you have to be on the cutting edge to really stay ahead of the curve.

Wright

I used to have to hang around the library when I was a kid. Now, I've got a 16-year old that can do a paper on almost anything in minutes. She's got the Internet and she can get the latest articles written by German Scientists or Japanese Poets. It's incredible, isn't it? The children are using the technologies. Are the people getting younger in your industry?

Green

I think they are. What happens is that, again, there's so much new technology that's being birthed almost daily—changing at a rate we never experienced when we were kiddos and growing up. When you grow up adapting naturally to new technologies, I think it's easier to learn how to take advantage of the speed of these changes. It's really just amazing. Some of the technology that's coming out—that's actually on the forefront—was almost unthinkable, even two or three years ago. You could never have imagined how it would work into the mix.

But, of course, it's not impossible for those who didn't grow up during this technology boom to learn new technologies. It's definitely not impossible to take advantage of them in a business sense, even if you don't understand them fully.

Wright

What have *you* done to keep up with these changes?

Green

Well, how it evolved for me is that when I started to realize that business marketing was moving to the digital world, I decided that companies above a certain size would actually communicate with CDs and DVD ROMs. I really thought that the idea of sending out a brochure for your business would probably eventually fade away. And, actually, if you look at the current state of the printing industry, you can see that it has started to happen. Marketing was going to need dynamic production tools, no longer just people skilled in graphic design and layout.

So, about six years ago, I developed a product called Digital Synchronization. This product is what synchronizes a CD ROM when you use animation, music, voiceover, 2D and 3D video all at the same time. It allows a multi-media presentation to run like a movie. That's all well and good, but this synchronization technology, with other new technologies being developed currently, is also going to allow engineers to create what they call a hundred-layer CD. The potential of this is overwhelming. Let's say that you had child born today and that child lived to be a hundred years old. Every event in that child's life—from infanthood, through adolescence, adulthood, and all the way up to the time that they actually pass away—every event in their life could be put on one CD ROM.

Wright

Things are getting smaller and faster.

Green

But, not all technological advances are good. There are some things that are happening due to the Internet and all this "availability" that I was talking about that I'm not real happy about. One is readily available personal information; I think we're starting to lose some of our privacy if you will. That is becoming a big issue.

Wright

I still don't understand the mentality behind someone who'd actually put a virus out that would stop people from using their equipment.

Green

I've often said that if someone would take that much time and put it into something that was useful, they probably wouldn't have to work very hard for very much longer.

Wright

Let me change the subject on you here for a minute. I'd like to pitch myself back to when you were younger. We're talking a lot about success today. I know that you're successful and I know that our readers will realize your success. Give us some kind of an idea. What was it like growing up for you? Who were some of your mentors, the people that you remember the most that might have done things that changed your life?

Green

I was born in Dallas, raised in a middle-income family. My mom and dad just celebrated their 61st wedding anniversary. Both are doing extremely well and living in Florida on the beach. When I was a child, growing up back in the '50s and early '60s, I was diagnosed with ADD and dyslexia. Now they've got a pretty good handle on overcoming the kind of learning obstacles that kids with these disorders face, but back then the schools were not prepared to deal with you. They just put you in the back of the classroom and said if you show up we're going to pass you. It was most frustrating for me. I wasn't learning, and I was getting passed over. In about the fifth or sixth grade I started to teach myself how to read and write. My grandmother and mother both had confidence in my ability to learn because I was able to memorize and remember things that most people couldn't, and that helped me. Many people who were diagnosed with dyslexia or ADD/ADHD as a child look back as adults and realize that part of the problem in their childhood was that they were rapid thinkers. The downside of being a rapid thinker is that as easy as your attention is to gain, it's just as easy to lose, and that is the challenge for teachers. It can be frustrating as an adult as well, even though there are no more classrooms. There's an upside to being a fast thinker, too, and there can be a payoff. When I look back I see the wonderful family I had growing up; they were most supportive. It just goes to show that anything can be overcome if you just stay focused on where you're headed, and have the support you need.

Wright

I had a friend that I grew up with who was so far advanced it was unbelievable. All the kids in the classroom knew how brilliant this kid was, but the teachers couldn't figure it out because he stayed in trouble all the time. We would do a Math test, and it would be an hour test, he would finish his in like 10 or 15 minutes. He'd have 45 minutes to create confusion and throw things. Of course, he made terrible grades, and he was always in the hall. I don't know how he ever passed anything because he was always in the hall. But he was just brilliant. The teachers just didn't know what to do with him, neither did the school system. So I can imagine how frustrating that might have been for you.

Green

It was definitely frustrating. When you're in that position you start to withdraw, and that can leave huge amounts of baggage in adulthood. At least it can if one doesn't keep their feet on the ground and stay focused. At a very early age you learn what rejection is about. Inside you feel as smart as anyone in the room, and yet you're the one having a difficulty. And other kids can't understand it. Today they really have a better understanding of what it's about, what to do about it and they seem to be more on top of helping other kids understand. It's amazing how many adults have pretty much gone through the majority of their life with learning difficulties. Some have done well and some certainly haven't. It's a real issue.

Wright

I have two friends who are speakers. If I told you who they were you'd know them, they're in the National Association. They've been speakers for years. Both of them were told they were dumb and stupid all their lives by almost everyone, including teachers. Both of them were diagnosed in their 30's as being dyslexic. So they basically taught themselves and got taught by other people after they were over 30 years old. Now they make a living teaching other people. Unbelievable.

Green

I had a teacher, I remember, in the sixth grade that was getting married. I'll never forget her. Her name was Miss Crack and she was kind of mean. There was another boy who sat in the back with me and she didn't like either one of us because we were, I guess, keeping her class from being where she wanted it to be. Anyway, to make a long story short, one day she told me that she'd never met anybody that was stupider than I was and that I would never amount to anything. I sure wish I knew where I could get a hold of her. But it's funny; sometimes those things tend to motivate me. When somebody tells me I can't do something that always tends to make me work a little harder.

Wright

You've got the choice, you can roll up in a fetal position or you can bow up and go stronger. Most people think of folks that develop things on the Internet and anything having to do with computers as kind of nerdy folks, sitting around in a room with blue jeans and their sleeves rolled up, not ever talking to anybody. I know that's not true all the time. In your adult life have there been any folks that have given you a helping hand, someone who you respected or has guided you?

Green

There was a gentleman along the way who fits that description. When I first got out of college I went to work for Club Med and the founder of that company was worldly and what someone else called "a free spirit." He was the most unconventional person I had ever met. He could absolutely do three or four things at one time and was inspirational because of it. I would have to say, in that business, early on, he had a profound effect on where we were going. He was what I would call a creator, and there really aren't very many of them.

If you remember, back when the Internet was just starting to come around you would see images of people in Silicon Valley, riding scooters up and down the halls of the offices. But even though there were a lot of people involved, and a lot of people making money, a very small percentage of them were really creators. Once somebody creates and develops an idea then the people who run with them are the programmers—people who basically have an order handed down to them—they are the ones that actually write the code. I learned early on to create, write and produce a product.

The other thing I learned is that no matter how big a company is, whether they are Fortune 1000, 500, individuals that have built companies, or just people that are working out of their homes, the one thing that most of them share is they all have issues with marketing. You either have to create a market share, or buy it, and most people don't have the opportunity or the ability to just buy it. That's why there has always been a need for marketing. It just happens that now there's another big channel to market through and that's the Internet. In principle, it's still the same thing. It still requires the ability to get the word out and get a response back. And that's what we basically work to do—create some effective marketing tools that really bring back results.

Wright

Do you find it frustrating to see so many talented people lose ground in the business world because of an inability to understand the new marketing world of the Internet?

Green

David, I have a thing I call these people, and I hope it doesn't offend anyone, but I call them "the big chief tablet and pen guys." You remember, back when we were younger, we would be in a meeting or in a boardroom and everybody would have their big chief tablet, you know, that big yellow pad, and a pen. We took notes and that's how we did business. That's how many people are still more comfortable doing business. And what is both amazing and unfortunate is that the resistance to change comes less from individuals than companies— whole companies. This is the real obstacle. They weren't brought up around the Internet, so in great part, they still just don't know how to work with it. They tend to want to shy away from it. It intimidates most people, especially people that have done business for 20 or 30 years the same way. They figure that they've gotten where they are doing business one way, and they're going to continue. Unfortunately, there's a group of what I call "people coming behind us," who if these business people aren't real careful, will leave them with just the feeling of a breeze going by because they're not trying to keep up. The Internet is a tremendous tool if used properly to propel and take your business into the next level. It's not something to be afraid of; it's something to embrace.

Wright

Is mentoring "the big chief tablet and pen crowd," as you call them, one of the ways you've found to give back to the community?

Green

I think that no matter what we do in life we have to give back. Most people think of "giving back" as giving of their money. But, that's only a portion of it. I really believe you have to give of your time, too, and we try to do a lot of that. I've talked to lots and lots of people who have had trouble in business, by losing ground to businesses moving faster, or by facing shifts in business climates and not being able to keep up. I try to do a lot of that. We actually give back in other ways as well; we participated this Christmas in feeding 10,600 underprivileged children in the poorest county in the US. I fed almost the whole school district. For a lot of those kids it was the only Christmas dinner they would get. I found tremendous inspiration from that.

Wright

Since you've been so successful in your business undertakings, what is it that continues to drive your success?

Green

As long as we continue to stay in the work stream, workforce, or just stay in the game, however we call it, we've got to stay ahead. Things have really changed and they will continue to change. I think that what drives me is the excitement of finding out how the technology, the media, just everything on the horizon and coming our way, is going to make our business different. Even more exciting is how it's going to make our lives different. I think it would be interesting to ask 100 business people from the junior executive level all the way up to CEO or chairman of the board of a major corporation how they would feel if someone was to take away their cell phone, or their PDA, or their computer, or their Internet access for the next 30 days. Let me just tell you, I think it's a very frightening thought for some people. And even five and ten years ago that wouldn't have been the case. We live in a very exciting time, and finding out what's around the corner, that's what really drives me.

Wright

What would you say to the next generation of business men and women to keep them motivated in such a rapidly changing field?

Green

I would say just stay focused on something you believe in, and that you can contribute to. Whatever that area is. Don't get frustrated because of the rapidly changing technology. Stay focused on where you want to be. I think what happens to most people is that they'll stay focused for a little while and then something distracts them. There's success in all of us, but unfortunately, we sometimes find ourselves listening to people who are not qualified to guide us, not qualified to tell us which direction we should be going in, and yet we sometimes follow them anyway. Listen to your own instincts and focus on where you want to be. And pay attention to new technologies. No matter what you're doing, there's a piece of technology that would probably fit in, and could really make a difference in what you're able to achieve in your time.

Wright

What a great conversation. I've learned a lot here today. The next time in Dallas I'd like to stop in and see your company.

Green

That would be great.

Wright

Today we've been talking to Glenn Green. After several building of company success and the success in Hollywood, Glenn's eye for business spotted the Internet wave and for the last ten years he's been developing cutting-edge marketing tools and technologies to help others ride that wave. I think we have found out here this morning that he actually knows what he's talking about. Glenn, thank you so much for being with us today on *Conversations on Success*.

Green

Thank you, David.

About The Author

Born in Dallas and educated in East Texas, Glenn Green overcame the hurdles associated learning disabilities and went on to spend the first 25 years of his professional life building two Fortune 500 companies that served the major motion picture and music industry.

After his production successes in Hollywood, Glenn sought to conquer the wide-open vistas of the Internet market. With his marketing and business development insight, he analyzed the nascent industry, and determined that what it needed most was the development of new tools and technologies to allow marketers to take advantage of this seemingly limitless medium. With true entrepreneurial spirit, Glenn created new companies to develop these cutting edge tools and technologies optimized for the Internet's unique channels, and has amassed a client list that includes names like MasterCard International, Ford Motor Company's Lincoln division, Jaguar Motor Cars, Lexus, the National Football League, GE Medical Systems, and Gulfstream.

While Glenn's Digital Synchronization technologies are coveted by the likes of Microsoft, his insight and thoughts are coveted by rapt audiences at technology conferences including COMDEX, and DV World. He enjoys consulting with major corporations on business trends and corporate turnarounds, but also takes pleasure in being able to deliver motivational messages to small companies and young entrepreneurs.

Glenn has returned to Texas and now lives with his lovely wife Starla in The Woodlands.

Glenn Green

6700 Woodlands Parkway #230

The Woodlands, Texas 77382

Phone: 832.754.3112

Email: glenn@nuvisionmedia.com

Chapter Fifteen

TERRY STROM

THE INTERVIEW

David E. Wright (Wright)

Today we are talking with Terry Strom. Terry started his career as an engineer with an MBA from the University of Southern California. Wanting to increase his income he signed up with an international network marketing company and rose quickly creating a significant six-figure income. He was instrumental in opening up businesses in Asia, South America; and Eastern Europe. He has spoken to over 250,000 network marketing professionals on stages with Tom Landry, Rudy Rutiger, Charlie "Tremendous" Jones, Oliver North, Wes Bevis, Tim Timmons, Willie Jollie and many others. He has been the vice president of sales and marketing for a software development firm and a technical consulting company. He has been a director of sales for an international medical service firm, and is a successful real estate developer. Terry does training, motivational keynote addresses and breakout sessions in the areas of motivation, sales, and communication skills. Also as a business coach/consultant he uses a five-step optimization program to help business owners/CEOs make their operations more efficient and effective, decrease costs, and lay the groundwork to take their businesses to the next level of profitability.

Terry, welcome to *Conversations on Success.*

Terry Strom (Strom)

Glad to be here David.

Wright

How did you get into network marketing?

Strom

I was working as civil engineer for a large public utility, and I was moving up the corporate ladder, but I was frustrated with the slow and inefficient corporate system, and I was looking for a way to make more money.

A fact that increased my need for more money was that my wife wanted to come home from work and raise our first son, but we couldn't afford to do that. Also, I was looking for a way to have more flexibility in my life; I wanted more time and more income, plus the ability to control my life. I also wanted the nicer things in life, a bigger house, a nicer car, better vacations, etc.

I just felt very stymied. I really couldn't move forward in the engineering world fast enough to make the income I needed to bring my wife home. In fact, I had been told by some of the managers to just relax, and wait and my promotions would eventually happen. However, I wanted my wife to be able to come home and raise my kids before they left for college, therefore, I had to do something different. That something was building a network marketing business that brought my wife home from work in one year, and created for us a significant six-figure income within a few short years.

Wright

So why do you say that when you started you were a reluctant network marketer and how can you help networking marketing organizations with their reluctant network marketers?

Strom

A very high percentage of all people who go into network marketing were contacted by a friend, family member, or an associate at work; then they got involved even though they had never planned on building a network marketing business. Many have never been in sales and have little or no sales or network marketing experience whatsoever. A lot of the network marketing presentations are very compelling, and the person gets excited and signs up but later many experience "buyer's remorse."

To answer your question, the reason I can help with reluctant network marketers is because the person I have been describing was exactly like me; I started out as a reluctant network marketer.

I had just finished my MBA from the University of California out in Los Angeles, and I was ready to move on in the corporate world. I thought I had a pretty good professional degree. I attended a seminar and when I realized it was presenting network marketing, the first thing I thought was: "What will my professional friends say when they find out I am in network marketing?" I was afraid they were going to think I had failed. The stigma surrounding network marketing would guarantee a skeptical reaction and I was worried about what my professional friends and family would think. As a result I was very reluctant to get involved.

Additionally, I'd never done any sales–I was an engineer. I was good at working with computers and calculators and numbers, but I had no networking experience at all. Therefore my belief level was very, very low; and it was just something I didn't have any background or confidence in.

Then because of the excitement and potential, I signed up; and immediately thought "what have I done!" I decided then that if I was going to do it, I was going to do it *my* way. However, for network marketing to work successfully, it is easier to follow a system that's already in place and has proven to work. I eventually learned that following a proven system is the best way to become successful. The best and most profitable network marketers have been willing to follow their organization's system.

At the beginning, however, I was not willing to follow the system exactly because I had the MBA, I had already been promoted a few times, and it turned out I was actually being a "little too big for my britches." At the time I wasn't willing to listen to my upline (my sponsor and those who had been in the business longer), and I wasn't respectful of my upline for what they knew or how they could help me. Until I was willing to follow the proven system, my attitude slowed down my growth.

I was the kind of person that sponsors don't like to work with in network marketing because I made mistakes such as I would call and cancel my first appointment, and I did not respect and listen to my sponsor. My sponsor and I quickly stopped working together because I was so difficult to work with. However, because I was a reluctant network marketer who changed his ways, I became very successful at network marketing. Therefore, I understand and know how to work with, train, and motivate other reluctant network marketers. I know how to get the important information into them, how to build their belief in themselves, how to build belief in their upline and their training system, and how to show them that even if they don't have sales or network marketing experience, they can still become very successful at network marketing.

As I built my business, I realized there was a very professional way to build a network marketing business that was positive, professional, and would not turn people off. I learned that if the business was built properly, some people still wouldn't be interested, but they could see that there was a very professional way to build it. Because I know how to navigate these treacherous waters, I can help someone who is a reluctant network marketer to see the benefit of building their own network marketing business.

Wright

So why do you think you were successful at network marketing?

Strom

Well, that's interesting. I remember hearing an ancient story about the captain of a group of fighting ships who went out to war in another country, and when he got his ships to the shore where his men were going to fight, he had them all get off the ships to build their camp. After all his soldiers were off of the ships, he had all his ships burned and sunk. You can imagine the soldiers looking back at the ships saying, "What are we going to do if we don't win? If we lose we're all going to all die out here!"

Then this captain came on shore and got up in front of all his soldiers and said, "We either win or we die." Well, as you can imagine, they fought harder then they had ever fought and won as a result of that. That's what happens when you don't allow yourself a plan of retreat. When you burn your bridges, sink your ships, and commit all to succeeding, your odds of success are much greater.

I remember I was coming up for a promotional exam where I could not be promoted unless I actually got a high score on the exam. That was not a problem because I had always received high scores on these exams. I decided, however, that I did not want the building of my network marketing business distracted by several months of studying for the exam. I also didn't want to give myself the opportunity to get promoted and be distracted from the goals my wife and I had set of bringing her home from work, getting myself free from my job, and becoming successful in my own business. As a result, I didn't take that promotional exam.

I had also just been offered my dream job at the time after a very long seven-month interview process. I remember finally being offered the job, but my network marketing business was just starting to take off. I thanked them, but turned down the job because I needed to stay focused on my primary goal of building my network marketing business. I gave myself no retreat, and that was scary, but it motivated me to working much harder on my business; which in the end resulted in my success.

Another reason I feel I was successful in network marketing was the fact that I was willing to be uncomfortable for a time—I would force myself to do the things I didn't want to do. My wife and I have a saying, "We will do today what other people will not do so we will have a life tomorrow that other people will not have." I realized that people go to a job every day and they may do things they don't like to do. They may be bored, and they may not like doing it at all, but it's probably not uncomfortable. It may not be fun, but it's comfortable to show up every day and just do their job. However, it may not be comfortable to go out and meet strangers and give presentations, or to share an opportunity and deal with the rejection that might result.

I decided that for one year I would do that which was uncomfortable and as a result I became very successful by the end of that first year, which also laid the groundwork for a very large international organization. I was also a person who had always been willing to forcibly push myself to do things I didn't want to do or that were difficult and uncomfortable for me. I was able to do this because I knew that if I did push myself, these tasks would eventually become more comfortable—or less uncomfortable—and as a result I would get better at them.

As a matter of fact, I remember during the MBA program taking the General Incongruity Aptitude Level (GIAL) test. It was used to determine the level of structure you needed in your life, your job, and your business to be successful. Therefore, the less structure you needed the higher up in management you were supposedly able to go, and the more you were suited for being an entrepreneur. This is because entrepreneurs and high level managers lead professional lives that are much less structured than the lives of those in lower levels of an organization where they tend to be much more micro managed, and structured.

Well, it turned out I had the lowest score in the class! This meant I needed the most amount of structure meaning I wasn't even good middle management material! This was very frustrating for me, so I went to the professor afterwards and asked him how I could move my GIAL score up to be able to handle less structure and more uncertainty.

He said, "Terry, it's like this, think of a rubber band. If you have a rubber band in your two hands and you were to pull it apart in the opposite directions very quickly, you would break the rubber band. But what would happen if you took that rubber band and just, a little bit at a time, kept pulling it a little bit more apart and then you backed off a little, and then you pulled it a little more apart and backed off a little, etc. If you did it gently enough with enough patience, the rubber band would continue to get a little bit bigger each time you pulled it a little further apart. If you kept doing this, that rubber band would continue to get larger and larger without breaking, because you'd kept testing and pushing its limits gently until you made it as large as you wanted it."

It's the same with human beings, if you keep gently and patiently pushing your limits a little bit more into the uncomfortable zone, then back off a little, and then push the limits again, you will grow and change; and in my case live successfully with much less structure. That's what I have continually done in my life.

To just give an example, I had done very little public speaking before I got into the network marketing world, therefore I was not that good at it yet and very uncomfortable with it. I can still remember the day I did my first presentation for nine people. I can even remember the street address—that's how much it impacted me and scared me. However, as a result of continuing to push my limits, over the years I've spoken in front of as many as 15,000 people at a time in major arenas across the country. Each time I had a great experience, enjoyed it, and was very successful at it. How did I get from nine people to 15,000 people? Well, the first time I spoke in front nine people it was very scary, but the next time I spoke in front of nine people it was not as scary as it was the first time. When I spoke in front of fifty people for the first time it was pretty scary, but after I did it once, it was never as scary to be in front of fifty people again. The same was true with 100 people, then 500 people. Then, when I went in front of 1000 people for the first time, I was really scared. But again, after I went in front of 1000 people the first time, it was never as scary to go in front of 1000 people again. I kept expanding that boundary until I was in front of 15,000 people and comfortable with it. The important point to understand about this is that you can only do something for the first time once. I've taught many, many, people how to give presentations and it's that first presentation or first sales call that just scares the heck out of you. But I tell them they can only do it the first time once, so get it done as soon as possible. Successfully doing what is scary and uncomfortable is all about stretching the "rubber band" without breaking it, which works the same as stretching your personal limits.

Another thing that helped me to be successful was saying to myself: "I hate personal growth but I love the results." It's important to realize that everything about your ongoing success is related to your continuing to learn and grow. You learn from others and even more importantly you learn from your mistakes. I'm a firm believer that you can read about something repeatedly, and still forget it; but once you make a mistake at something you rarely forget that mistake—it will become embedded in your brain. And yes, it's always better to learn from other people's mistakes if you can, but let's face it, we're human, and we're going to make mistakes.

Unfortunately, a lot of people like me beat themselves up when they make a mistake; which actually lowers their personal power and self-confidence. Fortunately however, I learned to force myself to learn from my mistakes. I remember when I started out in the network-marketing world; I'd give a presentation at someone's home or business and come back a few days later for a follow up appointment. Then, when I was driving away, I would remember the perfect thing I should have said that would have closed the deal. I call this "delayed intelligence" where you remember what you should have said when you are five or ten minutes away driving down the road. At the beginning, whenever I did this, I would get so mad at myself because I would think, "if I had just remembered to say that one thing the appointment would have gone so much better, and the presentation would have made so much more sense that the person would have signed up and started right away."

Eventually, after beating myself up mentally in the car several times I came to the realization that I should only be doing that which moves me forward. Beating myself up was not moving me forward but moving me backwards instead. Therefore, what I decided to do was say (at the beginning yell) to myself as I was driving away in the car,

"Terry, did you learn something from the mistake you just made?" I would answer, "Yes." Then I would say to myself, "Are you going to do something different in the future as a result of what you just learned?" Then I would answer, "Yes." Then I would say to myself. "Great, it was a positive experience because you learned from it, so forgive yourself and move on." From this, the end result of each delayed intelligence experience was I learned that anytime something negative happens or I make a mistake, if I can learn even one small thing from it, I can make it into a positive experience.

Another trait that made me successful in network marketing was the way I looked at showing the business plan, no-shows, rejection, and signing up people who eventually quit. Many network marketers sign up several people at the beginning and many of these first sign-ups don't get started or even quit very soon after signing up. Then when their first five, ten, fifteen people don't really get going they get frustrated and depressed, and in many cases may even quit at that point. The first eleven people I put into the business quit, but what I realized is that you need to keep putting in new people until you find your leaders. I also found that sometimes people who come into your business are there just long enough to keep you going until you do find the right people. Additionally, because I had continued to put in new people, by the time the first eleven had quit, I had all my leaders in place and realized that the first eleven who quit were actually there to get me started so I could find my "real" leaders.

Because network marketing is a numbers game, it's very important that you create momentum. If you keep putting in the numbers you are going to increase your odds that you will find the right people who are looking for you and your opportunity. Additionally, if you keep putting in the numbers you are going to get better at what you do and therefore, you're going to become more knowledgeable. Also, by going through the numbers you are going to increase your self-confidence which will make your posturing much stronger. When you are only talking to one person at a time and that one person says, "No" you're devastated because you lost 100 percent of your active market. However, if you have twenty people in process at any one time and someone says, "No", you have only lost 5% of your working market, and you just think, "Thank you very much, I haven't got any more time for you anyway, NEXT"–you're moving on to the next person. It's NOT a big deal.

Another important reason that I was successful in network marketing is because I learned that "life happens" and when it does, you have to move on anyway. Life happens to the most successful people and the least successful people. Because he is human, I am confident Bill Gates has had many problems come up in his life just as the most broke person in the world has had a lot of problems come up in his or her life. Additionally, you and I have had a lot of problems as well.

Problems will continually happen to all of us. It's not the problems that make or break you, it's whether you deal with the problems and move on or if you let the problems stop you. Success oriented people realize that "life happens" and you have to move on anyway.

My wife and I have had four kids, and we had three of them as we were in the process of hitting major goals in our network marketing business. I can remember so many people who quit network marketing because the wife got pregnant and the couple decided that they could not build their networking business because they were having a baby. Then, once their baby was born, they could not build the business because their baby had just been born and they needed to be there all the time.

We realized that by building our network marketing business, we were building a better life for our kids and for our family as a whole, so we moved forward even when Judy was pregnant. As a result, my wife, who wanted to be home to raise our children, has been home raising our four children since my oldest son was two and a-half years old, and now he is a young adult.

Another example of moving on even though life happens, came about on January 17, 1994. You might remember that was the day Los Angeles had the Northridge Earthquake. It was a big one. It was in the LA area; and the north side of LA called the San Fernando Valley was hit really hard. Most of the freeways were down for months. Many bridges were down. You could hardly drive around because traffic was so bad on the city streets. Many streets had big cuts in them from fires and explosions from gas mains that had been broken. It was amazing to see–it was almost surreal.

I was working on a major goal in our network marketing business, and the three leaders we needed to move on for us to achieve that goal lived in the San Fernando Valley. The people and the leaders we needed to move on all lived within a ten or fifteen mile radius of the epicenter of this earthquake. As a matter of a fact, one of our leaders lived within a mile or two of the epicenter, and couldn't move back into his house for ten days after the earthquake. The city put a yellow tape around his house and wouldn't let him or his family move back in. They had to camp outside in tents and cook from cook stoves. I could have easily given up on reaching that goal that year and said, "Well, not this year but next," and no one would have faulted me for it. But I had made a decision that we were going to reach our goal that year and those three leaders came along beside me and decided to hold strong to their commitments to meet their goals. As a result, I reached my goal and all three of those leaders reached their goals. My leaders and I succeeded because we moved on in spite of life happening to us. We realize that it was up to us, not our circumstances that determined our success.

Wright

So what are the most important ingredients for someone to be successful in network marketing?

Strom

It's important to realize that when you are working really hard at your network marketing business, you will hit resistance. It's just like when you drive your car–the faster you drive the more bugs your windshield will hit. In the same way, the harder you work in your network marketing business, the more negative situations you'll face–more rejections and more people who say they are definitely not interested. Just understand this point, and use it as a sign that you are doing the right things because you are hitting a lot of rejection. And remember, the more no's (rejections) you get, the more yes's you are going to get as well.

Another key to being successful in network marketing is to just *get started*. If you have ever wanted to start jogging to get in shape or lose weight, you will relate to this story. You want to start running and you set your alarm clock for 5:00 A.M. and that first morning the alarm goes off you hit the snooze button. Then you hit the snooze button again and again, and by the time you finally stop hitting the snooze button and start to get up, you don't have time to jog anymore. Then you say to yourself, tomorrow I'll do it. So the next night you set your alarm again and the next morning you'll only hit the snooze button two or three times. But day after day you continue this ritual, and eventually you get to the point where you get yourself out of bed and go out jogging. The first day is miserable–it's cold and you feel terrible. You end up walking part of the way, and you're out of breath and not feeling good. But you force yourself to do this the next day and the next day, and after a couple weeks, all of a sudden you're starting to feel good about jogging, and your pants are starting to get looser at the waist. You're starting to have some success and you're not walking anymore, but running the whole time. As a matter of fact, now when you hear the alarm, you *want* to get up and run. This empowers you because now some momentum has been built and you want to keep it going.

Well it's the same with network marketing. At the very beginning it's painful. You don't want to get out there and do it. You don't want to talk to people, it's uncomfortable, and you just don't want to do it. But once you get it rolling it starts to get exciting, and you start to enjoy some of the fruits of that success–you start to get people who say "yes." You have people who get excited about it and actually do something. Then bonus checks start coming in which empowers you the same way you would got empowered after several weeks of jogging. Therefore, to become successful, just get started and get past the beginning.

Another trait of a successful network marketer is that they are fanatical. This is interesting because this is one of the things I've heard so many times in a negative way about network marketers– they are fanatical. Someone who is outside of network marketing meets a successful network marketer or one who's on his or her way to becoming successful, says, "You're just too fanatical."

Well, I've realized that an employee is never fanatical about their job because it's not their business. They get paid a certain amount of money for doing a certain job and then they go home. If there's any additional profit for the company they don't get it, the owner does. Many times for the employee there's nothing to be fanatical about. But look at the business owner. He or she *has* to be fanatical about their business if they want to succeed. What "fanatical" means is you're always thinking about your business–how to increase profits, how to decrease costs, how to expand your customer base, how to bring in a better product or more product offerings, all these things. You may not be working on it all the time, but your mind's always thinking about it because it's something exciting, something you're building yourself. You're fanatical about it because you get it all if you succeed.

As a matter of fact I don't know of any business owner who is not fanatical about their business if they're successful or if they're on the road to being successful. I believe that to become successful in network marketing, you need to be fanatical about it. You need to be thinking about it all the time. How you can be better at it, how you can get more people exposed to it, how you can help more people become successful at it, etc. As I said, you may not be *doing* it all the time, but your *thinking* about it all the time, because it's your business and you get all the benefits of success if you succeed.

Another trait of successful network marketers is that they have or are developing strong communication skills. This is important in order to be successful in network marketing because network marketing is totally a people business.

You see a lot of people come into network marketing who have never been in sales or network marketing before. They have a certain personality style, and that is the personality style they think everyone should have.

There are basically four personality styles:

1. Driver (high energy–low relationship need, high information need)
2. Analytical (low energy–low relationship need, high information need)
3. Expressive (high energy–high relationship need, low information need)
4. Amiable (low energy–high relationship need, low information need)

To be successful at network marketing, you need to be where your potential future downline (prospect) is regarding personality style. It doesn't matter what personality style you are if you want to be successful. This means, if you're an "amiable" you need to learn when you're with an "expressive" to be expressive. If you're an "analytical" and you're around a "driver" you need to learn to be a driver. If you're an "expressive," and you're around someone whose analytical, you need to learn to be more informational based. You're not just going to stay in your own personality style. You're going to learn to be a chameleon and to be like the people who you're around and are trying to sponsor or sell to.

Think about when you were back in high school, and you didn't have to be with anyone specific. Instead, you surrounded yourself the most with people who were primarily like you. There was the drama club, the jocks, the swimmers, the chess club, the band, the partiers, and the people in choir. The people you most likely were with the most were the people most like you. You then go out into the workforce and you've got to be with whoever is hired to work in the cubicle next to you and you have to get along with them. It's important to understand that people like to do business with people they are comfortable with and whom they like, and in most cases people are going to like those who are most like them. The goal then is to be as much like the people you are communicating with as you can. That means you need to learn to mirror people. If they talk fast, you talk fast; if they talk soft you talk soft; if they want information, give them information. If they are more relational then you talk about what a great time you have with friends you have met while building your network marketing business. But most importantly, be observant as to what they (your prospects) are like and mirror that.

A very important part of communication skills is not only giving out information correctly, but also making sure that the information you gave is received by the listener in the manner you meant it to be received. This comes from a phrase I use a lot, "perception is reality." This means, it's not what you *said* that matters, it's how what you said is *perceived* by the person you are communicating with that matters. Therefore the onus is on you to make sure your listener receives the message the way you meant it to be received.

Many people in network marketing believe all they have to do is say what they are thinking or tell their prospect what they need to know. But proper communication is not only saying properly what needs to be said, but making sure what you said is perceived the way you wanted it to be perceived. It's very important to understand there are two sides to this communication picture.

One other trait to being successful in network marketing is that you have some sort of goal setting mechanism. You must set a goal to aim for and you must reinforce that goal. There were some very simple things I did. For example, on the mirror in my bathroom I taped up pictures of houses, cars, and vacation locations that I liked. Probably one of my favorites was of a little dirt path that went through a forest on a misty morning. It made me think of not having to work on a Wednesday morning and going on a walk with my wife through a forest. The freedom that picture represented empowered me. In the middle of those pictures and others that inspired me, I taped up my activity and timeline goals per week, month, etc.; showing the number of plans I was going to show, what follow-ups I was going to do, and etc. Then, every morning when I shaved and at night when I brushed my teeth before bed, I would see my goals in the middle of the pictures which would remind me of what I needed to do that day or the next day, and why I was doing it.

Many people in network marketing get excited about it, but then life gets in the way. They go to work, take care of the kids, pay the bills, etc., and they forget about building their network marketing business. All of the sudden it's the end of the day and they've done nothing towards their business. They just went home and watched television or whatever.

To help people not forget about their goals, I teach them to reinforce them throughout the day. I did this in my office by strategically placing several vacation pictures where I could see them throughout the day, which would keep me thinking about what my ultimate purpose was. At lunch and after work I was focused on building my business. In my car I had a postcard with my goals on it that would also remind me of where my focus was.

Goal setting is very important because without a goal, I can pretty much guarantee you won't reach it. For example, my children are very much into soccer and it would be hard to play soccer without a soccer goal wouldn't it? Or if you were in an airplane and the pilot says, "We're going to fly for about four hours at 35,000 feet and when we start to run out of gas we'll land," you would not feel very secure– you want the plane to land at your planned destination. The point is you need a target–a goal–to aim for, and you can't aim for a target until you know what your target or goal is.

I teach people in network marketing that there are actually three points that they will move through if they are going to be successful at network marketing. It's what I call point A, B and C. Point "A" is when you get in the business. Point "B" is when you decide to do what ever it takes to build your business, and point "C" is when you reach your goal. Now, the time needed to go from point B (when you decide to build the business and do whatever it takes) to point C (when you reach your goal) is pretty well defined according to your network marketing company's system. However, the time needed to get from point A (when you get started) to point B (when you decide to do whatever it takes to build your business), can be an hour, a day, a week, a month, a year, or years. So the sooner you get to point B where you have made the decision to do whatever it takes to build your business, the sooner you are going to reach your goal.

Wright

So what are the biggest obstacles people face in trying to become successful in network marketing?

Strom

Well I'd say that number one obstacle people face in building a network marketing business is rejection. Many people have never had to handle rejection before, and it's very uncomfortable for them–they don't want to deal with it. In fact, I don't think anybody really enjoys rejection; however the best network marketers have learned to minimize its negative affect on them so that it doesn't slow them down.

To help with rejection, I have a saying, "They either get in or I get great practice." Therefore, every time I work with a prospect at any point in the sponsoring process, I look at the time spent as gaining great practice on prospecting, showing the plan, following up, and dealing with objections. As a matter of fact, I have a little game I play–the higher the salary of the prospect I am working with, the better training I am getting. If I'm talking to a person who makes $300,000 a year and I'm going back and forth dealing with his/her objections, I think about how much it would cost me to get this kind of training from the person if they were to charge me for their time. Here I am, however, getting the training for free by being there refining my skills.

Another way to handle rejection is to not personalize it–understand that it's a numbers game and you need to keep it positive for the benefit of your attitude. You also have to understand it's not *you* they are rejecting; it's the business opportunity. When someone's not interested, just say, "Thank you very much for your time. I appreciate you, I wish you the best, and have a great day," then move on and forget them. The less negative you incur, the more empowered you will remain.

Probably the biggest reason people don't make money in network marketing is because they don't treat it as a serious business. A traditional business involves a large amount of initial monetary investment, has a lot of liability, and takes a lot of time. Many people have to take out a home equity loan or small business loan for hundreds of thousands of dollars, quit their job and work full time at their business, while paying themselves from their loan. During that entire time they are hoping they will make more money than they spend before their resources run out. People who do this are going to be very serious about their business. If someone has a birthday party when you need to be at your business, you're probably going to decline the invitation. Or, if you don't feel well one day—unless you are extremely sick—you are not going to take the day off because you cannot afford to. If you don't feel like showing up one day it doesn't matter whether you feel like doing it or not, if you have half a million dollars invested, you are going to be there. You are serious.

Well, the good and the bad of network marketing is that it doesn't cost very much money to get involved and it has very little overhead. It doesn't have a lot of the same challenges as a traditional business. Therefore, many times unsuccessful people in network marketing will say, "Well, I don't want to work it today, but that's okay because I only invested a little bit of money." Or, "I didn't put that much money into it so I don't need to take it seriously." The problem is they don't take it seriously because it did not cost them a lot.

However, what I tell network marketers who want to be successful is if you wouldn't take time off your job or from your traditional business, then don't take time off from your network marketing business. It's all about treating it like a traditional business. What I did, even though I didn't invest hundreds of thousands of dollars in my network marketing business, was that I built it as though I had invested hundreds of thousands of dollars in it. As a result, I made a lot of money in network marketing.

Some people look at how much time and energy they put into their network marketing business to become successful and they think it should be a quick fix—they should become rich quickly in network marketing. But I ask them, how long has it taken you to get as good as you are and to make what you make right now in your job? Did you have to get a degree? Did you have to go through training? How much time did it take you to get where you're at right now making what you're making, which isn't enough? Then I tell them if they expect their network marketing business to make them more money than they are currently making on their job and to actually give them more freedom and time than they currently have, shouldn't they expect to put in a good amount of time and energy to get their training and build their business? Shouldn't they have to invest some of their resources into it?

People have told me they will start working their network marketing business once they start making money at it. But I remember getting my degree in Civil Engineering, and I can just imagine telling the dean of my Civil Engineering program, "I'll tell you what Mr. Dean, once I start making money in Civil Engineering then I'll start studying, buy the books, and pay for the tuition, etc." If I would of said that, he would of kicked me out of his office.

It took me four years plus in college to get my Bachelor's degree in Civil Engineering and then I started making money. You have to understand that you must invest time and money in your business. The great thing about network marketing is you can build it part time and keep your job, therefore you don't have to have that crunch of being scared you're going to run out of money, because you can build your business part-time while you're still bringing in a paycheck. However, you still have to be serious about it, and build it (mentally) as a traditional business.

Well David, in this interview I have gone through several points that I believe can greatly help anyone who is working on building a network marketing business.

Wright

What an interesting conversation. I think our readers are going to get a lot out of this. I know I have—not only food for thought but I've also discovered some changes I might want to implement in my own life from some of the things you've said. I really do appreciate your taking this much time with me, Terry, to discuss this important chapter of *Conversations on Success*, and I really do appreciate all you've shared with me here today.

Strom

Thank you David, it was great being with you.

About The Author

Terry Strom is a master network marketer, executive business coach, author, and professional speaker in the areas of motivation, sales, and communication skills. He was instrumental in opening his network marketing business in several countries and has spoken in front of over 250,000 network marketing professionals. He is a successful real estate developer and has been the Vice President/Director of three different corporations. Terry has an MBA from USC, is a Certified Guerrilla Marketing Coach, and is a member of the National Speakers Association.

Terry Strom

Phone: 951.695.0192

Email: terrystrom@stromint.com

www.terrystrom.com

Chapter Sixteen

DAVID JAKIELO

David E. Wright (Wright)

Today we are talking to Dave Jakielo. He has over thirty years of management experience. His background includes twelve years in hospital patient finance and subsequently over two decades of managing physician practices nationwide. Dave has been speaking, consulting, and teaching business methods throughout the country and in England and India. He has extensive experience in sales, marketing, customer service, business startups, and turnarounds. Dave has been involved with numerous due diligence processes and acquisition assimilations. He is the co-author of three additional books, *The Sales Coach, Tips From The Pros*, and *Information Technology For The Practicing Physician*, and *Real World Customer Service Strategies*. He is also a regular columnist in *The Trade Journal Billing*. Dave is past president of the Healthcare Billing and Management Association and is past president of the National Speakers Association, Pittsburgh Chapter. He also holds memberships in the International Brotherhood of Magicians. Dave, welcome to *Conversations on Success!*

David Jakielo (Jakielo)

Thank you, David. I appreciate the opportunity to talk with you today.

Wright

After twenty-five years of corporate life, why did you decide to start your own firm and become your own boss in 1995?

Jakielo

That's an interesting question. I realized that I was learning and gaining experience throughout my corporate life, and I found that I was agreeing with my boss's ideas less and less. However, my boss was the one signing the paychecks, and I found that he was always the tiebreaker. I'm not saying that I was right and the corporate life was wrong, but the time had just come to become my own boss and be responsible for my own destiny. The one drawback that I have found about being your own boss is that when you call in sick, you know your lying.

Wright

Someone once told me one time that the difference between commissions and working for a company. In the company you have to live with the bosses imagination when he signs your check and when you work for yourself you live with your imagination. What do you consider to be the keys of success?

Jakielo

I've found that there are four critical areas that lead to success and we need to continue to work on these areas throughout our entire lifetime. It amazes me how many people feel that their education is over after they leave high school or college. I think being a continuous learner; especially in today's global economy is an absolute must. As Mark Twain said, "Plan for the future because it's where you are going to spend your life." The four critical areas that I think are important are: SKILLS we obtain, our STYLE relating to dealing with people, our continual DEVELOPMENT and our RESPONSIBILITIES to others.

Wright

Can you expand on the four crucial areas of success? For example, what skills are necessary?

Jakielo

In today's economy and environment, the foremost skill is communication. Whether you are talking about communicating electronically, such as email, or presenting and discussing your ideas in front of a group or in a meeting of your team members, the ability to communicate is essential. An important part of the communication process is the ability to listen. I find that listening is a skill set that most of us don't take the time to develop. Instead of sitting back and listening attentively to someone who's talking to us, we race ahead and begin formatting our answers in our mind. Think about your best friend and what your best friend does the best, usually that answer is listening to us and not giving us advice or instructions, but just being our sounding board. I think listening is another very important skill that contributes to success.

An additional skill that I wish they would teach us in high school is how to delegate. We are so busy being busy these days we have a tendency to not pass on work that could be done by others more efficiently and more effectively. Many times we fall into the trap of thinking, "I must do this myself because it is the only way that it will get done correctly." For any of us that have teenagers or youngsters at home, the analogy that I like to use is, "Have you ever played a video game against your teenager, and have you ever won?" The funny part is we sit down and read the manual on how these games are supposed to work and they just pick up the game controller and beat us without even opening the instruction manual. We need to keep in mind that there are people that can do things as well or better than us.

Another important skill that I feel is necessary is that we need to take the time to learn how to read people and situations. Knowing where people are coming from or what motivates them is an important attribute. Here's an example of reading people. You are driving down the interstate highway and you see a couple in the car next to you sitting so close together that you assume that they are glued to each other at the hip. What does that situation represent? Well, most people would respond, "Wow, they're really in love," or they will say, "You can tell they are not married." I've been married over twenty-eight years. I remember during the first year of marriage we were driving down the road and my wife was sitting in the car with me. We saw a couple almost sitting on top of each other and my wife turned to me and said, "You know, we used to sit like that." I turned to her and said, "Well who moved?"

I think the last important skill that we must have, is we need to be able to be creative and generate ideas. Tom Peters says, "If you're doing the same thing today that you did six months ago, it's probably wrong." We are in such a dynamic environment and economy you cannot afford to stand still. Plus with globalization and the other ever-changing facets, you need to be constantly thinking about how we can do things more efficiently, effectively and at less cost.

Wright

In your opinion, what is the most important thing about style?

Jakielo

Today we are facing a changing workforce. The workforce is no longer responsive to an authoritarian management style. One element that is important relating to style is, "Are you a negative or a positive person?" Attitude does have a lot to do with the success that we are going to realize in life. Almost everybody knows a negative person in his or her life and it's been a mystery to me as to why we tolerate that person negative behavior. It always fascinated me that one negative person can bring down an entire department, but one positive person can't pump up an entire department. I realize that staying positive can be a challenge today. We have more demands on our time and that can lead to an increase in stress in our lives. What things do you do to try to keep from falling into the "negativity trap?"

One practice that I adopted about eight years ago is I quit watching televised newscasts. I find that no matter what city I'm in, when I turn on the nightly news the lead story is always the same, who was murdered, who got robbed and a plethora of other negative stories. The way I look at it is if I'm still alive that's a positive. It doesn't mean that I don't stay abreast of what's going on in the world, but I'd much rather selectively read news stories out of magazines or newspapers than listen to the constant negativity coming across the airwaves. You can leave your home in a good mood in the morning and if you're listening to the news on the radio, by the time you get to your destination, it can make you feel like the world is going to end today. So, I think staying positive is a very important part of style.

Another attribute of style is that we have to be flexible. Things are changing dramatically. We all know someone who has been affected by mergers, acquisitions, outsourcing or globalization. I was born and raised in Pittsburgh, Pennsylvania and most people know that we used to be the steel capital of the United States. Now that's no longer the case. We've had to take a look at our economy and say, "Well, given that we're no longer an industrial manufacturing city, what can we do to replace the jobs that have been lost?" We have leaned more to medical and educational type of services, expanding our healthcare centers and institutions of higher learning.

Another important part of style, and I think we often overlook this, is recognition. Recognize the people that work with us, for us, or help us. You know, I always like the quote, I don't know whom it's really attributed to, but someone once said, "People don't care how much you know until they know how much you care." I think with us moving so fast today we take for granted the people around us that help make us successful. Success involves an entire team of people, whether its employees, associates, friends or neighbors, recognizing and thanking people for helping us is a very important habit to acquire. Remember there is no such thing as a self-made person. Everyone must rely on others for assistance.

Another facet of style is the integrity. Being a trainer, a teacher, a speaker and an author, I can teach a multitude of subjects. I can work with people to help them develop numerous skills, but the one thing that has always stumped me throughout my career is that I never found a way to teach people integrity.

The last but not least attribute of style is enthusiasm. I am a firm believer, if you do what you love and are enthusiastic about your career choice, the money will follow. As I travel around the country, and around the world I have the opportunity to meet many different people. It is surprising that most people don't seem to be happy with what they are doing for a living. If you aren't enthusiastic about your life choices or you don't love what you're doing every single day, it's very difficult to be successful.

Wright

So, what variables go into development?

Jakielo

Development is what I consider the third element that is very important relating to success. First and foremost we have to decide what our goals are. Goals are different for everybody. There isn't any one magical formula that's going to make you successful, but we have to decide about our goals. I'm a baseball fanatic, which is a hard thing to do coming from Pittsburgh, Pennsylvania (we have had a couple of rough decades here), but one of my favorite baseball players of all time was a fellow named Yogi Berra, who was a catcher for the New York Yankees. Yogi is credited with many quotes. He once said, "When you come to the fork in the road, take it." If you have adopted that attitude, then it doesn't matter really, what you do or where you go. However, if you have a specific place you want to get to then you know which route you need to take. Determining your goals isn't a one-time exercise. You'll need to establish a series of goals, and keep in mind, they may need readjusted from time to time. When I was young, I had the goal to be six foot four inches tall, now that I'm 50 plus years old and I stand five foot eleven inches it's time to abandon that goal.

Another development issue that is extremely important is presentation skills. When I'm in front of an audience I love to ask the question, "How many of you like to speak in public?" I'll see one or two hands out of a hundred go up. Then I ask the audience, "So what do the rest of you do, just talk to yourself?" I always feel the need to hammer home how important it is to be able to get your point across, whether it's to an individual or a group. If you cannot articulate what it is you want to have done or convince people to follow your directives then you will lack the ability to lead effectively. I like to remind people that it's not difficult to obtain presentation skills. Almost every major city has at least one chapter of Toastmasters International. A Toastmasters chapter is a great place to learn or improve the skills that are necessary for effective presentations. The dues are inexpensive, but the learning experience is invaluable.

Another question relating to development we all need to ask ourselves is, "How do you spend your time?" I know there are statistics about how many hours per day people spend in front of TV. However, I've never seen statistics relating to how many hours people spend daily investing in learning. Everyone needs to carve out a segment of their day for reading or listening to educational materials.

I fly coast to coast about once a month and it's great to have five hours on an airplane, with no cell phones (I hope they don't change the rule) and no pagers. I use those hours for my educational time. We all have choices of what to do with our time. Do we continue to learn? Do we continue to grow? Or are we just going to spend our time with mindless activities? You're in trouble if you can name the last three winners of the TV show *Survivor,* but can't name three popular business authors. Another important aspect of development is that you need to be networking on a continuous basis.

When I first started out in business someone said to me, "It's not what you know, it's whom you know." But I've heard a recent twist on that premise. "It is not only whom you know, but who knows you." We need to make sure that we're always building relationships with others. If I don't know the answers, I need to know whom I can turn to get the answers.

An additional strategy that is essential today is the formation of power teams. Its amazing what technology is allowing us to achieve, you and I can talk via cell phones or we can log onto our computers and within seconds talk to anybody around the world. We should be forming power teams not only locally and regionally but also globally. Communicating with "power teams" comprised of people that have similar likes or corresponding with people that are in our field and have different points of view is very important. Investing time in this type of networking will assist us in the learning and growing processes.

And lastly, we must be willing to commit ourselves to continuous learning. We must be willing to invest at least an hour per day in furthering our education. When I'm conducting a presentation, I always ask the audience, "How many dollars do you spend annually on your education?" I let them think about that for a minute and then I ask them if it is more or less than they spend on cable TV. It's our choice. We can spend our time learning or just vegetating.

Wright

Whom have you determined has responsibilities related to success?

Jakielo

I think we all do. In today's society there is a lack of accountability when something goes wrong. We have a tendency to say it's somebody else's fault. One of the responsibilities I find that is lacking in many environments is people have the tendency to not give the necessary feedback to help others improve. Here is an instance that happened to me a few years ago. I was riding down in a hotel elevator in Atlanta. The door opened and a young lady pushed her way into the crowded elevator. She was pulling a travel suitcase that was on wheels and had a laptop bag draped over her shoulder. It was close to Christmas and she had on a beautiful plaid skirt the type you see at the holidays. She must have thought she looked great in her holiday outfit and I'm sure she would have except for one minor detail. The back of her skirt was tucked into her pantyhose exposing her backside. Everyone in the elevator noticed but no one said a word. When we reached the ground floor and everyone exited I watched to see if anyone would tell the woman about her skirt. No one said a word or made an attempt to inform her of the situation they were just all snickering. I tapped her on the shoulder and informed her about her skirt. I'm sure she was embarrassed that she put herself in that position but she was a heck of a lot less embarrassed when I told her than if she had proceeded across the entire hotel lobby with her butt in full view. We always need to give feedback even if it makes us uncomfortable, we can't assume that people know the situation.

Another example that I've seen where two managers are talking about a problem they are having with one of their employees however, they didn't take the time to give the problem employee the feedback they need to improve. A good rule to keep in mind is, "Don't discuss a problem with someone who can't help solve it." I think feedback is a responsibility we all must shoulder to help people become more successful.

In today's society with companies downsizing and rightsizing, coaching and mentoring have gone by the wayside. We are so busy being busy, we don't seem to take the time to teach and share with others. One of the things that I find is that people seldom improve when they don't have a role model to follow. I've been blessed in my career; I've had three really solid mentors. These were people who took the time and interest to help me develop my skills. I think the most valuable lesson that I learned was from my third mentor. I remember that what he did most to assist in my development was he didn't give me all of the answers, he would let me work on a particular problem, present different solutions and if I was off track, he suggested an alternative solution. However, he would never shoot down any of the ideas I had developed. He took the time in the mentoring process to allow me to make some of my own mistakes, but to also point out some other ways of dealing with the issues at hand.

This helped me with another aspect of responsibility, I think that none of us should put our heads down on our pillow at night before we have taken the time that day to try to help teach or share ideas with somebody in an area that we know very well.

Another responsibility is that we have to respect other people's points of view. Many times we fall into a rut because we have done the same thing the same way for ten or twenty years. We sometimes assume that because we have been in the field for twenty years that we're experienced. However, I have encountered two types of people. People who have had twenty years experience and have become lifetime learners and can help teach and train others, and then I've come across people that have one year experience twenty times. They've never changed anything; they've never been open to other people's ideas or points of view and they don't invest any time in learning.

Wright

So why do you wear multiple hats? You're a speaker, an author, and a consultant.

Jakielo

My goal in life, as I talked about goals earlier, is to help people and companies become as successful as they want to become. I find that it takes the three modalities of being a speaker, author and consultant to be able to achieve that goal. I love to speak and teach that is one of my first loves. I enjoy getting up and effectively delivering ideas to audiences via a presentation. However, I also need to write, because some people don't learn just by verbalization, they would rather read my material at their own pace because they learn and absorb from reading rather from hearing. I also need to consult spending time inside a company and working with people on a one to one basis, keeps me topical. I've run into speakers and authors that are writing and talking about issues that have not existed for years. Consulting helps keep me grounded to make sure I really am addressing the issues that need to be addressed today, and I find that I can accomplish more working one on one with people versus them just attending one of my presentations or reading one of my books.

Wright

What are some areas that have helped contribute to your success?

Jakielo

As I look back on what has helped me with my success; networking is probably one of the most important items. We have all heard these saying, "Don't burn any bridges," or "be nice to people on your way up because you will meet them on your way down." It really is true. Networking and relationship building is one of the major keys and I think that you need to have the approach that when you are working with someone or networking with someone you need to give without any expectation of ever receiving anything in return. I know people that say, "Well, I don't want to talk to them because they are just taking from me all of time, they don't send me business, or they don't share ideas with me why should I help them?" But you just never know when a particular situation will pay off. I think that fact you treat everybody the same, you share as much as you can, you try to be a catalyst to help them become successful is very important. Another contributor to my success has been my relationships in trade and civic associations. None of us have enough time to learn everything. We need to have contacts we can rely on for answers when we are stumped. I heard a speaker say one time that, "The older I get the more I realize I don't know."

Wright

If you could go back ten years to the beginning of your own firm, what are a couple of things that you would have done differently?

Jakielo

I think focus would be number one. I remember reading books explaining that one must "develop and execute a plan," and I think that I was pretty religious about every October, November and December in developing and fine tuning my plan. But come March, April and June, I was off doing something else. For example, I remember my plan always was that, I would like to spend eighty percent of my time speaking and teaching and about twenty percent of my time consulting. But I have found that percentage sometimes flip-flops. I may have a couple of years in a row where that goes eighty, twenty, the other way. Then what I find is that the reason that speaking is down and consulting is up is because I was doing so much consulting I wasn't taking time to promote my speaking. So I think one of the things I should have concentrated on is staying focused; to make sure that I'm doing the right activities that will help me hit the targets and goals that I've set for myself.

Then the next area is that, I wished I had written a book sooner in my career. This is my fourth book in the past six years however; it took me about five years in my own business before my first book was published. The discipline of writing and getting published are great ways to ensure that I keep my research skills honed, and it gave me more credibility with my clients knowing that people were interested in what I had to say. I think if I could go back, I would say, "I should

244

have started working on getting published sooner than four years after I started my firm.

Wright

What do you think of the three most important ingredients that go into any success formula?

Jakielo

I think if I were to sum it up into three areas, first would be, you need to decide what your definition of success is. It's different for everybody. It isn't that you need to make tons of money, although that is a common response when the question is posed. For some people their definition of success is getting married, the definition for some is getting unmarried. You have to decide what success is going to be for you, because there is not one magical formula.

The reason I started my own firm is that I had gone as high as I could in the company I was working in, and when I had reached that plateau, I had no desire to become the president of the company. I was second in command, but I had no desire to be first in command and everybody just said, "Well, why don't you just stay with this firm, why would you go out on your own, because you have a shot at the top job, but that wasn't my definition of success, to have that top job.

Second thing is that you need to develop a plan to achieve your definition. Make sure you have the resources. Do you have the proper preparation? I remember one time asking a group, "How much money would you like to earn in your career"? This was a few years back and one fellow raised his hand and he said, "I want to make a hundred thousand dollars a year, I think that would be the ideal amount of money." O.K., so for the position and job that you have, how many people in that field make a hundred thousand dollars a year? He said, "Well, nobody, the top salary is about sixty-five thousand." And I said, well, how are you going to get to your goal? What position is it in your company that pays that amount of money? He listed about four of them, and I said, "What are you doing to get yourself prepared for those positions?" He hadn't thought of it that way, he had it reversed; he came up with a dollar amount, but hadn't figured out how he was going to get there.

You need proper preparation that will enable you to achieve your plan. We know that if we stop eating, eventually our bodies will shrivel up. It's the same thing when we stop learning. Our brain will react the same way, it will shrink. The last ingredient and a very important ingredient is persistence. You've got to stay the course. I remember reading in *Forbes* not too long ago, it said, "If you really want to do something, you'll find a way. If you don't you will find an excuse." It sort of hit home, because, staying the course and not giving up is a very important part of the success I have realized over the years.

Wright

Well, Dave, I really appreciate all of this time that you have spent with me today, and I've really learned a lot and I think our readers are going to learn a lot as well. I really appreciate you spending this much time with me.

Jakielo

Thank you David because, as I had mentioned earlier, sharing and mentoring is all of our responsibilities and hopefully, I have shared some ideas that can help other people in their endeavors to achieving success.

Wright

Today, we have been talking to David F. Jakielo. He is co-author of the books, The Sales Coach - Tips from the Pros, Information Technology for the Practicing Physician, and Real World Customer Service Strategies. He is also a regular columnist in the Trade Journal – Billing. He has extensive experience in sales, marketing, customer service, and business start-ups and as we have found out today, know a lot about success that we can use. Thank you so much Dave, for being with us today on Conversations on Success.

Jakielo

Your welcome and again I appreciated the opportunity.

About The Author

Dave Jakielo has over 30 years of management experience. His background includes twelve years in hospital patient finance and over two decades of managing physician practices nationwide.

Dave has been speaking, consulting and teaching business methods throughout the USA and in England and India.

He has extensive experience in sales, marketing, customer service, business start-ups and turnarounds and acquisitions assimilation.

He is co-author of three other books and is a regular columnist in the trade journal *Billing*.

Dave is Past President of the Healthcare Billing & Management Association and the National Speakers Association – Pittsburgh Chapter, and also holds membership in the International Brotherhood of Magicians.

David F Jakielo

Seminars & Consulting

86 Hall Avenue

Pittsburgh, PA. 15205

Phone: 412.921.0976

Email: Dave@DavidJakielo.com

www.DavidJakielo.com

Chapter Seventeen

HOLTON BUGGS

THE INTERVIEW

David E. Wright (Wright)

Today we are talking to Holton Buggs. Holton was born and raised in Tampa, Florida. Upon graduation from high school he was relocated to Houston to pursue a college degree. After finishing school in 1995 he realized very quickly that working in corporate America for a salary as an engineer was a dead end career for him. Thus he pursued a career in sales and started his own business in 1996. After four successful years in business, sales drastically declined forcing Holton to reevaluate his financial future.

His prayers were answered in the form of a phone call about a network marketing opportunity on the Internet. As a result, Holton retired from corporate America at the tender age of twenty-seven. Currently he has more than thirteen years of experience and has built teams totaling more than 40,000 distributors over the past five years. Holton is a master trainer and motivational speaker—sought after all across the globe for his business savvy and entrepreneurial expertise. Together Holton and his wife (his junior high school sweetheart) Earlene took the Network Marketing industry by storm. They were the number one income earners in a previous company and are currently among the top four income earners in their current company.

Holton, thank you so much for being with us today.

Holton Buggs (Buggs)
You're welcome David.

Wright
What are the top three contributing factors to your success?

Buggs
David, I believe there are four factors that have contributed to my success. I call them "The four philosophies of a seven-figure earner." The phrase, "seven-figure earner," doesn't only mean an amount of income. The term also applies to the inevitable personal growth that takes place within a person when success principles are applied. In one's pursuit of professional success, the *internal* growth that manifests inside of him or her is far more valuable and noteworthy than the monetary gain by itself. However, if it were not for the desire for monetary gain, the internal growth may never have taken place.

Philosophy #1 Picture Your Success. In life you don't get what you want, you get what you picture. Many people continuously set the same goals year after year confessing the things they want, and year after year they fail to achieve their goal—they still want those very same things. Once you *picture* success however, the brain's success coach (the subconscious mind) begins to chip away all that is not pertinent to the task at hand. It leaves only results based on instructions given by the picture.

I call it "the Michelangelo Principle." Michelangelo's greatest work of art began with a clear, detailed picture and a huge piece of marble most would have considered rubble. His brain's success coach (his sub-conscious mind) began to chip away all fragments of marble that were irrelevant to the picture he possessed in his mind. We now marvel over the illustrious beauty of the "Statue of David," that in my humble opinion might never have been possible without Angelo's ability to see that statue in his mind's eye long before it became a reality.

Personally I pictured health, wealth, world travel, and great relationships long before I possessed them. And now I live a life filled with perks only the rich and famous ever have the opportunity to enjoy.

Philosophy #2 The deposit is first, the withdrawal comes later. You have to decide what you're willing to give up temporarily to get what you picture. What I mean by that is success is not easy or convenient. However, I do believe success is very simple to obtain. I had to give up some time with friends, money, sleep, and entertainment activities so that I could totally focus on achieving my dreams and goals. Very few people are willing to do that. Most people want to have the cake and eat it too; but they've never even taken the time to bake the cake.

Philosophy #3 Pick a Champion. You have to find someone who's been there, done what you are looking to do and who is willing to teach you how to do the same thing. You must follow the path they are going to set for you. The best way to sum it up is with a term called "mentorship." Success is much more obtainable when you have someone who is more experienced than you are and who has accepted personal responsibility for your success in life.

Philosophy #4 Plan Your Work, and Work You Plan. After you have executed the first three philosophies, develop a business plan that leaves room for adjustments and then follow the plan until you receive the desired results.

Wright

Does a person's leadership ability affect his/her ability to achieve success? If yes, please share with us why.

Buggs

When I look at extremely successful people, their level of success is usually based on one major skill—leadership. In his book, *Developing the Leader Within You,* John Maxwell wrote, "Leadership is influence, nothing more and nothing less." If an individual lacks sufficient influence, they simply cannot impact the lives of very many people. Thus, success—as it pertains to that individual—will more than likely be short term or non-existent.

I believe that to become successful, one has to develop a major sphere of influence. Consider someone like Bill Gates for example. The fruits of his labor expand the globe and my guess is that society as a whole will continue to benefit from his accomplishments—directly or indirectly—for a very long time to come. When I evaluate an individual's success, I compare their success to the throwing of a stone in a lake and I ask myself, "Was there a small ripple effect or a huge one?" Bill Gates obviously threw a boulder and made a huge splash. In my opinion, his accomplishment was largely due to his ability to lead.

Wright

You alluded to it earlier, but tell me specifically, what sacrifices are most common among those who are ambitious?

Buggs

Well, you know I wouldn't even term them as sacrifices, I call them "investments." When you sacrifice something, you give it up for something better in the future. Sacrifices—investments—give a return in the future. For example, when I invest time, I eventually received more time in the long run. I gave up money—money I didn't have—and I invested it into my business. I gave up relationships as well—I didn't have a lot of time to be with my family and friends. I term sacrifices as investments because I expect more to come back later on and it did. It eventually came back ten fold, a hundred fold, and a thousand fold. But now, because I invested time and money, I have all the time in the world to devote to my loved ones and the money to do it.

I think the biggest investment people make is to be out of balance for a short period of time. Many people want to stay in balance and accomplish extraordinary goals all at the same time. Anything I have ever seen that stayed balanced eventually became stagnant, but anything moving and moving fast is out of balance for a short period of time.

Wright

Tell me, do you feel that one's educational background or social economic status has any bearing on his or her ability to achieve success?

Buggs

You know David, that's a great question. My answer to that question is both "yes" and "no." A person's socio-economic status and/or educational background (or lack thereof) is usually the reason they desire success in the first place. This point is abundantly clear in my life. I was motivated to obtain a college degree simply because no one in my family had ever done so. At the time, graduating from college was for me a measure of success because I was the first to do so in my family. Furthermore, there were no millionaires in my family. Here again, I was the first member of my family to become financially independent by the age of twenty-seven.

Lack of financial ability was the most prominent motivating factor for me in the early stages of my career. So to answer your question, yes, one's educational or socio-economic status may have a tremendous impact on their desire for success. But on the other hand, a person's lack of education or financial ability has never prevented them from achieving success, either.

In short, yes, a person's financial ability and level of education may very well play a part in their initial desire for success, but it is in no way the only determining factor for achieving success.

Is college necessary? Absolutely, I do believe that it can help an individual in many ways. The college experience really gives an individual the appropriate atmosphere needed to sharpen his or her leadership skills and to obtain experience dealing with people from all walks of life. But by no means does the possession of a college degree guarantee success of any kind. Many of my closest friends have never gone to college but are nonetheless, extremely successful and are leading hundreds of thousands of people in some of the most noteworthy professions in society today—"The facts simply do not count when you have a dream."

Wright

You spoke earlier of finding a mentor or someone you can emulate, what advice would you give to our readers on how to choose a mentor?

Buggs

Well the key thing to consider when searching for a mentor is to know exactly what you desire that person to be. Many people take the mentorship process for granted and are just looking for a coach more or less. There is a big difference between a coach and a mentor. A mentor is someone who will literally pour his or her life and life experiences into you. When you are looking for a mentor, it has to be someone who has the same moral values you have—you have to be what I call "equally yoked" in that sense. Also, when looking for a mentor, make sure that person has strengths in the areas of life that you do not have in those areas. It's not necessary to have a mentor who is weak where you are weak and strong where you are strong because there isn't much you can learn.

I think the third aspect of searching for a mentor is that you must search for someone you know is going to be accountable to you just as you are accountable to him or her.

I think the most important responsibility of a mentoree is to make certain that they are prepared to be the best protégé they can be. And whatever you do, do not take your mentor or the mentoring process for granted. This action could cost you a relationship that could have very well made you a fortune.

Wright

What qualities should an individual who is looking to be mentored possess?

Buggs

There is one major quality I look for when I am trying to determine whether or not I want to accept a person as a mentoree. To me, a mentor is like a cartographer, one who draws and designs maps. A mentor is there to design a travel route and point out landmarks and roadblocks along the way. If a mentor is a cartographer, I believe a protégé' must resemble a clean canvas. You must submit yourself totally to your mentor's philosophies because I guarantee you will frequently be given instructions and information that you may or may not understand or agree with [at the time] and as a result, you will be faced with the dilemma of following your own understanding versus your mentor's suggestions. If the decision to submit your ego totally is not made in advance, this dilemma could very well cost you the relationship. My view on this issue is non-negotiable. You must make a conscious decision to submit your ego entirely as it pertains to your mentor even when you do not like or agree with his/her position with respect to an issue. Always remember that you are in need of what your mentor has to offer, and they are not in need of what you have to offer. If you have chosen your mentor properly, then you can trust them with your life. In that case there should be no need for argument.

I realized very quickly during my early stages as a mentoree, that I didn't have to look for a mentor, so to speak. Rather, if I focused totally on being the right protégé', the mentor I needed and desired would find and chose me when I was ready, just like the old adage says, " When the student is ready, the teacher will appear."

Wright

Almost everyone I have asked to give me his or her definition of success has given me a unique answer. In fact, the number of times I have asked this question is equal to the number of different answers I have received. Nonetheless, I'm going to ask you the exact same question: What is your definition of success?

Buggs

You know David, my definition of success is quite simple. Success is defined as the progressive realization of a worthwhile dream or goal. In my humble opinion, success happens when an individual has impacted another person's life in a manner in which they could never be compensated. That is by far, the *ultimate* success.

Wright

Do you feel affirmations are important to one's likelihood of becoming successful? If so, why?

Buggs

I am a strong proponent of the positive affects of affirmations when they are used as a part of everyday life. One of the topics I have studied more than any course I ever took in college is the human brain, human behavior and how the mind works. As humans, we have the most precious computer ever designed right between our ears. I read something recently that said that the human memory has the capacity to fill eleven libraries the size of the Library of Congress. With that said, it is easy to envision just how much input the brain can handle.

I believe affirmations are extremely important because seventy percent of the conversation one has is with oneself. The subconscious mind can only project that which is consistent with its programming. If seventy percent of the programming is coming from within, positive affirmations are the key to elements in changing negative programming into positive programming. Most people ruin their chance for success with their spoken words of doubt, defeat, and failure. In short, affirmations assist the individual with changing that programming. Once a person's belief changes their actions change. Once a person's actions change their results will also change. But it all begins with the spoken word as well as internal communication. This process is what I have coined "The Raising the Bar Philosophy."

Change the beliefs and the actions will change. Change the actions and the results will change!

Wright

In your opinion what are some of the reasons people fail?

Buggs

There are many reasons why people fail. I think that the most significant reason why people fail is because they quit too soon. I realized many, many years ago that there is no time clock in the race to success. No one is keeping score. Each time I have experienced a less than desirable outcome in various situations, I have always maintained the attitude that regardless of how the world views my performance, I am a winner who simply ran out of time to show externally what I know to be true internally. The thing I love about living is that I am the gatekeeper of the time clock associated with my success in life. That said, it's my prerogative to reset the clock or restart my game of life at will and the great news is that I don't need anyone's permission to do so!

Wright

One of the most important points I have ever read said that ninety-eight percent of all failure comes from quitting. You are the second person I've heard say something similar. Many people believe that visualization is a vital aspect of success. I'd like to ask your opinion as to what role you feel visualization plays in one's ability to achieve success.

Buggs

I use visualization in just about everything I do. I played organized sports from grade school through college. One of the most common characteristics among great athletes is their ability to visualize a game victory long before the game is actually won—they see the victory in their mind's eye.

I had the good fortune of attending the final round of golf at the 2005 Master's Championship. For fifteen holes I watched Tiger Woods visualize each shot before he actually hit the ball. I was on the side of the putting green at the memorable sixteenth hole when Tiger visualized the shot that may be recognized as the most important of his career. The intensity of his visualization silenced over 10,000 people, and the execution of that vision lies permanently in the minds of millions who watched.

If this principle works in sports, it will also work in marital relationships; and if it works in your marital relationships, it will work in personal relationships; and if it works in personal relationships, it will within the community; and if it works within the community, it will work in your business; and if it works in business, it will work among cultures; and if it works among cultures it can transcend life as we know it.

Wright

What is a definiteness of purpose and how does one go about establishing one?

Buggs

A definiteness of purpose is, as defined by world renowned author and businessman Napoleon Hill, is one's chief aim or goal in life—it is the purpose for which an individual determines that he/she has been put on this earth to fulfill. I believe that so many people live life as a wondering generality when we all should strive to be a meaningful specific. A definiteness of purpose is the dominate driving force in the life of the individual who has accepted the responsibility of realizing God's purpose for their life.

My definiteness of purpose came to me as I was pacing my bedroom floor one evening over a year ago. I was contemplating what I really want to accomplish in a year. I also thought about my current goals and I began to visualize what 2004 would be like for me. I went further to ask myself (and God), "What am I here for?" At the moment when I realized my definiteness of purpose, it was as if time stood still. And my purpose became as clear to me as a glass of drinking water. I set a goal to positively affect the lives of 100,000,000 people financially, spiritually, and socially. For the first time in my life I had set a goal that actually frightened me. But the thought alone of a goal with such magnitude was enough to get my juices flowing rampantly.

Now almost everything I do is in alignment with making that goal come true. If nothing more, determining my definiteness of purpose has freed me from worrying so much about my own well-being. I know for a fact that no man has ever helped another without helping himself in the process.

Wright

Through the years when you have been forced to make significant changes in your life, how has faith played a part in that decision making process?

Buggs

Faith is a muscle that must be exercised daily. I believe that the greater your faith, the greater your accomplishment. Most people say, "Fake it 'till you make it," but one of the things I tell people during my Success Seminars is "faith it – 'till you make it." I learned that from a really good friend of mine from Dallas, Texas. When I heard him make that statement nearly five years ago, I made a decision to believe success was happening even when I didn't actually see it. At that time, I really began to understand how to use faith in my life and that provided me with the comfort of knowing that what I desired had already been done in the spirit long before the physical results would be revealed.

Wright

Finally Holton, if you had a soap box that you could get on or a radio station that would go out to everyone in the world—if you could say one thing that you think would help to make someone a better person, experience spiritual happiness, and become successful, what would it be?

Buggs

Jim Rohn, one of my "silent" mentors, encourages the individual to work harder on oneself than you would on a business and you'll create massive success. That's the one piece of advice I would give to someone who was looking to achieve happiness and success. Both of those characteristics can be quite elusive. I know because the same was true for me until I learned that happiness and success is determined by internal factors verses external ones. Most people try to do a better job, try to be a better engineer or try to be a better business owner. It is my belief that if they invested that time on themselves, they would undoubtedly do better in their jobs and success would come naturally.

Wright

Today we have been talking to Holton Buggs. He is a master trainer, motivational speaker, entrepreneur, and business executive and is sought after all over the world for his business savvy and his entrepreneurial expertise. He and his wife, Earlene, have taken network marketing by storm and are major income owners in the industry. We have found out today many reasons why that is the case. Holton, thank you so much for being with us today. I really appreciate the time you have given me.

Buggs

Thank you David and I really appreciate the opportunity to talk with you as well.

About The Author

Holton was born and raised in Tampa, Florida. Upon graduation from high school he was relocated to Houston to pursue a college degree. After finishing school in 1995 he realized very quickly that working in corporate America for a salary as an engineer was a dead end career for him. Thus he pursued a career in sales and started his own business in 1996. After four successful years in business, sales drastically declined forcing Holton to reevaluate his financial future.

His prayers were answered in the form of a phone call about a network marketing opportunity on the Internet. As a result, Holton retired from corporate America at the tender age of twenty-seven. Currently he has more than thirteen years of experience and has built teams totaling more than 40,000 distributors over the past five years. Holton is a master trainer and motivational speaker—sought after all across the globe for his business savvy and entrepreneurial expertise. Together Holton and his wife (his junior high school sweetheart) Earlene took the Network Marketing industry by storm. They were the number one income earners in a previous company and are currently among the top four income earners in their current company.

Holton Buggs

Phone: 281.831.0657

Email: holton@3kmg.com

Chapter Eighteen

THE INTERVIEW

David E. Wright (Wright)

Today we are speaking with Mona Thorpe, coach, entrepreneur and organizational consultant. Mona's blended background in industrial psychology studies and her proven coaching techniques provide a cutting edge approach in delivering success strategies to her clients. She has a unique and effective approach and is known for rapid results in improved performance for organizations and executives from leading companies such as IBM, Pfizer and Citibank, as well as individuals seeking personal transformation.

As an entrepreneur of five companies, Mona's diverse business background combined with her interpersonal studies brings a powerhouse of expertise to share with her clients that produce extraordinary results. Believing that everyone, no matter who they are, are capable of transforming their lives into exquisite creations of fulfilled dreams, she leaves each client enriched and powerfully endowed to do so.

In addition to being the founder and President of Creative Edge Coaching, she has been involved with charitable groups such as the ABC House—an organization set up to house and provide advanced education to inner city children—Meals on Wheels and the local Lions

Club. Some of her memberships include the American Management Association and The American Society of Training and Development. Mona, welcome to *Conversations on Success*.

Mona Thorpe (Thorpe)

Thank you, David. It's great to be here.

Wright

You have been working in the field of organizational development and individual transformation for more than twenty years. What drew you to this line of work?

Thorpe

I knew most of my life I wanted to work with people, but when I realized it distinctly was in second grade when two things happened. I observed a classmate leave the room for an hour every week to visit with a well-dressed gentleman. I knew he was helping her in some emotional way and thought that someday when I was grown up I would do that also. I don't think I have truly grown up yet, but here I am doing what I love to do. The second thing was when a teacher asked me what all the lines were on a picture I had drawn. I told her they were maps of bridges showing people how to get anywhere they wanted to go. To this day, I have never stopped enjoying the feeling of being part of a process that helps to provide people and organizations with a picture of the clearest and most effective path to achieve the success they seek.

Wright

Mona, you are known for producing rapid results in helping your clients to achieve success. What do you attribute that to?

Thorpe

It is getting to the core issues. I can remember as early back as grade school, I frequently felt and looked at things differently than the other children and even adults. One instance a classmate was crying while we were attending a showing of the movie, *101 Dalmatians*. The teachers could see no reason for her crying and after many times asking her to stop with no success, they told her she would have to leave the theater. I leaned over and saw that the railing in front of her was blocking her view and preventing her from seeing the screen. She was missing the movie. I would have cried too,

I thought to myself. I asked her if she wanted to change seats with me. We did and there was no more crying until that evil villain Cruella Deville appeared on the screen and then we decided to hold hands and cry together. Of course, we were then both made to leave the theater and sit in the lobby where we struck up what turned out to be long friendship. So to answer your question, most definitely, it is the ability to look at things at their deepest, most core level and address a solution from that stand point.

Wright

How do you get organizations or top executives to be open to addressing these core level issues?

Thorpe

It is a matter of showing them that no matter the situation or the time in which an individual or group has been non productive or just not working at their peak, no one is to blame. There is no need to make anyone wrong in order to find solutions. The cause is merely not having the right information to turn things around. Once the correct information is in tact, perspectives that need to shift fall into place and the path forward is rather easy at that point. I find that where there is blame included in the mix there is great resistance in addressing issues and is a huge factor in slowing down any process that is looking to seek productive structure. The answer is that I offer a no fault policy.

Wright

What does success mean to you?

Thorpe

To me, success is an ability to keep authenticity prevalent in one's life. When we so bravely embark upon a human experience and enter into the world, we encounter many factors that pull us from our authentic selves. From parenting, schooling, the media, to just about everything in our environment is designed to make us feel that in order to be valuable we must be something other than just ourselves. This is a misnomer and an underlying factor that keeps us from experiencing our full power. Once we reunite with our authenticity and choose to keep our integrity around it, we gain access through a gateway into a space that holds unlimited possibilities. It is in this realm of being that gives us the power to attract success. Even in the corporate world it is important, but even harder to stay authentic. There is a lot of pressure to please others and integrity can wear thin, especially under those conditions. Corporations that do the best in the market are the ones that set a climate that encourages authenticity in their employees. My coaching and consulting are geared around this premise. Imagine thousands of staff members working for your company motivated and inspired to each generate authentic new ideas. These are the companies that have their finger on the pulse of the business environment and find continued success through each new phase of their company's growth.

Wright

That is very interesting and I agree with you, but give me your definition of authenticity.

Thorpe

The dictionary's description is as follows: having a genuine origin; and the definition for genuine is: being what it claims to be or appears to be. If we go a little deeper and explore how being authentic actually impacts our lives, we find several things to be stead fast. We always feel better when we have expressed our true feelings about something; we always have a complete feeling when someone else has been real with us; we always get more accomplished when we face the real issues; we have closer, more satisfying relations with others when we are ourselves; and we always feel more comfortable when we are with people that accept us for who we truly are.

Look at the rose. It does not try to be a tulip, nor does a lion try to be a tiger, nor does wind try to imitate fire. All the natural elements that have remained themselves have been appreciated throughout the centuries for exactly what they are, but as humans we are encouraged by our cultures to go against our nature and try to be what is accepted by the masses. This way of living has gotten us in a lot of unwanted situations, such as religious wars, territorial disputes, gang wars and so on. The list of positive effects that being authentic produces is endless. Unfortunately, so is the list of negative effects when we are not being authentic.

I would say my definition of authenticity is staying true to what you feel in your gut, not second guessing yourself and drawing on your courage to remain yourself, even in the face of that almost unthinkable affliction, "being different." It's not to say going out and buying a name brand pair of shoes or suit is betraying your authenticity. What you want to keep in mind is that being yourself is the best place you could be and you might have to put yourselves back on track every śo often.

Wright

How do you help people to get back on track?

Thorpe

I help them to discover where it was that they initially got off track. I remember when I started on my transformation journey there were several areas I was unsatisfied with. I found it helpful to be aware of them, but what really helped give me momentum toward my goals was the discovery of why. When I actually saw the reasons why I was repeatedly off track, I felt free from the unconscious pull they had on me. What we don't know will hurt us, and a little bit of the **right** knowledge goes along way.

Wright

How do you coach and consult others to be successful?

Thorpe

Many of my clients are successful and look to expand their levels of success, while others experience being blocked in certain areas. The first step I take is to identify the core issues that stand in the way of successful endeavors. I do this by observing an organization's or individual's present situation or existing climate, using one on one interviews and assessment tools. The information is delivered to the client. I then make recommendations for a new climate or reorganization, along with coaching, consulting sessions, group meetings and workshops. Sometimes working with one executive in the company to help them reach their potential or grooming a staff member for a management position is a more desirable approach verses looking to bring someone from the outside to improve an organization. I provide individual coaching sessions to obtain these results. As you can see, David, there are many ways in which to supply these services and it is really a customized approach depending on the clients' goals and needs.

Wright

In your opinion, what does it take to be a success whether operating as a corporation, as a private business owner, an entrepreneur or an individual looking to live life to the fullest?

Thorpe

It takes, first and foremost, an extraordinary outlook and approach to life. With that in tact, you are in the driver's seat to choose any area and to what extent you want your success to soar. To give you an example of this, when I was in college I was recruited by Carvel Franchising to work in their sales and marketing department, and shortly after that to a large recruiting firm. I worked at the firm for a little over a year and realized I had developed the business on my own and managed it myself. It was my first experience of working autonomously. I decided to start my own recruiting company. This was in the early seventies. I broke many unspoken rules such as, youth is not responsible to manage and operate independently in business, women are not suited for running and developing companies, small companies will not make it in corporate driven environment and so on.

The spoken broken rules sounded like this, you are not old enough, therefore, no one will respect you, no business will get off the ground in a recession; I was even told I was just too petite and wouldn't be taken seriously. All this came from friends and family. Well, with all that wonderful support, I thanked them all for their good intentions. I weighed each consideration and the first thought I had about being petite at five feet was, "Hey, what about Gandhi?" I then proceeded to conclude that my age, the recession and the fact that I was petite had not hindered me from becoming the top producer in the company I was working for, therefore, my chances were exponentially greater at succeeding. Succeed I did. I took the business to profiting $40K per month, while creating winning situations for my clients. The first year of the business, in the 1970's when the country was in a recession, I did better than all my preceding years. My mantra became, "The person's opinion that I value most is my own." That doesn't mean I don't listen and assess what others have to say, but when all is said and done it is my evaluation of all the data that is presented to me and my opinion on what is included in my final decisions, which are most important to me. Starting my first business was one of the best decisions I made in my life and it set a powerful direction for me. So to be successful, in my opinion, you need to follow what is in your heart and stay true to it.

Wright

How do you get clients who do not have an extraordinary approach and outlook on life to develop one in order to be successful?

Thorpe

David, I believe each and every one of us is born with inherent gifts. Each of us has the ability to create miracles in our lives. The only problem that exists is we don't know that we can. We are born with such courage and curiosity. But we are side tracked by the beliefs and values of all that surrounds us. As children, we are like sponges absorbing everything. This means the bad along with the good. A few of us, by some grace, are able to not choose to listen to the doubts that are created for us. What determines this attitude is not known, but there is no one that can not acquire this way of thinking. If we learned to go against our natural grain it means that it exists and we can certainly reunite with it. It is in this reunion that sparks our extraordinary qualities. By exploring the misperceptions that cloud my clients' abilities and strengths they see the full extent of their talents. It is like walking through a dark room. You don't know what you will bump into so you travel slowly and cautiously. But when light starts to brighten the room you see the obstacles. Knowing how to maneuver around the obstacles frees you to explore the extraordinary talents that exist within you. My clients find their extraordinary approach to success on their own. I just help to clear the path.

Thorpe

Transformation and working at achieving success can be tedious and tough work. How do you keep your clients focused when dealing with these issues?

Thorpe

Fun and excitement, of course! It is really all about discovery. People have an endless desire to know more about themselves and how to get the most our of life. It is the whole premise of our existence. We have been working at this since our first day here. We were in this discovery process as infants thru to toddlers, to teenagers and now adults. When we were infants, a gurgle and a half smile went pretty far, as toddlers a tearful pout or a hunger strike had the potential to attract a more interesting food plan, and the teens today can wear down even the toughest parents by a few strategically placed body rings and some orange hair.

As adults, we seek to find the really sophisticated processes that will provide not just what we think we want, but a whole way of being that produces a sense of ease and grace in our lives. Whether we are part of a large corporation, small business or an entrepreneur, under our ambitions lays a desire to be ourselves and contribute to our lives an authentic existence that produces our personal best. The process to find this can be incredibly exciting and rewarding. This is the path I provide for my clients and I can assure you the process getting to the goals is as fun and exciting as living with the success.

Wright

Once success has been achieved, does the fun and excitement end?

Thorpe

Success is progressive and can fluctuate. There is really no end to success. When any level of success is achieved it is important that you know exactly what steps you took to get there so when times waver, and they do, you will know your way back. Having a good view of the big picture that surrounds your goals gives you the next level to aspire to. If you only focus on the smaller view you may spend time working on projects that have not taken you where you want to end up. Most important is that the success you achieve leaves you feeling uplifted and joyful. Success does not mean hard work, long hours, deprivation, nor surrendering your blood, sweat and tears. There is nothing more disheartening to spend you life at work that is grueling, that you have to pull yourself out of bed to get to, all so that at the end of it you will have something to show for it. Every minute of life is a cherished moment, one that we will not get back. We can and deserve to have each of them filled with what we love to do, be and experience. Success is moment to moment and constantly evolving, therefore, learning to choose fun and excitement at every moment is an important ingredient to success.

Wright

When you are consulting with clients what kind of questions do companies and individuals present you with when they look to successfully achieve their goals.

Thorpe

There are all kinds of questions. It has a lot to do with what it is they seek to accomplish. Sometimes clients will come with a certain issue, and after exploring it we discover it was a stepping stone to something different. For instance, one company wanted to increase the motivation of there sales department in order to produce more business. While examining the overall picture we discovered that they were very motivated, but what stood in the way of their productivity was more a matter of communication. Many avenues were clogged with missed communications effecting orders, leads, work sheets, and necessary information was being delivered through the wrong channels. In other cases, there are clients that have a clear view of what it is they want to accomplish and their questions are geared around how to find a direct and rapid process to get it done.

When working with individuals on transformation, the questions range from, what do I want to transform, to I know what I want to transform to, but how do I get there? As many people as there are, is equivalent to the range of different questions that exist.

Wright

What distinguishes your coaching and consulting from others when helping clients to achieve success?

Thrope

I feel I can best answer that by sharing one of my coaching experiences with you. I had a woman set an appointment with me who had been seeing a psychologist for 12 years and a psychiatrist who was prescribing medication for her. Upon her first meeting with me, she informed me that she had been diagnosed as having a personality disorder, bi-polar disorder and several other disorders. I don't handle problems that are beyond my scope of expertise, but something compelled me to finish the meeting with her. We met for 1 1/2 hours. When we were done my gut feeling told me she had none of the disorders. I agreed to see her under the conditions that she would continue with her psychologist and her psychiatrist and she would acknowledge that my services would be strictly on a coaching basis. When we started she could not finish one complete sentence, nor keep a succinct thought, in addition to having very low self-esteem. Within eight months of working with me she had pulled much of her life together. We discovered that she was living up to many of the diagnoses she had been labeled with, as well as other expectations from her childhood and her marriage. When she saw this clearly she began to regain and trust her own perspectives. Over the following year and a half, she ended some unhealthy relationships, started a business and was making continual trips to Ireland, where she, to this day, writes and participates in the Irish peace movement. Trusting and following my gut feelings in order to look beyond the obvious and using strength to make a call that may not be the most popular, but one that will produce productive results is how I work. I will not sell any of my clients short by provided a service that is based methods that are designed for the sole purpose of appearing popular. I believe these are the distinctions that make my service invaluable to my clients.

Wright

Mona, I have one final question for you. How do you measure success?

Thorpe

This question is really simple. I measure success by how many times one smiles each day. All the money and fame can not make you happy. If you have achieved all the goals you think you wanted to and you are not smiling, it is not success you have achieved. At the end of the day, if your goals are met and you're smiling, then, David, you've won the gold.

Wright

Mona, I have thoroughly enjoyed talking with you today. I find your ideas and approach to success refreshing, enlightening and innovative. Through just this conversation I have gained several new ways to enhance my success strategies. It is clear why your clients are so impressed with your services. Thank you for taking this time to share them today.

Thorpe

It has been my pleasure.

About the Author

Mona Thorpe is founder and president of Creative Edge Coaching. She in an entrepreneur of 5 companies and for more than twenty years has provided individuals and businesses with coaching and organizational consulting. Her clients include mid-size companies to corporate executives from fortune 500 businesses in a wide variety of industries as well as individuals. She continually puts passion and energy into developing her work in order to provide clients with the best and most productive services, which includes coaching, consulting, speaking assignments, workshops and customized programs.

Mona Thorpe

Creative Edge Coaching

Phone: 203.894.8784

www.creativeedgecoaching.com

Chapter Nineteen

WILLIAM "T" THOMPSON

David E. Wright (Wright)

Today we are talking to William "T" Thompson, one of the country's leading consultants and speakers on the science of achievement. While others theorize about success, "T" speaks and consults from both a personal and practical perspective. As CEO of the Summit Group Companies, "T" built a company whose interest included residential and commercial real estate, technology, engineering and food service franchises. A multi-unit owner of Subway Sandwiches, Dunkin Donuts and TCBY Yogurt, his units received national awards for both the highest increase in sales and the most innovative marketing program in Subways 22,000-store system. His business achievements also garnered a nomination as *Inc. Magazine's* Entrepreneur of the Year.

A decorated Air Force veteran, "T" has been a pilot for Delta Air Lines for 25 years and serves as an International Check Captain. He is also an attorney, member of two state bars and the bar of the Supreme Court of the United States.

A former Commissioner of Aeronautics for Massachusetts, "T" was appointed to five consecutive four year terms by three different

Governors and has the unique distinction of serving in both Democratic and Republican administrations.

He has been featured in numerous media outlets including the Wall Street Journal, the New York Times, and the Boston Globe, NBC, CBS, PBS and Black Enterprise magazine.

A member of the National Speakers Association, "T" has brought his blue print for personal, professional and organizational achievement to numerous organizations including Verizon, State Street Bank, the American Cancer Society and the Security and Exchange Commission.

"T," welcome to Conversations On Success

William "T" Thompson (Thompson)

Thank you, David. It is a pleasure and honor to be speaking with you today.

Wright

"T," you have a very interesting background. You began your professional career as a pilot. What motivated you to become an attorney and businessman?

Thompson

David, it was 1977, and I was a young Air Force Instructor Pilot. I had just flown a mission and was walking back to my squadron when I picked up a magazine entitled, *Entrepreneur*. I began to flip through the magazine and came across an article on unique ways to sell flowers. A young Canadian fellow was selling flowers on street corners and making $100,000 a year. To say that I found the article interesting would be an understatement. I was flying a multi-million-dollar jet and making $24,000 a year. I became very excited about the possibilities of increasing my income and I can honestly say that the magazine changed my life. I began to develop a budding, but serious interest in business. The more I read and the more I studied, the more I realized that the principles that determined success in business, mirrored the principles that determined success in aviation, and in many ways, accounted for success in life. These were principles such as leadership, vision, planning and execution. I decided that to be seriously committed to business, I should go back to school for formal education and decided to get a MBA. Upon further investigation, however, I decided that a law degree with an emphasis in business, tax and finance would give me a solid business foundation and, ultimately, more flexibility. So I enrolled in law school at night, while I still continued to fly my Air Force missions during the day.

Wright

That is quite an eclectic career, flying jets, practicing law, running a significant business, a governmental agency, and doing it all simultaneously. You must really excel at time management?

Thompson

David, during my first few weeks as a cadet at the Air Force Academy, I discovered that to be successful, I would have to master the concept of time management. I was suddenly in an environment where I was given more than I could possibly accomplish and yet, I was responsible for getting it all done. It forced you to learn to organize and prioritize or you were going to fail. You see, we all have the same 24 hours. It's both what you choose to do with that time and the amount of time doing what you do, that is important. Of course, we all have different priorities at different times. Let's be honest, most people spend more time watching TV or doing other fun things than they do spending time on working to improve themselves. So over the years, I've focused on doing things that I've enjoyed but that would also improve my life experience.

The second thing that I do is to focus on doing the most important things that need to be done at the time. You can seldom accomplish all the things that you would like to on a daily basis. This is true even when you have written them down on a "To Do List," which I have done for many years. But I have prioritized the 3 or 4 most important things that I needed to get accomplished that day and focused on achieving those in a laser-like way.

Wright

You have been quoted as saying, "I am not the smartest guy around, I have just had a pretty good plan." Can you elaborate on that?

Thompson

Well, David, I have always worked hard, and though I have had my disappointments, for the most part, I have done well in my endeavors. But I have never ceased to be amazed at the number of truly brilliant people that I have been fortunate to come into contact with. And some have been extremely talented and blessed with tremendous gifts. Yet for all of their talent, all of their intelligence, and all of their brilliance, many have not been able to go out and successfully accomplish the things that they have expressed a desire to achieve. And in talking to some of them, it became readily apparent that they either didn't have a plan or didn't have a very good plan. Now what I mean by a good plan is one that is well thought out, simple and, most importantly, that can be successfully implemented. My entire aviation background has been built on planning. We never fly a mission without a plan. In fact, in the Air Force, we had both a flight plan and a mission plan. This was a very definitive process, which took you from the very beginning of the flight, through a series of specific objectives and way points, which were all designed to get you to your final destination and to accomplish your mission. So, I used that planning background and experience in aviation and decided to apply it to my own life. I created my own personal "flight plan," which I have consistently used to help me achieve the things in life that I have desired.

Some years ago, I discovered that my plan was transferable. A couple of close friends who were aware of some of the goals that I had set and eventually achieved, asked how I had been able to accomplish what I had. I shared my personal "flight plan" concept with them and they were able to apply the principles and achieve some remarkable results. I also found that the principles of my plan, or "way points" as I call them, worked very well in an organizational setting. So I used my "flight plan" as the basis for my involvement in civic associations and in my business ventures and have shared them with other businesses and organizations, as well.

Wright

Can you share with our readers what the" way points" of your "flight plan" are?

Thompson

I would be happy to. If I may, I would like to use the aviation analogy of an airline flight to illustrate. At the beginning of each flight in the "new generation" commercial airliners that we fly today, we go through a process called "alignment," which uses global positioning satellites to determine, with pinpoint accuracy, where the airplane is. Accomplishing this "grounding" process is absolutely essential before we will be able to successfully program the computers that will control our flight.

In life, it is also essential that you first go through an "alignment" process if you are going to successfully program your journey to achieving the things that you desire. This personal "grounding" process requires that you define what I call the "way point" of your "Core Values." These are those things that are most important in your life. Both defining and then prioritizing your "Core Values" are absolutely crucial to being able to soar to great heights in life because your "Core Values" determine so many critically important things about you. For example, your "Core Values" will influence how your family and friends, fellow workers and clients perceive you. Your "Core Values" will also determine the things that you place a priority on and will go out and do. In short, your " Core Values" determine, fundamentally, who you are.

In the airplane, after we have finished the "alignment" process, we can then begin to program our flight control computer. We'll first program our departure point. Then we will input the arrival city. We'll program the jetways, the navigational facilities and intersections that define our route of flight. We will choose the arrival procedure, select the right approach and pick the specific runway that will get us to our final destination.

That same detailed programming is required with the process of personal achievement. You have to take stock of where you are and determine where you want to go by defining your destination. You'll have to establish a way to get there by determining the specific steps that will have to be taken along the way. In effect, what you are doing is creating, the "way point" of "Vision."

When our programming is completed and our destination is defined, we then shift to the way point called "Focus." This is the process of studying, learning and attempting to predict all of the factors that could affect our flight. In the airplane, for example, we begin by studying the mechanics' log to educate ourselves about its current maintenance status and prior history. We then pull out our charts and review our route of flight. Even though we can't control it, we study the weather environment along the route because it can have a dramatic effect on the flight. The temperature at altitude will affect the power available from our engines. Headwinds will require more fuel and time and crosswinds can push us off course. And when you are flying at 10 miles a minute, being off course for only 5 minutes can have you 50 miles from where you need to be. We'll check for turbulence or thunderstorms that we need to avoid. And we'll check the weather conditions for landing to determine a backup plan if we have to proceed to an alternate destination.

David, to achieve success in business or in life you will also have to "Focus" on your organizational or personal "Vision" and closely scrutinize your plan. You'll have to study and educate yourself to determine what you'll have to do to achieve. Begin by accessing the things that you already have and then "Focus" to determine what else you will need. In business, you'll have to study the economic environment and try to predict the direction of the economy, interest rates and other factors over which you have no control. You'll have to identify the trends that might affect your business and how that might alter your plan. Who is your competition? What are their strengths and weaknesses and what are they likely to do in reaction to your moves? And, finally, what is your back up if things aren't happening the way you want them to? What is your alternate if, because of the environment or the competition, you have to change your plan?

In the airplane, we are finally ready to take off. But it is crucial that we use the correct runway, which will get us headed in the right direction. Using the proper runway gets us airborne in the shortest distance and insures that we gain altitude as soon as possible to avoid obstacles on the ground.

The same is true in life. It's critically important that we are mentally headed in the right direction. We insure that this happens by developing, what I call, the "way point" of a "Positive Attitude." A "Positive Attitude" enables us to keep things in the proper perspective and to see our challenges in their most favorable light. It helps us to maintain a positive outlook and to soar above the obstacles that we will most definitely face. A "Positive Attitude" keeps our feelings up and enables us to fly high rather than to sink low and risk a crash. A "Positive Attitude" is the jet fuel of your flight to success.

Back in the airplane, it's time to get things going. We have planned and studied and we know which way we are headed. Now we are ready to take "Action." We push up the power, set the thrust, pull back on the controls and get that giant metal bird into the air. We intercept the proper course and set the drift correction to counter the effects of the crosswinds we know we'll have. We then begin our climb to 41,000 feet.

Achieving great heights in life requires taking "Action," as well. In business you have got to overcome the inertia, and execute your plan.

For example, you may have to bring your product to market, tighten-up the distribution system, energize the sales force and insure that the customer is satisfied. In your personal endeavors, you have got to conquer the procrastination and do the things that will need to be done. Taking "Action" is the jet engine that gives you the power and propels you toward achieving your goals.

But no flight is ever perfect. You'll almost always have challenges to overcome. Turbulence, thunderstorms, mechanical or passenger problems will arise. But we don't let these obstacles stop us. Once we are airborne, we don't have the option of parking the airplane on the side of the road. We keep going because we are determined to get you to your destination. Now we may have to change altitudes. We may deviate to the left or to the right of the storm. Sometimes, we'll even have to penetrate the weakest part of the storm. But we do what we have to, to reach our final destination. This is the "way point" of "Determination."

Achieving, in business and in life requires that you develop that "Determination," as well. It requires that same persistence. It requires that dogged perseverance. It requires doing whatever is necessary to ultimately achieve your goals.

The final "way point" is "Belief." Having the "Belief" that something both can and will happen even when you don't know when, where or how. The experience of aviation, more so than anything else that most people do, so aptly illustrates this fact. Most people don't understand how an airplane flies. In fact, most think that it is utterly amazing that this huge mass of metal, heavier than air, can even make it off the ground. Yet when they get on that airplane, they believe that it will take off. And they believe that they can fly for hours and over thousands of miles and safely arrive at their final destination, and every time they do.

High achievers have that same self-confidence and that great personal "Belief." Even when the "how" is not clear, their "will" to succeed is 100% sure. The evidence is overwhelming. The research is clear. People, who believe that they will achieve, most often do. These are my "way points": Core Values, Vision, Focus, and Positive Attitude, Action, Determination and Belief. These are the "way points" of the "flight plan" of achievement and success.

Wright

It is clear to see how these concepts come together for the flight to success. Are all of the "way points" that you have described of equal emphasis or would you say that some qualities are of greater or particular importance?

Thompson

They are all very important because they are inextricably intertwined. They are logically sequenced, just like that airplane flight and build on each other like steppingstones. But I will emphasize the importance of "Determination" because I think it is a quality that we all intuitively have, although it sometimes manifests itself in a negative way. In its negative connotation, it evidences itself as stubbornness. The challenge is to transform and channel the stubbornness that we all sometimes have, into the positive quality of "Determination." You see, " Determination" is that mental toughness. It is that ability to "stick to" something. "Determination" is going the extra mile when you would really rather not. It's being professional at what you do even when you are having a "bad day." David, if you and your family were going on vacation and you came on board my airplane, wouldn't you want me to do my job in a professional manner? And you wouldn't care, nor should you care, that I had spilled coffee on my shirt, had a flat tire on the way to work and locked my keys in the car. Even though I would be having a terrible day, your expectation would rightfully be that I perform my job in a very professional way.

It has been said that some people are successful in life because they are destined to be. I can tell you from personal experience, that most people are successful in life because they are determined to be. All you have to do is look to history and you'll find numerous examples of people who through persistence, perseverance and sheer "Determination" have changed the world into what we know it as today. We can look to Nelson Mandela in politics, Walt Disney in business and entertainment or the Wright brothers in science and technology. These are all great examples of ordinary people who endured great personal hardship or tried and failed on numerous occasions before ultimately achieving monumental success.

Wright

You are absolutely right about that "T." In one of your magazine articles you said, "Achievement is self-sustaining, that it feeds on itself." How does that work?

Thompson

That quote came from a discussion on my "way point" of personal "Belief." As I've said, the evidence is clear that people, who believe that they will succeed, most often do. The research shows that strong personal "Belief" creates high self-esteem and people with high self-esteem have a tremendous degree of self-confidence. Self-confident people have usually already experienced success in some way or in some other endeavor. This is often the motivating factor for believing that they will succeed again. The more you achieve, the more you know you can achieve and the more you know you can achieve, the more you want to achieve. And that's what I mean by achievement being self-sustaining and feeding on itself.

Wright

As well as speaking, you have done organizational consulting, particularly at the senior executive and board level. Can you share with us what you feel are some of the key challenges facing business leaders today?

Thompson

David, there is the cacophony of external issues that we hear and read about every day; a sluggish economy affected by high energy prices, rising interest rates, the cost of homeland security, and the effect of terrorism because of the situation in the Middle East. And there are always the continuing internal challenges of increasing productivity, successfully integrating new technologies and effectively managing employees. In fact, the employee issue will be particularly challenging, especially as the economy begins to pick up steam. A recent survey conducted by Accenture reported that 50% of 500 middle managers polled were looking for or planned to look for new employment when the economy turns around. In a similar poll conducted by the Society for Human Resource Management, 83% of employees polled said they were likely to look for a new job when the job market got better. But I think that there are three key foundational issues that companies will have to address if they are to build successful, sustaining organizations.

The first issue is one that we have already touched on, but only from a personal perspective. It is just as important organizationally, however, and it is the issue of "Core Values." We find that many companies spend considerable time and effort creating mission and values statements. Unfortunately, these values are seldom integrated or infused into the organization's culture and norms. They are not monitored by boards of directors, practiced or implemented by management or adopted by employees. You will see senior executives taking huge bonuses while asking for sacrifices from frontline employees. And, of course, we are all familiar with the financial manipulations that have hurt employees and investors, alike. The tragic result of this failure to incorporate and live by worthy values produces the World Coms, the Enrons and the Tycos of corporate America. The connection between bankrupt values and bankrupt companies appears to be clear.

A second issue is what I call "Mission Alignment." This is the principal of understanding why and what you are in business for. Many companies fail to grasp this simple fact.

And the third issue is what I call "Congruency." This is the process, which insures that an organization's purpose, direction, plans and planning processes are synchronized in the most effective way.

Wright

Can you elaborate on "Mission Alignment" and "Congruency?"

Thompson

David, when I was in the Air Force, our mission was simple: To Fly, To Fight and To Win. Now the actual mission statement was a little longer than that, but this is what it essentially boiled down to. Now please note what the mission was not. For example, it was not to have the most advanced fighter in the world, though the Air Force did. The F-15, which was the best performing fighter ever built and is still the backbone of our fighter force, was just coming on line to replace the Vietnam era F-4. Interestingly though, the National Guard pilots, who were flying the F-4, often bested the active duty pilots who were flying the F-15 in mock dogfights. Why? Because many of the National Guard pilots had flown the F-4 in Vietnam and their superior skill and combat experience negated the F-15's technological advantage. So having the best fighter in the world did not necessarily guarantee mission accomplishment.

Now, I'll go into an organization and read the mission statement where a company wants to have the best bakery products in the business or build the greatest computers in the world or be the company of choice in one field or another. Statements about satisfying the customer often appear to be an afterthought, if they are even mentioned at all. Yet the customer is the boss and pleasing the customer has to be the core function of any business. This is fundamental and the only reason for a company's existence. A company will only become great by bringing superior value to the customer. It won't happen or be sustained by building a great organization or providing jobs or by positively impacting the communities they serve. None of these things can exist for long if you are not focused on providing superior service to the customer. So your mission statement, which is your reason for being, should be primarily "aligned" with the interest of the customer, and secondarily focused on building the organization to support this goal.

Now, "Congruency" simply means that your strategic plan should further your mission and your business plan should support your strategy. That is a very simple concept that most executives would agree with. But the implementation of this principal in an organization often proves very difficult.

It is not uncommon to find that the strategic plan encompasses elements or seeks to achieve objectives that have nothing to do with the mission and if followed would take the organization in a completely different direction. Yet, the test for "Congruency" of the plan is amazingly simple. You just ask the question, "How does this further our mission?" If you can't readily and easily answer that question, then you have got a problem with your strategic plan.

Sometimes the strategic plan is what I call a 3C; complicated, complex and convoluted. An organization's strategy should be simple, clear and easily understood. It should define where the business is now, where it is going and the route that it's going to take to get there. Again, I'll use the aviation flight plan to illustrate my point. The flight plan gives me a departure point. It lays out my route of flight and the way points that must be crossed. Finally, it gives me my arrival routing, which takes me to the final destination. It is clear and understandable. But just as important, it is usable and can be implemented. A good strategic plan should possess the same qualities.

The annual business plan should be "Congruent" with the organization's strategy. Very often, however, it is not. The chief reason for this incongruency is that the business plan, which I'll call BP1 is often driven by the budget process, which we will call BP2. And BP2 can be, and often is, arbitrary and unrealistic.

Think of BP1, the business plan as the plan for how the organization will actually move along the route of flight. This is the plan for how to go from way point A to way point B. But if BP2, which drives BP1, is arbitrary, it will have the effect of a strong crosswind, and can easily blow the organization off course.

The dictionary defines arbitrary as—*determined by individual preference rather than knowledge of the intrinsic nature of something.* Given that definition, let's look at how BP2 sometimes operates. The CEO or the senior management team decides that they will have to drive an earnings increase of 12% next year or increase fund raising by the same amount in the non-profit sector. This number may come from what the CEO feels is doable or in the public sector, what the CEO thinks the competition will do, or what Wall Street expects. A revenue target will be imposed and expenses will be adjusted by the rate of inflation. The pronouncement comes from above and all the business units will be tasked to meet the new goals. But often there is limited knowledge of the "intrinsic nature" of what each business unit can actually do and, no objective evaluation of whether the business can actually deliver on the plan. So because the budget process and the business plan are not "Congruent," it ultimately has a detrimental effect on the company's strategy.

Wright

It is clear that "Congruency," as you have explained it, is important. Would you say that it is one of the primary reasons that some organizations are more successful than others are?

Thompson

There is a lot of things that a company must do and do well to be successful. It clearly depends on the type of business and the things that must be done can range from research and development to marketing and sales. It is also critical to have not only good people, but the right people in the right positions, so the human resources function in the organization is key. But let me give you what admittedly is an overly simplistic example of the effects that a lack of "Congruency" can have to illustrate the point.

Let's say that we are looking at an Atlanta based company whose mission is transportation that represents superior value to the customer. They have traditionally been a ground transportation business, but have decided that some synergies and opportunities exist in aviation. They have also looked at different city pairs and decided that Atlanta-New York represents the greatest profit potential. So, in effect, they have developed the very basic components of their strategic plan. They know where they are, where they are going and how they are going to get there. Now let's overlay the business plan on the strategy. They will need to lease an airplane and some gate space and obtain some FAA approvals. They will need to negotiate with the airport authorities to secure their landing slots. They will need to contract for fuel, and buy food and other supplies. The CEO instructs the accounting department to begin to develop a budget and in this company, as in many, the budgeting process drives their business plan. The budget includes the airplane and gate space in Atlanta, but not enough funds for gate space in NY. There is money in the budget for food, but for only a limited amount of fuel. There is no money in the budget for the meteorological services necessary to track the wind and temperature conditions at altitude, which will affect both, time and fuel. And to top it off, your HR department hires a Captain, who is very experienced and extremely well thought of, but who has been piloting cruise ships for the past 20 years. What are the chances that this budget will help the company achieve its strategy? None. When the budget process is arbitrary and drives the business plan, it puts the organization's strategy at risk. So these are the types of issues that we can help companies work through.

Wright

So, in effect, you are helping an organization to undergo fundamental change. Do you find that to be a significant challenge? Aren't most organizations resistant to change?

Thompson

I have discovered over the years that the most effective way to get someone to change is to focus on the benefit or the value proposition associated with the change. The other important aspect associated with change is to make it as least disruptive or seamless as possible. I have also discovered that most people are really not afraid of change. But they are afraid of one or two things associated with change. The first thing that they are usually afraid of is that the change will leave them in a worse position than they were before. I don't know of too many people who are afraid of what they would consider to be positive change. There aren't too many people who would be upset if I took their 1985 Ford and gave them a 2005 Mercedes.

The second thing associated with change that people are afraid of is the process of change, not the change itself. They are afraid of what they will have to go through, even when the change itself is good.

I was sitting in the cockpit one day at LaGuardia airport. We were about to fly to Ft. Lauderdale and were going through our preflight procedures when this businesswoman stuck her head in to say hello. "Good morning, Captain," she said. I'm on my way to Florida with you because I'm going on a cruise. I'm really looking forward to it," she said. " I've been working on a business deal for the past 5 weeks without a day off and I'm really burned out. This cruise is just what I need." Then she said, "But I'm a very nervous flyer. I get terrified sitting in the back of a plane so I always come up to meet the crew because it helps to put me a little more at ease." We had a nice conversation about the flight, what we were going to do and what she could expect. She then went back to the cabin and, of course, made it through the flight.

Now the point of the story is this. The lady wasn't afraid of change. In fact, the change she sought, being on that cruise ship, was good. But the process of change, sitting in the back of that airplane for three and one half-hours, had her terrified, even though there was very little for her to worry about. When I am dealing with a client, I address and deal with these change issues right up front.

Wright

I understand that you will have a new book coming out next year entitled *Pilot Your Way to Success; A Flight Plan for Personal and Professional Achievement*. Can you tell more about it?

Thompson

Sure, David. The book essentially goes into depth and detail on the "way points" that I have mentioned today. Again, those principals or "way points" are Core Values, Vision, Focus, Positive Attitude, Action, Determination and Belief and the book approaches them from an aviation perspective. The book is somewhat biographical, totally informational and most importantly, gives the reader a clear plan to achieve personal, professional or organizational success. It is filled with great illustrative stories but more importantly, proven steps to help the reader achieve desired, concrete results. Feedback has been positive and we are very excited about the prospects.

Wright

We can't wait until it comes out. It has really been a privilege and a genuine pleasure talking to you. I have learned a lot about commercial aviation and the process of achieving success. I appreciate the time you have spent with me today and I hope we can do it again very soon.

Thompson

Thank you, David. I really enjoyed our conversation, as well.

Wright

Today we have been talking to William "T" Thompson. He is an airline captain, attorney, businessman, consultant and a powerful speaker. "T" speaks and consults to major corporations, government agencies and universities on leadership and the science of achievement. The best thing about "T" is that he speaks from a personal, diverse and unique perspective. Thank you "T" for taking the time to be with us on *Conversations On Success!*

Thompson

The pleasure was mine, David. Fly high, fly fast and fly safe.

About the Author

A dynamic and powerful speaker, William "T" Thompson has brought his message of achievement and success to thousands of people and organizations across the country. An expert, who speaks from experience, "T" is an accomplished businessman who has received many accolades and awards. He has been featured in numerous media outlets including the *Wall Street Journal* and was nominated for *Inc. Magazine's* Entrepreneur of the Year.

Currently a Captain for Delta Air Lines and an attorney, he was Commissioner of Aeronautics for Massachusetts for 18 years and was on the short list for Secretary of the Air Force. He has served on the board of directors of numerous for profit and not for profit organizations including the national board of the American Cancer Society, Northeast Health Systems, The Bank of New England and Eastern Bank.

He thrives on helping organizations achieve maximum results and individuals achieve their greatest potential.

William "T" Thompson

627 Belmont Crest Drive SE

Marietta, Georgia 30067-9124

Phone: 770.952.1813

Fax: 770.984.8736

Cell: 978.828.7307

Email: tairlaw@aol.com

Chapter Twenty

JOHN GRAY, PH.D.

THE INTERVIEW

David E. Wright (Wright)

John Gray, Ph.D., is the author of 15 best-selling books, including *Men Are from Mars, Women Are from Venus*, the number one best-selling book of the last decade. In the past ten years, over 30 million Mars and Venus books have been sold in over 40 languages throughout the world.

An expert in the field of communication, Dr. Gray's focus is to help men and women understand, respect and appreciate their differences in both personal and professional relationships. In his many books, CD's, DVD's, tapes, workshops and seminars, he provides practical tools and insights to effectively manage stress and improve relationships at all stages and ages by creating the brain chemistry of health, happiness and lasting romance.

Dr. Gray has appeared on *Oprah, The Today Show, CBS Morning Show, Good Morning America, The View, Politically Incorrect, Larry King,* and others. He has been profiled in *Newsweek, Time, Forbes, USA Today, TV Guide, People* and *New Age Journal,* among others.

In addition to being a Certified Family Therapist, Dr. Gray is a consulting editor of *The Family Journal,* and a member of the Distinguished Advisory Board of the International Association of

Marriage and Family Counselors. In 2001, he received the Smart Marriages Impact Award.

John, it seems like every time I turn around I see you or one of your exciting books or programs on television or on radio somewhere. What in the world have you been up to lately?

John Gray (Gray)

One of the secrets of success is to always have many goals; it seems very natural to me. I'm always staying in touch with what's important to me and continuing to stretch myself and as I've gotten older in my 50s, one of the things that's interested me most is staying healthy and vibrantly healthy. I see so many of my friends waking up with aches and pains and getting sick and some even at this age starting to die which is absurd because our body lifespan should be 120 years. So I've been focusing on helping myself and others stay young and healthy.

I've found that the secret of health is learning to produce an abundant supply of brain chemicals. As we get older we tend to produce less dopamine in the brain if you're men and tend to produce seratonin in the brain if your women. In terms of my expertise and gender differences, this was very fascinating to me because when you start producing healthier amounts of brain chemicals your stress hormone, cortisol, begins to come back into balance. For most people, as they get older, the stress hormone becomes elevated and that inhibits digestion, inhibits the immune system and so forth.

So I've spent about the last 10 years developing a nutritional profile for men and for women which is unique and different to help balance brain chemicals which certainly makes their relationships more passionate and interesting over time. Also it makes the body healthier.

Wright

Before we dive into your latest projects, I want to talk with you about some of the big picture issues surrounding your life. People all across America are looking for ways to be successful. You turned your first book into an industry in of itself. Did you ever imagine things turning out the way they did when you wrote your first book *Men are from Mars and Women from Venus*?

Gray

No, I could never imagine how many things were going to happen as a result of that. I did think that that particular book was going to be a big bestseller and was going to touch the lives of millions of people. Already I had been doing the work for over 10 years on gender differences and felt the book would be very successful since my seminars had been very successful. But it's certainly gone beyond my imagination.

Wright

Looking back are there some success principles that you've relied on as you built your career and things our readers would enjoy hearing about?

Gray

Well, I think for me the number one thing is to be true to myself. Always do that which I love to do, that which is most interesting to me, that which excites me in term of my passion. It doesn't mean that everything along that pathway is enjoyable. I mean, there's sacrifices you make, there's bumps on the road, but you feel the truth in your heart that this is what you're here to do and you just keep following that.

I remember a famous artist who once was quoted this way, he was saying that an artist came to him and showed him his work and said, "Well, do you think I have what it takes to be an artist?" And the famous artist replied, "If there's a choice, then don't bother being an artist."

As you become more in touch with who you are by being authentic in your life, what occurs is, while you're free to be yourself because you're now choosing your life, you're making choices based upon what's important to you instead of what's important to other people, you have this freedom which can create a tremendous amount of stress because you have more choices – stress always arises when you have more choices – and feelings of regret certainly emerge when you have more choices. But excitement and passion can arise when you're coming from a place of choice.

As you come closer to really your true self, however, you find that really you find that you have no choice. You really have to do what you have to do and that's what you're here to do in this world. When you find that place, there's always passion and you love what it is that you do, particularly in terms of the outcome.

First you imagine yourself achieving your goal and just feel the passion and the joy and happiness that comes from achieving that goal; that's what feeds you. Gradually, as you get closer and discipline yourself to do those things necessary to achieve your goals, those things that sometimes you don't like to do become just as enjoyable because you're aware that they're necessary to achieve that goal.

It looks like this: I'll be flying to South Africa in a couple of weeks. The thought of flying to London and then South Africa – maybe an 18 or 20-hour journey in an airplane – is certainly going to be compromising to my health, which is something very important to me, it's not very fun, etc., etc. But when I think about being able to help a whole segment of society I've never been to and the plan and program which is waiting for me and what a difference I'll be making for these people, that's very exciting to me.

I think this trip can be a negative or a positive because it's bringing me closer to that goal and I can make it very enjoyable. I can bring books to read, I can take the time for myself, and I can pack some extra nutritional goodies to take along the way. I can make sure I take along ingredients for a salt-water bath for use when I get there to help wash away some of the radiation from being in the plane. I can make this really fun. By adjusting my attitude I have just made the trip a complete win.

Even during this process I already know that life always has its little bumps along the way but those bumps are there to just challenge us and help us recommit ourselves to our goals. Often people say, "Oh, I want something," and that's what I want to accomplish, that they really don't have strength around that. It's the challenges; it's the disappointments that really build the strength. It's like if you want muscle strength you have to go to the gym, that's always one way to do it, and you challenge those muscles and those muscles will grow stronger.

People who have bigger goals will tend to have more challenges. Fewer "big goals" will have less challenges and that's a choice we make.

Wright

I have to admit that I'm one of your web site junkies just to see what's going on. I get so much free information there too. I was visiting your web site recently – the www.marsvenus.com -- and it is really loaded with some great stuff. The first thing that caught my eye was the 9 Day Relationship Makeover. Could you tell us a little bit about that?

Gray

Having been a teacher of personal growth for 35 years, I put all that together in a "blue box," I call it. It's a 9 Day Relationship Makeover and you can do it in nine days or you can do it in nine weeks. It's a series of videotapes or DVDs and CDs with talks. I've edited my best talks – they're very entertaining and fun – and they all focus on how our relationships can stimulate the production of dopamine in the brain for men and seratonin for women to increase our sense of passion and happiness in life and, in addition, to create lasting romance. Then I included nine different CDs which you take turns using and playing before you go to bed at night. They are guided visualizations which ask certain questions to stimulate different parts of your brain that need to be awakened and stimulated if we're not to grow older.

People don't realize that men always start out with bigger brains than women but when men die, their brains have shrunk smaller than women's. The adage is true: if we don't use it, we lose it. This is true for both men and women – that there is more brain shrinkage – but it's just more in men. It's important that we stimulate the brain.

I've developed these exercises to stimulate the brain as well to produce more dopamine and seratonin an endorphins in the brain which are the important brain chemicals for happiness, well being and health. They are goal-setting exercises, they're reflective exercises on issues in the past, on how we can do things differently, they challenge your thinking on things. But they're done very easily and in a very relaxed manner. People enjoy them.

There are those which I have developed over the years and put into the "blue box" and then there are three DVDs wherein I explain the relationship of food to healthy brain chemistry; to brain chemistry as it relates to romance and sex, as well as how our relationships are affected by what we eat and how we exercise.

Then I have two DVDs on really super simple exercises that are designed to stimulate brain chemicals in the brain that stimulate health in the body by oxygenating the cells and stimulating fat burning which most exercise neglects to do, which is why most exercise doesn't help people who are overweight lose weight. People who use this program will tend to lose weight very quickly as well but it's done in a whole new and different way.

We have brain-boosting exercises that help stimulate spinal flexibility in a rhythmic motion. We have glandular stimulation to increase the amount of hormones in our body – another important principle for slowing down the aging process, or restoring normal aging, let's put it that way.

This is the whole program. There's a little diet book for people to follow and what I do is help restore sanity to people's lives in terms of their eating program which is to give up all diets basically. I point out a few important points that show people how to eat reasonably. There are a few foods out there that taste really good but that are very, very toxic to the system; I explain that as well.

There are just a few things to either minimize or give up. One example of that would be a diet drink. Diet drinks have never been proven to help anybody lose weight and, particularly for women, the sweetener, aspartame, lowers seratonin levels. Women already have low seratonin levels, the cause of the majority of the stress in their lives, so drinking diet drinks will just cause more stress, more food cravings and won't help lose weight at all.

I give a few tips like that but basically I explain to people how to balance their diet just with proteins, carbohydrates and fats and point out how women's bodies are different than men's, so we can make a few intelligent choices based upon that difference as well. Men typically need to take in a bit more protein; women typically need to take in a bit more of the good fats. I talk about what are the good fats, the good carbohydrates and the good proteins.

So, that's the Nine-day Relationship Makeover, it's a very exciting program and what I do is present one of the centerpieces of how to provide the extra nutritional support to promote dopamine and seratonin in the brain so that we feel healthier and happier. This centerpiece is a super nutritious, delicious smoothie to be added as a supplement to your regular diet every day to replace breakfast or any other meal. I include all the ingredients for the smoothie in the blue box with the Nine-day Relationship Makeover because people were saying it's too hard to get all the ingredients. It can now just be ordered. The cost is less than about $2 to $3 per day. You'll save money on your food bill but you get all the nutrition you need which will take away food cravings and help you lose weight very quickly if you need to lose weight, build muscle mass if you need to increase weight and the same program does it – it just gives your body what it needs for your body to do what it needs to do to heal itself and to stay young and healthy.

Wright

My wife and I are both dieting and we're having some real success. At my age, health has become a real priority topic. I noticed a link on your web site to Mars Venus Health for Happiness and Romance. You have to ask my wife about the romance department, but I could stand a little more happiness. Could you tell us about this project?

Gray

The wellness project is at my ranch in Northern California in Mendocino. It's about three and a half hours north of San Francisco. I have a wellness center and I teach weekend seminars (three-day) or five-day seminars. At these seminars we serve people gourmet food. It's in a beautiful setting surrounded by a million acres of redwood forest, and it's a thousand feet up along the California coastline. It's absolutely a stunning and beautiful setting.

I teach the various oxygenation exercises – fat burning exercises – together. We do emotional exploration work as well. There's a lot of information about health, wellness and relationships presented. Half the time we spend at the spa. We have a special oxygen spa which is one of a kind. It's taken me the last five years to build and develop. What it does is to help oxygenate the body so that the cells can regenerate themselves. This year, after the first treatment I had at this spa – the first five-day course I taught – all my allergies went away! That was amazing to me. It just seems so normal now it didn't seem like a dramatic change except that now I don't have to take allergy medicines or nutritional support because of allergies; it was just gone in one week.

We have people coming up there with all kinds of sicknesses and they find dramatic improvement in just three or four days of the oxygen treatments.

There used to be about 50 percent oxygen in the air. In Antarctica you can measure the ice from 1,000 years ago and find air pockets that will show the measurement of oxygen in the air back then. About 100 years ago it was around 35 percent, so it is lessening. Now, in the forest, it's down to 23 percent. In cities it's down to 17 percent. On a bad day in cities like Tokyo it can be as low as seven percent oxygen in the air. Oxygen is really the only nutrient we can't live without; it's so, so important. It helps the body to activate every cellular activity necessary and it gives the body energy to operate. When the body doesn't get enough oxygen, then to get energy, it requires more sugar. Then the body goes into what's called "sugar-burning mode." To get energy from sugar you don't need oxygen in the muscles. But, unfortunately, this is just a back-up system the body has in case there's not enough oxygen. The brain requires sugar and that's very healthy but it's not healthy when the muscles burn sugar. When the muscles burn sugar the byproduct is excessive acid which then gets stored as fat which is why so many people become fat as they get older, around the gut or in the thighs. These are places where the body will try to store that excess acid because acid irritates the body and blocks oxygenation of the cells. The cells need oxygen to produce energy and do their jobs.

A German scientist who discovered this process and I convinced him to come to America and help me build my spa. It's quite amazing. We have these large hot tubs that are filled with oxygenated water. One is a "lithium pool" with minerals, particularly lithium. Millions of people go to healing places like Lourdes in France every year. We measured the water there and found a high content of lithium. Lithium is a brain mineral that helps the brain stay relaxed. We oxygenate our lithium pool which causes the body to release massive amounts of toxins while it oxygenates and rejuvenates the cells. We have a salt-water pool to which iodine is added. The Romans used to add kelp, which has a high iodine content, to their salt-water baths. We've improved on this and added the oxygenation. In our oxygenated baths, the body begins absorbing extra oxygen that it's been missing so it can do its natural healing process. It literally reverses the aging process. People look younger, feel younger, they can safely go off their drugs and medications quite rapidly. Diabetics notice their blood sugar balancing; people with hypertension find their blood pressure returns to normal; cholesterol levels go down in literally a matter of a few hours. We've done tests on our oxygenated water and found that in one hour your cholesterol level come down 30 points.

This is a phenomenal health break-through. We have steam rooms where we pipe in oxygenated steam. We use crystal benches and tables for people to sit so their bodies go into more of a harmonic resonance with the earth's frequency. This can be compared to if you were to spend a month on a mountain. Your body feels so much healthier because you're in the frequencies of nature as opposed to on concrete. The body requires resonant frequencies to do its job so we provide ways to accomplish this. We have low heat, infrared saunas in cabins which are oxygenated. We have an oxygen dome where people lie on a crystal table. There's red light therapy – we use different kinds of light therapy on the body to stimulate cell regeneration. When people need to lose a lot of weight, they lose weight so quickly that we put them on the crystal table to help stimulate cell regeneration so that the skin is not hanging down when they lose four to five pounds in a day. It's quite phenomenal. We have a crystal chamber that includes oxygen mists, we have oxygen showers, oxygen bathhouses, and we have public baths with just pure highly oxygenated water that helps to detoxify the body.

This is quite amazing – after I had gone through this process many times the ring on the tub was about three inches wide and it was all some kind of blue, oily substance that had come out of my body which was actually some heavy metals gradually being taken out of the brain. As they get older, most people get Alzheimer's which is the result of aluminum poisoning and heavy metals that go into the brain. This is also true for children with autism. Children are very susceptible to the heavy pollution around us which will also cause brain problems. We also find this kind of toxicity when we get vaccinations and shots which all contain heavy metals.

The body is designed to get rid of those metals and toxins as long as it gets enough oxygen, the right kind of exercise and the right kind of nutrition. We teach people how to do that, we provide this wonderful oxygen therapy and the entire experience is an excellent vacation.

One of the simple tests we give to people when they first arrive is a blood oxygen level. In a few days we do another test and they can see how it has come up to normal. What would happen on a normal three- or four-week vacation is achieved in three or four days.

Wright

In everything I read, scientists say every cell in the human body regenerates or renews itself in different cycles but each is completed within seven years, so why do we get old?

Gray

That's exactly right, why don't we regenerate healthy cells? And the reason for that is DNA becomes damaged through oxidation. This means we don't get enough oxygen to our cells and the damage continues. One of the most damaging factors to the body is chlorine; people are drinking it every day, they're taking showers in it. Maybe a little chlorine here and there wouldn't be so damaging but every day we're being exposed to this irritant. It damages the cells, irritates the body which then tries to protect itself by producing cholesterol and this is why people will tend to have high cholesterol levels. Certainly cholesterol is involved with heart disease but it's not the cause. The cause is the chlorine and the body's healing mechanism is designed to produce more cholesterol which eventually turns to plaque which can cause strokes. We can get to the real cause of the problem by eliminating chlorine which means getting water filters and drinking purified water. Very soon, at the marsvenus site I will have available the Marsvenus Oxygenated Water. In the meantime, one company that carries the best water I've been able to find is a company called Aquarius Water – www.aquariuswater.org. That water is so pure and so oxygenated that just by drinking a couple of liters a day your cholesterol levels begin coming down right away. Now, that's just by drinking the water. If you have normal cholesterol the levels will stay fine.

This is a wonderful alternative for people and it's been exciting for me to teach people about the importance of oxygenating exercises that are included in the blue box. This includes the importance of getting Omega-3 essential fatty acids. Your Omega-3 used to be in milk, in cow's meat but when the cows are fed corn and grain instead of grass, what occurs is the animals stop making Omega-3 essential fatty acids. These acids are vital for the production of brain chemicals. They're actually what are called "oxygenated fat lipids." So, again the fat, which is oxygenated, is most the most important to the body. As we've found, the lower the oxygen intake into the body the higher the chances of creating all kinds of health crises.

Wright

I see you do some relationship testing. How does that work and how do people benefit?

Gray

There again, I think that's one of the activities shown on the web site. In the testing available there, if you're single you can help identify your priorities and the type of relationship you want. The test can help you become aware of what's important to you, who you are, how you're different from others, what your values are, what your goals are, and what your likes and dislikes are. As you become sharpened by just taking time to look at the answers to the questions we ask, what occurs is that your mind now becomes sharper and you begin to look for what you really want. You begin to feel more motivated to achieve what you want. You begin finding clever strategies to get what you need. You begin understanding why things work for you and why other things don't work for you.

A tremendous amount of insight results from taking 10 or 15 minutes to take one of these tests. You can then gain self-reflection. I think the wisdom of the ages has always been "know thyself." Some people think, "I know who I am, I know my name," but "to know thyself" is to know how you are unique, to know how you are different from others, to know how you are like others, to know how you relate to others, to know your place in the universe, how you're here to contribute, to know what your needs are, to know what other people's needs are which are different from yours. It's all about knowing who you are and how you fit in with others, to knowing how you are seen by others, to recognize how you are needed in this world.

As you get to the truth of these different answers, you're sense of well-being dramatically increases. It's a wonderful, wonderful process. It's a life unfolding process and from time to time this kind of evaluation is important to do. About once a month I'll do some exploration – take time out to explore where I am in my life, what my goals are, and what my needs are. Each day, of course, to some extent I'm doing that. It's a discipline of learning to continue developing an awareness of who you are and how you fit in.

Wright

What an interesting time. I always enjoy talking with you John. I know you're busy and I've got to let you go.

Gray

It's such a pleasure to talk with you and what where we've just arrived is one of the fundamentals of success – recognizing that life is an ongoing process of self-discovery and exploration and learning.

There are three things that actually stimulate cellular growth in the brain: The most important is learning. If you're on a learning curve and you're learning new things you actually grow brain cells. Most people don't grow new brain cells. As people grow older their brain cells are dying and their brains are shrinking. Not everybody, however. My brain is growing and your brain can grow. If you're on a learning curve, you're passionate, you're interested in new things, then that always stimulates brain cell growth which is always going to stimulate health.

The second thing is pleasure. If you're doing things that are pleasurable to you, that will stimulate brain growth.

The third thing that stimulates brain growth is pain – not that you do things that are painful but that you challenge yourself. There'll always be some frustration, there'll be some anxiety, there'll be some emotional reactions to life but the difference is that you're able to feel it and release it. That's the key to it – is to be able to feel the natural pain of life and then release them. Anyone who is conscientious has to feel pain sometimes because the world is a mess. When you put your attention on some of the problems of the world you feel that pain and then you release it through compassion and motivation to do something about it.

Many people medicate themselves to feel numb so they're not interested in anything new, they just watch television shows, they eat themselves into numbness so that they don't feel the frustration in their lives. They feel if they're not making a difference in the world and they're numb they can't feel great pleasure either, nor can they feel accomplishment, achievement, sharing, loving, giving and receiving and all those wonderful things that are part of life.

Children are so good at those positive things; they can't manage themselves but at least they're in touch with the authenticity of how they feel. That's a big part of feeling healthy and young and that's what I help people to relearn what to do at my wellness seminars. They relearn how to be in touch with their feelings and how to achieve their goals and managing their live while also staying young and healthy which is the spa aspect of it.

So you can see I'm very passionate about all that I do and I think that is the key, over and over – being true to yourself, keeping the passion, staying dedicated, and working hard. That is the key to success.

Wright

We've been speaking with relationship expert and best-selling author, Dr. John Gray. John, you just can't imagine how much I appreciate you spending this much time with me on *Conversations on Success*.

Gray

I look forward to doing it again. I love sharing with you and I invite people to come to my web site www.marsvenus.com and explore more all the information we were just talking about.

About The Author

John Gray, Ph.D., is the author of 15 best-selling books, including **Men Are from Mars, Women Are from Venus**, the number one best-selling book of the last decade. In the past ten years, over 30 million Mars and Venus books have been sold in over 40 languages throughout the world.

An expert in the field of communication, Dr. Gray's focus is to help men and women understand, respect and appreciate their differences in both personal and professional relationships. In his many books, CD's, DVD's, tapes, workshops and seminars, he provides practical tools and insights to effectively manage stress and improve relationships at all stages and ages by creating the brain chemistry of health, happiness and lasting romance.

Dr. Gray has appeared on *Oprah, The Today Show, CBS Morning Show, Good Morning America, The View, Politically Incorrect, Larry King*, and others. He has been profiled in *Newsweek, Time, Forbes, USA Today, TV Guide, People* and *New Age Journal*, among others.

In addition to being a Certified Family Therapist, Dr. Gray is a consulting editor of *The Family Journal*, and a member of the Distinguished Advisory Board of the International Association of Marriage and Family Counselors. In 2001, he received the Smart Marriages Impact Award.

Dr. Gray lives with his wife and three children in Northern California.

Dr. John Gray

www.marsvenus.com

Chapter Twenty-One

ART DOAKES

THE INTERVIEW

David E. Wright (Wright)

We're talking to Arthur Clifton Doakes Jr. Art is an International Certified Chemical Addictions Counselor. Art has devoted his life to serving mankind. He is a decorated military veteran, school counselor, coach, community activist and more. He hosts radio and TV Talk shows providing solutions to real life issues. This dynamic, highly sought after keynote speaker and trainer holds a Master's Degree in Divinity and Christian Psychology, a B.A. in Behavior Science and an A. A. S. in Optometric Technology.

Art is a devout husband and a father of four daughters and holds the distinction of being a key member of the Les Brown Speaker's Network. Arthur, welcome to *Conversations on Success*.

Art Doakes (Doakes)

Thank you, David.

Wright

Art, what do contribute to your having become a Motivational Speaker?

Doakes

Definitely it is the desire to really deliver a message. I realized this when I was about 11 or 12 years old. I was having a conversation with my mother and she was comforting me during a tough time. I was feeling down on myself at the time. You see, I'm one of 10 children and all of my brothers and sisters are very talented. I felt that I didn't get any of the skills that they had received. My oldest brother Greg, is able to configure just about anything with electronics, and lettered in 4 sports while in High School. My oldest sister, Jean, is a masterful storyteller and a teacher extraordinaire. She also was an outstanding athlete in high school and college. My brother Carl, speaks about 6 different languages, is a master chef, and yes, you guessed it a great athlete and student. My sister Debbie could do it all; she is movie star pretty, and Einstein intelligent. My brother Rodney is a jack of all trades, and a master communicator. My younger sisters Madelyn, Patty, Aretha, and Stacey are equally talented. Madelyn is the greatest organizer you ever met, Patty is an accomplished Pianist and Aerobics Instructor, Aretha can draw anything in sight and teach you how to do it too, and Stacey can excel in anything she touches. I felt like I didn't measure up. I played a lot of sports and did well in school, but that just wasn't enough for me. I wanted to find my niche. My mother looked at me and said these words to me: *"Son you've got something that none of the others have." "What's that," I asked with tears welling up in my eyes. Little did I know at the time that her next words would change my life.* Mom said, "Son, you have the ability to share a message of hope and encouragement, to empower people to become the best that they can be!" The rest of this story is penned in my book, *"When God Calls" He Says Come Hear!*

Wright

Wow, Art that's quite a story. I have to ask you, what was it like for you growing up in the sixties?

Doakes

First, let me say that we had lots of fun. Being 1 of 10 children certainly has its advantages as well as its challenges. I'm the 6th of 10, so there I was right in the middle.

We had a lot of chores to do and being in the middle I got pressure from both ends. My older siblings passed some of their chores down to me and made sure that I did them, while the younger ones sort of depended on me to keep the heat off of them. We knew the bread man, the milkman, the grocer, mail man, and all other delivery persons. Yes, that's right, I did say milkman. You see, I grew up in the sixties and seventies, and that's how things were. I learned first hand about racial discrimination and prejudice. You learned to pay close attention to your surroundings and develop a keen sense of awareness. One of the best things I remember about my youth was our close family ties. My mother would teach us constantly; everything we did revolved around an educational process. We would develop our own games and they motivated us to utilize mathematical, spelling, and comprehension skills to be competitive. We shared many hours helping others, which I believe has made the most impact on my life today! I knew at a very early age that there was something special for me to do, I just didn't know what, where, or how to do it. My brothers and sisters set great examples for me by excelling in academics as well as athletics.

We later moved to Chambersburg, Pa., where I graduated high school. It was there that I began to develop the skills and talents that were given to me at birth by my mother and father. So growing up for me was a great experience and I honestly believe that my upbringing has helped me develop into the person that I am today.

Wright

Art this keeps getting better and better! It's obvious that your family has greatly impacted you. Who else has played a major role in your life?

Doakes

Yes my family has had and still does have a tremendous impact on my life. There are so many others I could name, and it would probably take up two or three books (Smile!). My mother would have to be number one, though. The reason is she never, ever quit. My mother is relentless at getting a job done. She has this saying, "Where there is a way, there's a will." I would say to her; "No mom, you mean where there's a will there's a way." She'd respond, "No son, where there's a way there's a will. You see if there's a way to get something done, I will find it out!" That statement changed my life and still has a fresh impact on me today. I believe that there is a way to do whatever God has given us to do. **Philippians 4:13 says, "I can do all things through Christ who strengthens me."**

Next, would be my father. He overcame many obstacles, is a decorated United States Marine, and treats everybody better than they treat him! That, David, is real impact. Now there are those like Nelson Mandela whose stand for justice is arguably unparalleled and Dr. MLK Jr., who labored for all mankind. Dr. Robert Schuller and Dr. Norman Vincent Peale, whose contributions to Positive Thinking and Possibility Thinking have inspired me to go deeper within my own personal belief system and emerge with hidden treasures. Those are some of the many people that I haven't had the opportunity to meet, though one day I do hope to meet with Dr. Schuller and be on his Hour of Power broadcast. I remember my elementary teachers in 2nd and 3rd grade, Ms. Ruda and Ms. Hofner, who treated me with such kindness and believed in me. My middle school English teacher Mrs. Anderson helped bring out the communicator in me. My athletic coaches who pushed me to accomplish more than I thought I could or wanted to try. I can remember playing basketball, baseball, football, and track and the coaches John Burgoon, Dick Nye, Barry Purvis, and others would push me to no end. I developed such a tenacious competitive spirit to do my best, and it is still with me to this day. There were many times that I got very discouraged and wanted to give up, but I would hear the words of those who inspired me to keep going, just echoing in the heart of my mind. I'm glad that I listened.

Wright

Art, now that's impact! What do you do when discouragement strikes, as it sometimes does?

Doakes

Yes it does. It's tough sometimes, and after you put your head down and cry and ask, "why me," you then reach down on the inside and you look for the number one reason why you're here. I had to ask myself that so many times, "Why are you here Art?" Strangely enough I really began to look for the answer. The answer is I'm here to be the best son that I can be to my mother and father. I'm here to be the best sibling that I can be to my brothers and sisters, the best friend to my friends, the best husband to my wife and the best father to my children. When I've accomplished this, I will be the best person that God has created me to be to serve my fellow man. When I get discouraged I look back at those reasons and those reasons empower me. It is this type of empowerment that enables me to press through even the darkest moments. I believe that you must have dreams to fight through discouragements. An old German Proverb says, *"A dream grants what one covets while awake."* So I would say to those who face discouraging moments, "Stop and look at your situation. Know that it is not as bad as it seems at the moment. You will get through it. Tap into your passion; focus on all the good things and people around you. Know that it's the rain that gives the sun a reason to shine and cause your life's garden to flourish." Say to yourself, "I have greatness within me and I will overcome this." Help somebody and help yourself. Always know that there are those who are worse off than you are. Your best days are ahead of you. You have too much time invested in your dream. Keep the fire burning! Get around people who celebrate you and your dreams. Plunge into something bigger than your situation and be thankful it is you and not your loved ones who are struggling. Yes, that's right, in all things give thanks! I have found that this last one really helps you fight off life's greatest challenges.

I recall a very discouraging time in my life when I took a $50,000 hit! Yes that's right $50,000! I had used my good name and reputation to help someone fulfill their dreams. It ended up costing me nearly twice my annual salary. I had to repay all those who invested in me to help someone else. That was a tough time for me. It was hard to give thanks during those days. Tough as it was, I did it. And to my surprise, soon I was in position to earn that same $50,000 on a monthly basis! Unbelievable wouldn't you say? That is what happens when you align yourself with those who can inspire you and believe in you and your dreams. Find your passion and your dream, and then watch your team appear. So when discouragements come, and they will, keep on moving. It was Will Rogers who said, "Even if you're on the right track, you'll get run over if you just sit there."

I hope this helps all of you reading this right now as much as it helped me.

Wright

I felt the passion in you come to life. Could you elaborate on PASSION?

Doakes

Sigh.... PASSION, to me is very personal. I really take this word to heart. Each letter stands for something special. I say that PASSION is a PERSONAL, ATTRIBUTE SECRETLY, STATED, IN, OBVIOUS, NORMALCY! I believe that what you do every day is a strong indication to where your strengths lie. I find that passion is something that most of us think is just a burning thought or a desire to do something. Those that truly focus in on their passion find this hidden secret. Passion becomes the thing that wakes us up in the morning. It is what we love to do so much that we would do it seven days a week, and do it for free. Since we love it so much, we do it so well, that people are willing to pay us for it. John Lancaster Spalding said, "What we love to do we find time to do." For me it is speaking. I would speak to dogs and cats and anybody that would listen to me. I just have a passion to speak, and I love it. I have and still do speak a lot for free, but one day someone heard me speak and decided to offer me some financial compensation for my encouraging words. Isn't that an awesome opportunity to get paid for what you love to do? That is the epitome of PASSION! Passion is also an opportunity to find your niche. The love of family and friends has inspired me to develop a burning desire to find my niche in life. People ask me all the time, "Art how can I find my niche?"

I teach several workshops on **Pursuing Your Passion, Investing In Your Passion, Producing Your Passion, Promoting Your Passion, and Perfecting Your Passion.**

There are (3) main keys to developing this type of self-knowledge. First, be fully persuaded. Second, Get Committed People Around You. Third, Keep Your Eves Moving On Your Vision. Passion will mean something different to each individual; however the outcome will be the same for all of us. You can see that I love to talk about this subject called PASSION. This is the reason that I've devoted an Entire Tape Series on the Matter. Everyday I breathe a new breath of air I become more passionate about life.

"Passionate people prevail." **Art Doakes**

Wright

Art, I'm impressed with your level of passion. Tell us, what you think life would be like if you were not pursuing your passion?

Doakes

I honestly believe that life would be motionless. I would imagine myself as one stuck in a rut and couldn't get out because of a lack of motivation. If Art Doakes were not speaking to empower others he would be miserable. Henry David Thoreau said, "Oh to reach the point of death, only to realize that you haven't yet lived!" Living without passion is not living in my book. Passion is like the pot of gold at the end of the rainbow, the silver lining in the cloud, the cherry on top of a sundae, and the icing on the cake! Passion is the highest level of inspiration known to mankind. It is my firm belief that inspiration without education leads to frustration! Those who live without passion have not taken the time to educate themselves on the areas of their dreams. I come to the conclusion that in life we're either in the way or on the way. Those who live with passion are on their way to greatness. I know from experience that you beat 50% of the people just by showing up. You beat another 40% by working hard. The last 10% is going to be won by who wants it the most—it's a true dogfight! Passionate People plan so that they don't fail. The reverse is true for those without passion; they fail to plan.

Wright

Folks, now that's passion. Art, a man told me many years ago that a rut is a grave with both ends kicked out. What do you say to those who are stuck in the rut of life?

Doakes

That's a good question. I go back to that individual and ask, "What is it that you really want to do? What will make you get up and move?" You know Francis Bacon said, "A wise man will make more opportunity than he finds." I try to find an opportunity in that individual to stimulate them. I have a quote for people in a rut, "When I invest in my passion it stimulates my hunger and raises my level of expectation, and enhances my performance." When we stimulate ourselves, creative juices begin to flow and opportunities arise all around us. Getting out of the rut of life takes commitment to ones goals. Write down your goals; make a list of those who can help you. List three reasons and three ways you can and need help. You see, you must know that your rate of return will equal your level of commitment and conviction. Time well spent committing to your goal and being convinced it's worth it pays great dividends. Life is full of people who have turned lemons into lemonade. I like the challenge of people who are in a rut. I use deliberate tactics to unleash their hidden potentials. I become constantly tenacious to find something that will motivate a person. Remember the bible story of King David? He was old and on his deathbed. His people wanted to bring him a young virgin to comfort him. Nothing would move the king. He was then told that the Ark of the Covenant was taken from Israel. Fire was lit and he arose from his bed, summonsed his Armour bearer and was ready to go to war! There was a great man, a King, Warrior, great leader, stuck in a rut and giving up his life. He turned it all around when he heard of the Ark being stolen. He was passionate about his conviction to his God! Show me a person's greatest desire, and I'll show you how to stimulate them to action and get out of the rut of life. Sometimes in life it may take a team of people to get you out of the rut. These people are your Dream Team. King David had this kind of team at his side when he returned to his passion. This is what we all can expect to happen when we are stimulated to action and Pursue Our Passion.

Wright

Art, you've got me motivated now! How do I find my Dream Team?

Doakes

First you must believe in the Dream, and want help from the Team. *The Dream Team* is comprised of those people around you that will inspire you, and not let you quit on yourself. There are a lot of battery drainers out there waiting to smash your dream. These are the ones that will always pull you down, and away from your dream. My friend Melvin Colbert calls them Dream Smashers! Now the *Dream Team* are those folks that you can align yourself with, they are doing what you want to do. They will encourage you to do it too. These people will take the time to show you how to alleviate some of the negativity and the problems that you may encounter. These are people that are committed to the commitment of helping you. Sometimes the team may be family members, friends and co-workers. I believe that 90% of the people on your team to be, you haven't even met yet. You need people who will cheer you on, others will constantly push you to achieve more, still others will provide you with information you need, some will just be there to comfort you, while still others will be there to guide you and mentor you. I developed a Master Mind Group. I used to see myself talking to the likes of Martin Luther King Jr., Nelson Mandela, and Malcolm X. These were men who developed a passion of serving people and enhancing the lives of humanity. Once I developed the character of these great men in my mind, I began to call forth my **Dream Team!** You will need different people to help you with a multiplicity of tasks and challenges. You'll have to sacrifice a lot to develop your dream team.

Take the time to wisely choose them and be specific when it comes to the role that they will fulfill on your team. Get as many experts as you can because they will find the time to help you help yourself. They will also challenge you to achieve far greater goals than you ever imagined possible. Know this; they are waiting for you to contact them! *In the multitude of counsel there is WISDOM!*

Les Brown is my speaking mentor. **Melvin Colbert** is my compass man. **Cynthia Hargis** is my professional counseling advisor. **Chy and Wade Stewart** are my Dream Sharers. **Arthur L. Andrews and John Nani** are speakers who share ideas and concepts with me. **Bishop T. D. Jakes** provides spiritual guidance. **Gary Johnston and Carl Chubb** are my prayer partners. **Dwayne Kilgo** is my production engineer. **Melissa Smith** is my graphic designer. **William Frazer** is my technology support. **Robert Perry, Edward Charles Jones, William Dickerson, James & Laurabelle Hope, James Tazwell, Mike Robinson, Robert Williams,** and their families provide encouragement. **Donna Satchell, Mark Garrett, Roy Smoothe** and **Jason & Janantha Pollock** are business colleagues. **Mike Hall, 5 Time World Super Heavy Weight Power Lifting Champion**, helps keep me physically fit and strong. **My wife Karen is my biggest supporter and comforter, her contributions are priceless and too numerous to count! My daughters DaRue, Shannon, Jasmine and Shamariah,** *give me hope, inspiration, purpose, and love*.

I am so very blessed to have these individuals on my dream team. God, of course, is my Captain! There are going to be more folks added to this list as my dream grows. I like the way that Jesus said it best, *"He that is greatest among you, let him be your servant!"* Matthew 23:11. That keeps things in proper perspective for me. I believe that committed people love to help and they thrive on being a help to others.

Wright

Art, that's an extensive team with plenty of shoes to fill, and consequently a lot of hats for you to wear. How do you juggle it all, fatherhood, husband, entrepreneur, speaker, pastor, coach, author, and I'm sure there's more.

Doakes

Yes, it is a lot of hats to wear, and I only have to wear one at a time. You see, I must remember why I'm here. There is a scripture in the Bible that says to whom much is given, much is required. I feel like I've been given quite a lot in the fact that I get up every morning and I'm able to breathe and move about on my own free will. I can think clearly and my mind is not bogged down with negative thoughts. I do not need any medication to get me through the day, and I'm not controlled by outside stimuli. **The truth of the matter is: juggling these hats is really a part of who I am to be for those I need to serve!** Remember my Dream Team; I've learned to delegate a lot of responsibility and authority to those in place to handle situations in their areas of expertise. This frees me up to do what I do best—SPEAK!!

My family has such a significant part in helping me juggle those hats by making life easier for me; they take away a lot of the stressors. My wife Karen, the love of my life, does an astronomical amount of things for me, as I said before, and this enables me to concentrate on being a servant to mankind. So juggling all these hats isn't as hard or demanding as it may seem to be. I love the challenges and the joy that it brings to the lives of those I serve is priceless. Pastoring is a gift from God, so I allow Him to direct all my efforts in this area especially, and the rest falls into place.

Speaking is something I love to do. It is fun, therefore, I look forward to every opportunity to speak and encourage others. My business is Customer Service, and again, my love for people makes this an easy and enjoyable endeavor to pursue. Being an Author is absolutely stimulating, especially when I get to work with a company like Insight *Publishing*, and Co-Authors like **Dr. John Gray, Jim Rohn, and Brian Tracy. The part of Husband and Father, now that is just pure JOY!** With my Dream Team in place, juggling these hats and more is welcomed and appreciated. I am truly thankful for being chosen to fill all the roles I've been given. It truly is humbling, and I consider it an honor to serve my fellow man. I hope that answered your question, David.

Wright

Yes it does. However, I'm sure our readers are curious about the sacrifices you must have had to make down through the years to become who you are today. Could you share them with us?

Doakes

The greatest sacrifice was on a hill called Golgotha, where a man named Jesus was crucified on a tree called a cross for the sins of mankind. When I think of my sacrifices, they somehow don't seem to compare with that of Jesus from Galilee. Nevertheless, I have had to make considerable sacrifices, as I'm sure you have David and all of our readers too. **This is by far the most humbling question that I have ever had to answer.** There was a time when I thought that giving up my seat in an auditorium for a senior citizen or a mother with a child was a sacrifice. I can remember staying late at work, and this was after arriving early that morning, and not getting any overtime, or getting up in the middle of the night to help a friend in need, stopping on the highway to pick up total strangers struggling with duffle bags and suitcases in the blistering Texas summer sun. I've served my country faithfully for over 14 1/2 years taking care of the soldiers and their families' medical needs. Giving my hard earned money to feed the hungry and clothe the poor. Giving up my vehicles to those who didn't have transportation, and taking family members into my home when they had nowhere else to turn. Giving students rides when they had no other means of transportation, even though it meant going miles out of my way. Volunteering my time, money, and talents, to all those who would ask and whenever they would ask. Yes, I used to think that all of these things were sacrifices. Even giving blood, donating my clothes, and shoes, and vehicles, and furniture to worthy causes to make sure someone else's life was easier. Giving up my gym time to listen to the problems of others, or missing family engagements to go to trainings, and seminars to get certified and licensed to practice my counseling skills. I did all of these things in the name of sacrifice. Were they sacrifices, yes I'd say that they were. What's the catch you might ask? Once I realized what a servant really meant, and what it truly costs to Pursue Your Passion, I soon realized that my many sacrifices, was really my reasonable service to mankind!

Remember the many hats? Let me elaborate on what wearing those hats have taught me and how they have molded me into the person who I am today. Reflecting on some of the places I've been, some of the things I've seen has given me a broader vision. I've seen neighborhoods where plumbing was insufficient and raw sewage was displayed openly. I've been inside of houses where dirty clothes and dishes were piled up knee high, while animal feces lay in the middle of the floor amidst children's shoes. I've seen the sick and afflicted lay in severe pain, dying from terminal diseases and illnesses that were treatable and preventable. I've seen the wear and tear of illegal drugs on the bodies and minds of men and women that literally changed their countenance and disfigured their anatomical structures, people eating out of garbage cans, and sleeping under bridges and on park benches and cardboard boxes. I've seen the mentally handicapped mistreated, families devastated by the loss of a loved one after serving their country faithfully and people denied privileges because of the color of their skin, the social and economical background, and the clothes they wear. I've seen all of this and much more. Yes, I'm humbled and I've learned that life is too short to sit idle, too precious to put in the wrong hands, too beautiful to hide in a closet of despair, too interesting not to share it with those you meet everyday, and most of all it is affordable to give freely to everyone who asks for some of your time. **SACRIFICE!** This is what our Seaford High School Lady Jays Basketball Team says when we break from our team huddles. Yes, I've made some, but so many others have made many, many more. The real heroes are sometimes not mentioned in our history books, they are our parents, teachers, civil servants, soldiers, health-care providers, and our children. Those we see everyday, day in and day out who keep life moving and make it safe and enjoyable for us all. This is the greatest impact we can get from our sacrifices.

Wright

Art you certainly have given our readers a new way of looking at sacrifices. With all that you've shared, what impact would you like to leave on the world?

Doakes

This is unquestionably the second most humbling request I must fill. First, that I lived a life pleasing to my God and helpful to my fellow man. I hope that being there for my children and my wife has touched them with a love that is everlasting; a love that will be passed on to my children's children and so on. That the service I rendered to my fellow man was a service that provided some good to them. I would like to have said that the son of Arthur Clifton Doakes Sr., and Florence Mary Colbert, lived his life with PASSION, and gave us all he had. I would like to encourage everyone to live a full life, an enjoyable life, and reach the full potential that God Almighty has placed within them. I believe that if a person looks at what they do and they begin to develop their purpose, they leave something behind that grows deeper than a legacy. They leave something in the Universe that says the place is better because I stopped by here. I want to leave the thought that every encounter I had on this earth had been better because I was here!

When I depart from here I'd like my epitaph to read, **"WELL DONE!"**

Wright

Art, I've had a great time. This has been one of the most interesting and empowering interviews I've had the pleasure of doing. You have motivated me today, and I'm **sure that you will be getting plenty of requests for your services as a speaker, trainer, and consultant**.

Doakes

I'm deeply grateful for the opportunity to share this message with our readers, David. I'd like to leave this quote to everyone who wants success. *"Pursue Your Passion With Purpose, and Provision Will Be Provided for Your Plan!"* This is Art Doakes, The Dynamic Dreamer, saying, "Have a Dynamite Delightful Day!"

Wright

Today we have been talking to Arthur Clifton Doakes Jr., a motivational speaker, which is key, if you desire to stimulate change. He causes participants to step outside of themselves and look within. The goal of this insight is the betterment of the individual and his environment. He does this through quality speech content coupled with his dramatic and inspiring presentation style as we have found this morning. Arthur, thank you so much for being with us today on *Conversations on Success*.

A motivational speaker is key if you desire to stimulate change. He causes participants to step outside of themselves and to look within. The goal of this insight is the betterment of the individual and his environment. Arthur Clifton Doakes Jr., The Dynamic Dreamer, does this through quality speech content and a dramatic and inspiring presentation style.

Arthur is an Internationally Certified Chemical Addictions Counselor serving the Delmarva area. Art's life is devoted to serving mankind. He is a decorated Military Veteran, School Counselor, Coach, Community Activist and more! He hosts Radio and T.V. talk shows providing solutions to real life issues. This dynamic, highly sought after keynote speaker and trainer holds a Masters Degree in Divinity and Christian Psychology; B.A. in Behavioral Science and an A. A. S. in Optometric Technology. Art is a devout husband and father of four daughters, and holds the distinction of being a key member of the Les Brown Speaker's Network.

Art Doakes

Phone: 302.249.5740

Fax: 302.337.7741

Email: dynamicdreamer@juno.com

www.thedynamicdreamer.com